# THE
# MOTHER COURT

Tales of Cases That Mattered in America's Greatest Trial Court

## JAMES D. ZIRIN
*foreword by Robert M. Morgenthau*

Cover by Elmarie Jara/ABA Publishing.

Printed in the United States of America

18 17 16 15 14   5 4 3 2 1

**Library of Congress Cataloging-in-Publication Data**

Zirin, James D., author.
    The mother court : tales of cases that mattered in America's greatest trial court / by James D. Zirin. — First edition.
        p. cm.
Includes bibliographical references and index.
    ISBN 978-1-62722-322-5 (print : alk. paper)
    1. United States. District Court (New York : Southern District)—Cases.
2. United States. District Court (New York : Southern District)—History. I. Title.
    KF8755.N9Z57 2014
    347.73'2209747—dc23

                                                            2013036466

Discounts are available for books ordered in bulk. Special consideration is given to state bars, CLE programs, and other bar-related organizations. Inquire at ABA Publishing, American Bar Association, 321 North Clark Street, Chicago, Illinois 60654-7598.

www.ShopABA.org

*To Marlene*

# CONTENTS

FOREWORD      IX

INTRODUCTION      XI

**1**   OF THE MOTHER COURT      I

**2**   BOB MORGENTHAU—THE BOSS      13

**3**   I, THE JURY      25

**4**   THE LOST ART OF CROSS-EXAMINATION      41

**5**   U.S. V. US: THE RED SCARE      53

THE SMITH ACT CASES      57

THE TRIAL OF THE COMMUNIST LEADERS      59

THE STRANGE CASE OF ALGER HISS      63

IRVING R. KAUFMAN AND THE ROSENBERGS      74

*Of the Rosenberg Case*      75

*The Rosenbergs: What Happened Later*      83

*Of Judge Kaufman*      89

**6** U.S. V. SEX                                                                   93
    *ULYSSES*                                                   98
    THE CURIOUS CASE OF *I AM CURIOUS—YELLOW*                    101
    *DEEP THROAT* OR HOW FAR DOES A GIRL HAVE
        TO GO TO UNTANGLE HER TINGLE?         104
    THE OFILI CASE—SEX IN THE MUSEUM                             107

**7** U.S. V. THE PRESS AND THE
REMARKABLE CAREER OF
JUDGE MURRAY I. GURFEIN                                                              111

**8** U.S. V. THE MOB                                                               129

**9** U.S. V. OFFICIAL CORRUPTION                                                   141
    THE MANTON CASE                                              142
    THE KEOGH CASE                                               145

**10** U.S. V. THE ACCOUNTANTS                                                      153

**11** OF THE LIBEL CASES                                                           171
    PEGLER V. REYNOLDS                                           174
    GOLDWATER V. GINZBURG                                        176
    SHARON V. TIME, INC.                                         179
    WESTMORELAND V. CBS                                          187

**12** U.S. V. ROY M. COHN                                                          199

**13** U.S. V. THEM                                                                 213

## 14 SOME OF MY FAVORITE JUDGES                    229

### SOME OF THE BEST                                230

*Edward Weinfeld*                                   230

*Thomas Murphy*                                     238

*Walter Mansfield*                                  246

*Harold R. Tyler, Jr.*                              249

*Edmund Palmieri*                                   252

### SOME OF THE REST                                259

*Irving Ben Cooper*                                 260

*Lloyd MacMahon*                                    269

*David Edelstein*                                   275

*Constance Baker Motley*                            278


## 15 THE COURT TODAY                                283

### THE LAUNCH OF THE DIGITAL COURTROOM             284

### TWEETING, FRIENDING, AND THE JURY               289

### SENTENCING BY GUIDELINES                        292


## CONCLUSION                                        303

## ACKNOWLEDGMENTS                                   309

## INDEX                                             311

# FOREWORD

The U.S. District Court for the Southern District of New York is undoubtedly the preeminent trial court in the nation. It is a veritable "crucible of justice." Its story goes back to the dawn of the Republic when Congress created the court in the Judiciary Act of 1789. But the court elaborated its reputation for excellence in the 20th century as America became more industrialized, and New York City emerged as a more densely populated commercial, cultural, and financial center.

The Southern District conducted some of the most important trials of our time transparently, fairly, and with rigid adherence to due process of law. The historic cases that unfolded in its courtrooms in the period following World War II represent a metaphor for what was going on during a time of radical transformation, and even hysteria, in American society. Lawyers call the Southern District the "Mother Court," not only because it is generally acknowledged to be the best in the justice business, but also because of the excellence of its judges, the quality of the lawyers who appear before it, and its fierce traditions of prosecutorial and judicial independence, and because it's the oldest court in the country, antedating even the Supreme Court.

I had the good fortune to serve as U.S. Attorney for the Southern District of New York in the decade of the 1960s. The outstandingly able young lawyers attracted to my office represented the government in some of the most important cases of the period. Our lawyers struck hard blows for the government, but they were always fair ones. We prosecuted high-profile cases without fear or favor, featuring the fields of organized crime, official corruption, white-collar fraud, Swiss bank secrecy, and narcotics, as well as criminal cases brought for the first time against senior auditors in nationally known firms. All these cases enforced and vindicated the rule of law. It was here that the rubber truly met the road.

Jim Zirin is a talented trial lawyer, an able writer, and a keen observer. It is not surprising, therefore, that he has crafted an extraordinary behind-the-scenes story, describing many of the people, cases, and events of the Mother Court. The reader will have a ringside seat at some of the major trials that unfolded in the Southern District in mid-20th century America. In a well-researched and highly readable chronicle, laced with some memorable and often hilarious anecdotes, he has captured the essence of what went on in Southern District courtrooms. He has made a valuable contribution to the history of the court that will be of interest to all citizens, not just judges, lawyers, and law students, but not excluding them either.

The book pushes forward the reader's knowledge of the American justice system. For those wishing to acquire a deeper understanding of why the Southern District is the special place it is, Jim Zirin's *The Mother Court* is both guidebook and testament.

Robert M. Morgenthau
New York
June 2013

# INTRODUCTION

*We had the experience but missed the meaning.*
—T.S. Eliot, "The Dry Salvages"

This book is about the U.S. District Court for the Southern District of New York, known to lawyers and judges as the "Mother Court," about what went on inside its courtrooms during a crucial era in the nation's history, and about some of the remarkable people and trials that helped shape its special character.

Volumes of documentary evidence usually aid those who venture to write a personal history, and there was a time when I had a veritable mountain of records and memorabilia, photographs, trial transcript, diaries, and letters from judges and public officials that recorded significant aspects of my many years of professional experience in the Southern District. On September 11, 2001, at 8:46 a.m., Mohamed Atta and his team of four hijackers, traveling at a speed of 490 miles an hour, flew American Airlines Fight 11 into my law office on the 54th floor of One World Trade Center. Thankfully, I wasn't there, but the attack totally destroyed my office. Lost in the charred ruins of the building were the documents that reflected a lifetime of professional experience. Remaining were only my memories, and you may find some of them here.

The Southern District is the court where the big trials occurred, where the big stories went down, where legendary lawyers argued, and where legendary judges ruled.

Some may see this book as "New York-centric." 9/11 was New York-centric; so was the 2008 financial meltdown. They both fired a shot heard round the world. The Mother Court happens to be located in New York City, but some of the things that went on there are of global dimension. The federal court in Manhattan is interwoven and interconnected with the fabric of America.

Many Americans sadly take little interest in our legal system, and even less in the history and role of the courts. I say sadly because what I describe as having happened in the Mother Court is about justice, law, and order, which profoundly affect the daily lives of all of us. And I would argue that what went on in this greatest of courts is a metaphor for changes in normative standards and attitudes as America emerged from the post-World War II era. Each case I consider is like a navigational dot on a mariners chart. Connect the dots, and we see the directional course and distance travelled in a vibrant and evolving society.

A trial is a powerful microscope for inspecting the soft underbelly of human nature; it reveals a slice of the human condition and vindicates the greatness of our institutions and the rule of law. From my perspective, a trial is where the rubber of government truly meets the road.

The American legal system is the envy of the world. Even the British, from whom we obtained our common law tradition, now look to our cases when a problem arises involving some regulatory complexity unknown at the time of Magna Carta.

The great legal historian F.W. Maitland wrote, "Such is the unity of all history that anyone who endeavors to tell a piece of it must feel that his first sentence tears a seamless web."[1] The American paradigm

---

1. *A Prologue to a History of English Law*, 14 L. Q̣TRLY. REV. 13 (1898).

of how justice should be administered is the Mother Court, and I will here "endeavor to tell a piece of" its history, knowing both that we are tearing a "seamless web," and that there is no real beginning and no real end.

The Mother Court is the court that sentenced the Rosenbergs to death for espionage. It is the court where Judge Harold Medina tried the 11 Communist Party leaders for conspiring to advocate the violent overthrow of the government, and, at the end of trial, held their lawyers in contempt. It is the court that convicted Alger Hiss of perjury.

It is the court that freed Joyce's *Ulysses*, the sexually explicit film *I Am Curious (Yellow)*, and the Pentagon Papers from the censor's numbing grip.

It is the court that convicted mafia figures Joseph Bonanno, Carmine Lombardozzi, Vincent Rao, Vito Genovese, and Anthony "Ducks" Corallo of racketeering and conspiracy. It is the court where a defendant in a drug conspiracy case, while being cross-examined, threw his 15-pound wooden chair at the prosecutor, and spent the rest of the trial gagged and manacled.

It is the court where, in an overcrowded courtroom, Judge Pierre Leval presided over the longest trial in American history, the marathon "Pizza Connection" case, involving New York mafia kingpin Salvatore Catalano. The trial, a mammoth $1.6 billion narcotics conspiracy case lasting 17 months, involved an international drug ring that used pizza parlors as fronts for illicit operations. It was a daunting challenge to trial management, and the jury convicted 18 men of over 100 acts of racketeering.

Official corruption cases abounded in the Mother Court. A Southern District jury in 1939 convicted Chief Judge Martin Manton of the Court of Appeals for the Second Circuit of bribery, and in 1962 convicted New York State Court Judge J. Vincent Keogh and U.S. Attorney Elliott Kahaner of corruption. And justice reigned on a host of other corrupt public officials, ranging from state senators to political leaders such as Tammany boss Carmine DeSapio, to New York City commissioners, to IRS revenue agents.

This story covers a tumultuous era in our collective consciousness, an era when so many serious national issues found their way into the federal courts. We will meet some of the extraordinary characters that gave the Mother Court a special role at a time of dramatic upheaval and transformation in our society. We will see some of the iconic judges and flamboyant trial lawyers of the Southern District, who did "strut and fret their hour upon . . . [its] stage," and were its soul.[2] We will view the humor, the drama, the people, and the war stories that were rife in that Depression-era classical revivalist Foley Square courthouse, where so much momentous judicial business made history.

All this was prologue to my own adventure before the Mother Court, as it attempted to dispose of contentious issues in a free society during the half century that I practiced there.[3] I hope to capture much of that in these pages.

First, I describe the origins and traditions of the Mother Court, and how my love affair with that great old place began. Then, I discuss my all too brief three-year journey with legendary prosecutor Bob Morgenthau, who brought me to the Southern District as a young lawyer.

We will meet some of the more memorable Southern District judges before whom I appeared, a Pleiades star cluster of judicial luminaries, and some of the more impressive and amusing lawyers with whom I had cases and whom I got to know. Many of my perceptions are unflattering to the human beings involved, and may not

---

2. *Macbeth*, act V, sc. 5.

3. I came on the scene in 1967, but as is always the case with folklore and history, I heard or read about what had happened before. The entire saga adds up to about 65 years.

be shared by all who knew them. I can only say that I have tried to be fair in my depictions.

In passing, I will discuss trial tactics: how we select juries, what they consider, and how they reach verdicts, even when deeply divided. I will then turn to the lost art of cross-examination and give some examples of how effective it can be as the best method ever conceived to get at the truth. Finally, as lawyers always do, I will move on to the cases that left an enduring impression.

The chapter U.S. v. Us—The Red Scare[4] discusses internal threat cases, set in the hysteria-driven first decade of our nation's postwar history, in which the government sought to prosecute alleged Communists, all accused either of conspiring to overthrow the U.S. government or of spying for the Soviet Union. The next chapter, U.S. v. Sex, explores instances in which the government tried to censor various forms of expression it deemed to be obscene. This is followed by U.S. v. The Press, in which the government sought to restrain the press from publishing material considered to endanger national security; U.S. v. The Mob, in which the government did battle with the organized criminal families; U.S. v. Official Corruption, in which the government prosecuted venal public officials, who sold power and influence for money and personal gain; and U.S. v. The Accountants, in which the government used criminal sanctions to rein in large accounting firms that turned a blind eye to corporate skullduggery and peculation.

The chapter titled Of the Libel Cases discusses Goldwater, Westmoreland, and Sharon, really freedom of expression cases that challenged the media to verify the truth of defamatory content they published, in which honor and truth were either vindicated or left for further trial in the court of public opinion.

---

4. Cases brought by the government are typically styled "U.S. v. someone—or something."

The chapter U.S. v. Roy Cohn explores the government's failure after four trials to nail the infamous witch hunter of the McCarthy era. Then, in U.S. v. Them, I discuss the external threat cases, in which the government prosecuted al Qaeda terrorists for attacking our people, our military, and our institutions.

My final chapter, The Court Today, explores how the Mother Court has or has not adapted to the innovations of the digital age.

In conclusion, we will have some observations on the state of the Mother Court today, what has been achieved over the years, and what has been irretrievably lost.

A little about me. I am a trial lawyer, and proud to be so. I have spent almost half a century of my professional career trying cases in the Southern District of New York, first as an Assistant U.S. Attorney prosecuting criminal cases, and later as a practicing lawyer involved in commercial and securities litigation fields, where I helped make some of the law that stands as controlling precedent to this day.[5]

During my time in the U.S. Attorney's Office, I prosecuted drug dealers and fraudsters, tax evaders and accountants, public officials and businessmen. Later, I defended accountants charged with breach of their professional standards, crisscrossed the country and the world taking depositions to be read into evidence in New York. I even took the deposition of Margaret Thatcher in a London conference room that was videotaped and later played back at a trial in the Southern District. My practice was exciting, lucrative, and intellectually challenging.

---

5. *E.g.*, Bersch v. Drexel, 519 F.2d 974 (2d Cir. 1975), on the extraterritorial reach of the federal securities laws); FOF v. Andersen, 567 F.2d 225 (2d Cir. 1977), elaborating ethical standards applicable to lawyers; Chem. Bank v. Arthur Andersen, 726 F.2d 930 (2d Cir. 1983), on the "strong family resemblance" standard governing what is a security); DED v. Andersen, 924 F. Supp. 449 (S.D.N.Y. 1996), on the reach of the Racketeering in Corrupt Organizations (RICO) law to professional auditors.

But my three thrilling years as a prosecutor in the Southern District, during which I tried over 36 cases to a jury that went to verdict, were the most rewarding of my professional life. I learned, I laughed, and I remembered. I knew all of the judges and most of the lawyers. I observed their idiosyncrasies and foibles, and saw how they approached a variety of legal problems. It has been said that some lawyers know the law; others know the judge. In my experience, both are important.

Attempted here is not a comprehensive history of the jurisprudence of the Mother Court over the past 50 years. Every year the Southern District hears congeries of complex cases involving a regulatory and legislative thicket of admiralty, patent, labor, copyright and trademark, food and drug, antitrust, tax, employment, civil rights, and a host of other fields, which I do not even touch upon. That will be left to the historians and the academics.

The art of being a trial lawyer is the art of telling a story. This story is about what occurs at trial in an American courtroom before a federal judge and a metropolitan jury, where the ranging issues before the Mother Court inevitably reflected the temper of the times. It is about the big trials and the smaller ones, the courtroom stratagems, the maneuverings, the mirth and the power plays that were the backdrop to the evolving case histories. It is about the larger-than-life people and the important cases that most impressed me, mindful, as Judge Weinfeld so aptly put it, that "every case is important, and no case is more important than any other case."

# OF THE MOTHER COURT

*[N]or shall any person be deprived of life, liberty or property*
*without due process of law.*
**—Fifth Amendment,**
**Constitution of the United States**

No one quite knows when the name "Mother Court" originated, or who first coined the phrase. This is perhaps because the court traces its origins to the Judiciary Act of 1789, and antedates by a few weeks the organization of the U.S. Supreme Court. One of the first lawyers admitted to practice before it was Aaron Burr. Whatever the provenance, the name stuck.[1]

In our system, U.S. trial courts are organized into 94 federal districts, including at least one in each state. Judges of the Mother Court, like all federal judges, are appointed by the president and confirmed by the Senate. There are as of this writing 33 men and

---

1. When Judge John Keenan, who prior to his appointment to the Southern District bench had been the president of the Off-Track Betting Corporation, took his fellow judges for an "outing" at Aqueduct, he succeeded in having one of the races named "the Mother Court Stakes."

15 women serving as judges on the court. While the Southern District is a trial court, occasionally judges of the Mother Court sit by designation in the Second Circuit U.S. Court of Appeals. Article III of the U.S. Constitution provides:

> The judicial Power of the United States, shall be vested in one supreme Court, and in such inferior Courts as the Congress may from time to time ordain and establish. The Judges, both of the supreme and inferior Courts, shall hold their Offices during good Behavior, and shall, at stated Times, receive for their Services a Compensation which shall not be diminished during their Continuance in Office.

The term "good behavior" is interpreted to mean that federal judges may serve for life, although they may resign or retire voluntarily. This, together with the provision that the salary of a federal judge may not be "diminished" during his term in office, gives us the crown jewel of our federal system, judicial independence.[2] A judge may also be removed by impeachment and conviction. Although this has happened 14 times in history, no judge of the Southern District has ever been impeached.

A number of outstanding judges of the Mother Court, however, have resigned. I remember some of them. Judge Simon Rifkind resigned for financial reasons. Mother Court judges were and are paid a pittance, in many cases about as much as the starting salary of a brilliant graduate of a first-rate law school.[3] Rifkind went on to found the Paul Weiss law firm, an institution. Judge Arnold Bauman also resigned for financial reasons in 1974, citing the runaway

---

2. I use throughout the indefinite pronoun "his" with total gender neutrality to refer to both men and women. I intend no discourtesy to anyone who may feel she is not possibly covered by the description.

3. Starting salaries for associates at large Wall Street law firms can be $160,000 a year or more; federal district judges receive a salary of $174,000. The Chief Justice of the U.S. Supreme Court receives only $223,500.

inflation that had gripped the country. Judge John Martin resigned to protest the federal sentencing guidelines that, he argued, stifled the discretion of judges. The guidelines were later rendered advisory and nonmandatory by decision of the Supreme Court. The brilliant Judge Abraham Sofaer, frustrated that he was not appointed an appellate judge, resigned to become legal adviser to the State Department under Secretary of State George Shultz. Judge Harold Tyler, one of the youngest judges ever appointed at age 38, resigned to become deputy U.S. Attorney General. Marvin Frankel, who had been a law professor, resigned to join a large law firm and became an advocate for human rights. Tyler's former associate, Judge Michael Mukasey, who was chief judge of the Mother Court, resigned to accept appointment as Attorney General of the United States in the George W. Bush administration.

The jurisdiction of the federal courts depends on acts of Congress, which determine what cases, civil and criminal, they may take. State courts have an independent and sometimes overlapping sovereignty, with jurisdiction over matters that may or may not be brought in the federal courts.

Thus, admiralty, antitrust, trademark and copyright, patent, and securities cases are normally tried in a federal district court, while divorce, probate, medical malpractice, automobile accident cases, and the like are generally tried in the state courts, where outcomes may dramatically differ.

The same is true of criminal cases. Congress has given the federal courts criminal jurisdiction over terrorism, racketeering, bank robbery, securities fraud, narcotics, and interstate theft cases, to name but a few. Some of these crimes may be tried in the state courts, but the major cases are normally prosecuted in the district courts, where the presidentially appointed judges are thought to be better, more sophisticated, independent of the political process, and not subject to venality and external pressure.

A mother court needs a home. Since 1936, the Southern District has been housed in the United States Courthouse, an imposing WPA building in Foley Square, a short distance from the southern tip of Manhattan. The architect Cass Gilbert designed the 30-story building, now a national historic landmark. Gilbert crowned the building with a pyramidal roof adorned by gold leaf.[4] The trappings of justice are supposed to be impressive—and in Foley Square, they are.

The Southern District is a trial court. Lawyers call it a court of original, as opposed to appellate, jurisdiction. Its job is to find the facts and apply the law in the first instance or, as Mother Court Judge Marvin Frankel used to say facetiously, "Get the issue erroneously decided and on its way to the Court of Appeals."

The Mother Court's jurisdiction, its power to act, comprises Manhattan and the Bronx, as well as six upstate New York counties. In establishing the Southern District in 1789, Congress had in mind primarily a maritime court. Its scope enlarged, however, as New York grew to become the economic, commercial, and cultural epicenter of the Nation. Today, its boundaries embrace America's financial markets, stock exchanges and principal banks, the Broadway stage, performing arts centers, and museums.

We think of the Southern District as the Mother Court for many reasons beyond seniority and geographic significance. Nationally recognized for the outstanding quality of its judiciary, the excellence of the advocates who appear before it, its authoritative opinions grounded in real substance, the sensitive management of its docket, and its relevance to the rule of law, the Mother Court is the gold

---

4. In 2001 the building, long known as the Foley Square Courthouse, was renamed the Thurgood Marshall United States Courthouse after the Supreme Court Justice who had served in the building for four years as an appellate judge. The building has just completed a six-year, $230 million renovation. The renovated building houses the Second Circuit U.S. Court of Appeals. Since 1996, the Southern District has enjoyed new quarters, named for the late New York Senator Daniel P. Moynihan, a stone's throw away at 500 Pearl Street. The Southern District also hears cases at satellite courthouses in White Plains and Middletown, New York.

standard for trial courts around the United States. It is the country's crucible of justice in the continuously unfolding history of our Nation.

Addressing the singularly outstanding quality of Southern District judiciary, the late Chief Justice Charles Evans Hughes said:

> The Courts are what the judges make them, and the District Court in New York, from the time of [District Judge] James Duane, [President] Washington's first appointment, has had a special distinction by reason of the outstanding abilities of the men who have been called to its service.

I began my love affair with Southern District trials when home from Princeton on school vacation. I became an avid courtroom spectator, watching mostly criminal trials, because they were both more interesting and easier to understand than their civil counterparts. How I stood awestruck, transfixed with the drama of it all, when I heard the two knocks on the robing room door heralding the appearance of the judge in the courtroom! "ALL RISE," cried the bailiff.

Then, he recited the venerable incantation announcing the beginning of the judicial business:

> Oyez, oyez, oyez. The United States District Court for the Southern District of New York is now in session. All persons having business before the United States District Court for the Southern District of New York, draw near, give your attention and you shall be heard. God save these United States and this honorable court.

The epicenter of the Mother Court's criminal business was Courtroom 318, United States Courthouse. That was the place where each morning they called the calendar.[5] There were rarely trials

---

5. The Southern District later went to an individual calendar system so that cases were assigned to a judge for all purposes at the time the indictment was filed. This ended the bazaar-like proceedings that transpired in Courtroom 318.

in Courtroom 318, but much could be learned from viewing that crowded scene of lawyers, defendants, and prosecutors all milling about in a cartoonlike atmosphere reminiscent of a Hogarth painting.

There I took measure of the immense stature of the judges, which stood in stark contrast to the ridiculousness of some of the lawyers. The Mother Court was not without its absurd characters. Otto Fusco of the Bronx, the few times I saw him in action, was one of my favorites.

Defense lawyers always wanted to delay things on the principle of "no trial, no conviction." The best in the business was Fusco. Fusco doubtless tried many cases, but I never knew of one. His technique, as I saw it, was never—or hardly ever—to go to trial, pleading his clients guilty after delaying the day of reckoning as long as possible. Fusco rarely even appeared in Foley Square. He was otherwise occupied in the Bronx. So he normally sent one of his many satraps. A typical Fusco scenario in Courtroom 318 went something like this:[6]

THE COURT:[7] United States v. Ramon Grasso.

THE PROSECUTOR: Ready for the government, your Honor.

A MAN [SPEAKING IN RAPID STACCATO-LIKE TONES SO AS TO BE
ALMOST UNINTELLIGIBLE]: Application, your Honor. I am
from the law offices of Otto Fusco. With apologies to the court,
Mr. Fusco cannot be here as he is actually engaged in a jury trial of
a leg-off case, Trial Part in the Bronx.[8] In addition, Mr. Fusco has
round trip tickets to Puerto Rico for a much-deserved vacation
with Mrs. Fusco and so requests a six-month adjournment.

---

6. The judge presiding in 318 would fix bail, set a date for pretrial motions, hear argument on defense motions which were mostly denied, adjourn the case, or send the case out for trial, either to himself or usually to another judge. The defense strategy was to avoid having the case sent out for trial, so it would languish on the 318 calendar.

7. In the stagecraft of the courtroom, when the judge speaks, the reporter always refers to him in the transcript as "The Court."

8. A "leg-off case" is evidently a personal injury matter where the plaintiff, represented by Mr. Fusco, lost his leg in an accident.

If pressed as to why the case was really going over, the Fusco office would inevitably present this excuse:

FUSCO'S OFFICE: Mr. Fusco is with all due diligence looking for a percipient witness to the matters involved in the indictment, a Mr. Green, lately of the Bronx [a transparently veiled reference to collecting his fee].

An adjournment, half of what Fusco requested, would inevitably be granted. Mr. Fusco completed his leg-off trial; Mr. and Mrs. Fusco went to Puerto Rico; and on his return to New York, his fee secured, Fusco would plead his client guilty. In Courtroom 318 Mr. Fusco was an indispensable cog in the slow but certain wheels of justice.

I relished being in the old courthouse; listening to the Runyo-nesque hangers-on discuss the evidence, the issues, and the per-sonalities involved. The courtroom buffs, the regulars, liked to call me "Stoo-dent," and the student attentively watched the lawyers wrangle, observed what arguments impressed the judge and the jury, and learned what kinds of silly arguments almost had the lawyers laughed out of court.

I remember the template of the prosecutor's opening statement:

Ladies and Gentlemen of the jury. I am an Assistant United States Attorney for the Southern District of New York, and it is my privilege to present to you the government's case. You are welcome to a court of justice,—justice to the defendant, to be sure, and justice to my client, the United States of America.

Clever, I thought to myself, how he wraps himself in the flag. He would have immediate credibility with the jury.

The opening statement continued:

The case is brought because a federal grand jury consisting of 23 citizens drawn from the community, just as you have been drawn from the community, returned an indictment.

Really clever how he invites the jury in the box to identify with their community, the grand jury that returned the indictment.

Now, ladies and gentlemen, an indictment is not evidence, it is merely the accusation that sets forth the various federal crimes that the government intends to prove.

I always loved this one; an indictment is not evidence, to be sure, but that's not why he said it. Rather, by power of suggestion, the prosecutor subtly encouraged the jury to believe *just the opposite*—that it was indeed evidence of something. He also said it because he anticipated that the judge, the jury's alter ego, would later repeat and reinforce the same boilerplate words. What a powerful way to create a psychological and intellectual bond between the jury and himself that he hoped would carry the day for the government.

Cicero used this oratorical convention on his political enemy, Cataline. It is called *praeteritio*, where the speaker asserts a proposition by denying that it should be invoked.

My senior partner in private practice, Charles H. Tuttle, was a master of *praeteritio*. Tuttle was a great advocate. He was astonishing in the way he could summon righteous anger to his cause. Once, one of his adversaries was so taken aback at this that he told Tuttle he was worried he might have a heart attack or a stroke. "Never fear," Tuttle said. "My ire is for hire."[9]

---

9. The only lawyer I knew who was Tuttle's equal in the righteous anger department was Sam Gates, a superb trial lawyer and name partner of the Debevoise Plimpton firm. At appropriate moments in the proceeding, Sam seemed to be able to make the vein in his forehead throb on command.

Tuttle served as U.S. Attorney for the Southern District of New York. President Calvin Coolidge appointed him to the post in 1927. Fond of a well-shaken cocktail, Tuttle seemed an incongruous pick to prosecute bootleggers at the height of the prohibition era, but throughout his career he earned a great reputation as an anticorruption crusader. He resigned in 1930 to run for governor of New York against Franklin Delano Roosevelt. He was shellacked.

Tuttle was an old warrior. For him litigation was what he liked to call the "drama of the law." Long before Edward Bennett Williams claimed the title, Tuttle was the "man to see" if you got into criminal difficulty in New York.

One of Tuttle's criminal clients was Richard Whitney. Whitney was a tall, ruddy man with a patrician Groton cum Harvard pedigree. He was president of the New York Stock Exchange, principal in a "white shoe" Wall Street investment bank, and treasurer of the New York Yacht Club. He had a wealthy wife and a wealthy older brother. Sadly, his tangled financial affairs unraveled in 1938, and it came out that he had stolen millions from all of them. He was the Bernie Madoff of his day.

Whitney called on Tuttle, and Tuttle, a born raconteur, spoke to me of the encounter. "Richard Whitney came to my office. An imperious man, he wore the Harvard pig at his navel.[10] He said, 'Mr. Tuttle, I am a traitor to my caste and want to pay the consequences.'" It doesn't get much more dramatic than that. Tuttle pleaded Whitney guilty. The fallen banker served three years of a five-to-ten-year term in Sing Sing before his release on parole.

Back to *praeteritio*. Tuttle won a legendary jury trial in a divorce case where the issue was the wife's adultery. In summation to the jury, he used *praeteritio* to great effect:

---

10. Whitney was a member of the elite Porcellian Club, a men-only final club at Harvard founded in 1791. The Club's emblem is the pig.

Forget about the testimony of the private detectives, trained investigators, licensed by the state of New York who testified under oath
that they saw the co-respondent enter the hotel with my client's wife.
*That's not important; that's not important.* [Of course it's important; it's
eyewitness testimony.] Consider the testimony of the co-respondent
when I asked him whether he had sexual relations there with this
woman, and he answered 'to be honest, Mr. Tuttle, I was so drunk,
I don't remember.' Well, ladies and gentlemen, I am an old, old man,
and I may be the only person in this courtroom, who can honestly say,
'I don't remember.' But I will tell you one thing that I do remember.
When sex happened, I remember it.

*Praeteritio* won the day for Charles H. Tuttle. An advocate's job is
to persuade, and words are "his quiddities ... his quillets, his cases, his
tenures, and his tricks."[11]

Little did I dream that after a law school education, a stint in the
army, and a few years in private practice, I would be standing in front
of real juries and a real Southern District judge. It was not lost on me
that the Southern District was a very special court, and the lawyers
and judges who did "strut and fret" their hour on its stage venerated
its majesty and tradition. To appear there was to know a special calling—that something special was expected of you. Judge Weinfeld
captured it all when he recalled a lawyers' dinner as a junior district
judge, during which he was asked to share the dais with Supreme
Court Justice Harlan and the legendary Second Circuit Chief Judge
Learned Hand—a daunting situation for any human being. Learned
Hand's scholarly and well-reasoned opinions today remain so influential that he has been called the "greatest jurist never to have been
appointed to the Supreme Court." Throwing caution to the winds,
Weinfeld rose to make the following comment:

---

11. *Hamlet*, act V, sc. 1, in the graveyard.

Meaning no disrespect to these outstanding jurists whom I venerate, or to the great courts on which they serve, I think the greatest court of the United States, barring none, is the Southern District of New York.[12]

He took his seat, fearing the worst as Hand rose to speak. As Weinfeld recounted the story, Hand followed him to the rostrum, and could not have been more gracious or more accurate:

Ed, you never rendered a more solid judgment and if from here out, all your rulings are as sound, you will never be reversed.[13]

Hand went on and talked about his 15 years of service as a district court judge until his appointment to the court of appeals, and wound up as follows:

I do not hesitate to say before this audience that with the exception of appointment to the Supreme Court of the United States, which for reasons that are not important I did not achieve, I wish I were back at the district court—it is indeed a great court.[14]

And a "great court" it always has been.

---

12. Address by Judge Edward Weinfeld accepting the 1985 Fordham Law School Stein Award, November 1, 1984, reprinted at XIII FORDHAM URBAN LAW JOURNAL 515 at 523.
13. *Id.*
14. *Id.*

# BOB MORGENTHAU—
# THE BOSS

*The rain may never fall till after sundown.*
*By eight, the morning fog must disappear.*
*In short, there's simply not*
*A more congenial spot*
*For happily-ever-aftering than here*
*In Camelot.*

**—Alan Jay Lerner, *Camelot***

In 1961 President John F. Kennedy appointed Robert M. Morgenthau U.S. Attorney for the Southern District of New York. He could not have conceived of how great Bob would be as a prosecutor. Bob, the scion of a distinguished German Jewish family, proved to be a totally dedicated public servant. Public service was embedded in Bob's DNA. His father, Henry Morgenthau, Jr., was secretary of the Treasury under Franklin Delano Roosevelt. His grandfather was Woodrow Wilson's ambassador to Turkey. As a young man, Bob met Roosevelt and Churchill when both visited his parents' home. When Churchill came, Bob made the drinks.

I first met Bob Morgenthau in 1967, when he was about to appoint me as an Assistant U.S. Attorney. Interviewed for the job by seasoned prosecutors Peter Fleming, Mike Armstrong, Larry Vogel, and Paul Grand, I had already experienced a rigorous vetting process. This "Sanhedrin" put me through my paces on criminal, civil, and constitutional law. Defending a PhD dissertation could not have been more daunting. They cared not what positions I took, but only that my answers were well grounded in fact and reason, and expressed with some degree of clarity. For months I heard nothing and then Bob's secretary, Jo Guercio, called me at my law firm. Jo guarded the kingdom that was the suite of offices occupied by Bob, Chief Assistant Silvio Mollo, and Executive Assistant Al Gaynor. "I am calling for Robert Morgenthau," she said. "Mr. Morgenthau would like to see you."

Peter Fleming became my great mentor in the office. He was a character. My favorite Peter story: When Attorney General Robert Kennedy visited Foley Square, he spoke with the Assistants in the library. Going around the table, he asked each Assistant why he was there. One said, "public service, General." Another said, "To put the bad guys in jail." Fleming's plucky answer evokes laughter among underpaid prosecutors to this day: "*For the money, General.*"[1]

Bob Morgenthau called Peter "one of the best lawyers around." Later, in private practice, Peter successfully represented such high-profile defendants as boxing promoter Don King and former Attorney General John Mitchell. He knew not only how to cross-examine but *when* to cross-examine. He had incredible poise in front of a jury,

---

1. As Attorney General, Bobby Kennedy had administrative responsibility for the U.S. Attorney's Office, which he looked upon with some affection. When he was assassinated in June 1968, I was one of the Assistants who stood in the honor guard around his bier at St. Patrick's Cathedral.

standing tall at six feet, six inches. He spoke without notes, although he was meticulously prepared. Peter had courage and imagination, coupled with the Irish gifts of gab and emotionalism. Trying a case was a personal thing with him. His father often came to watch him in court.

Occasionally Peter even wept during his closing argument. Lots of defense lawyers cry as they ask a jury for leniency, but I never heard a prosecutor cry (and get away with it!), with the exception of Peter Fleming.

I was thrilled. First, I met briefly with Gaynor, who spoke of the important work of the Office. Movie-star handsome, with a lantern-jawed face resembling that of Mitt Romney, Gaynor spoke in stentorian tones. He described his job as "doing whatever Mr. Morgenthau asks me to do." Then, I met with Sil Mollo. An iconic figure in the U.S. Attorney's Office, Sil was a career prosecutor who had seen just about everything there was to see in the Southern District. Sil had watched U.S. Attorneys come and go, but his loyalty to Bob Morgenthau assumed an almost religious zeal. He served Bob as chief of the Criminal Division, Chief Assistant U.S. Attorney, and later as Chief Assistant District Attorney of New York County. "You will become a partner in the best law office in New York. Your partners are all excellent lawyers. You will appear before the greatest court and the finest federal judges in the Nation," Sil said. He was right.[2]

---

2. A short man with a birdlike countenance, Sil was often the butt of satire in the office. At the annual dinner the Assistants gave honoring Bob Morgenthau, a quartet of prosecutors feeling no pain would serenade Sil with a ditty that the hilarious Hugh Humphreys, with a sense of humor second to none, liberally adapted from the *Mikado*:

On a tree by a river a little tom-tit
Sang "Mollo, Sil Mollo, Sil Mollo"
And I said to him, "Dicky-bird, why do you sit
Singing 'Mollo, Sil Mollo, Sil Mollo'"
"Is it weakness of intellect, birdie?" I cried
"Or rather dyspepsia in your little inside"
With a shake of his poor little head, he replied
"Oh, Mollo, Sil Mollo, Sil Mollo!"

After my chat with Sil, I met Bob Morgenthau and the magic began. He spoke of the independence of the Office, and his vision of its excellence. "We would love to have you with us," he said. "It *will* be the criminal division." I gulped, to which Bob nodded, "Yes."[3]

"I accept," I declared without hesitation. I didn't even ask the salary. And my adventure began.

First, the FBI investigated me, and the background check ran true to form. If a candidate lived in an apartment, they invariably started the inquiry with the building superintendent. They thought the superintendent would surely know where the bodies were buried as he lived in the basement. I was living then with my parents in Brooklyn Heights in a small apartment building overlooking the East River and lower Manhattan.[4]

One night, I returned home rather late, and the superintendent, Lopez, called to me from the darkness. "Mr. Zirin," he said, "the FBI was here asking about you, but I tell them nothing, NOTH-ING!!" I was flabbergasted. Notwithstanding Lopez' reticence, I got the job. My mother and father came to the courthouse to attend the induction ceremony on May 17, 1967, and it was Bob who swore me in.

Everyone in the Office called Bob "the Boss" out of affection and admiration—not because we were subordinates (though subordinates we were), but because he was the guiding spirit in a collaborative enterprise to which we were all totally dedicated. In fact, Bob well understood that no lawyer really has a boss. He

---

3. The office was divided into the elite criminal division, consisting of about 50 lawyers who prosecuted federal crimes, and the smaller civil division that represented the United States in civil matters.

4. Through the large picture window in our living room, we could see giant passenger ships passing by as they sailed from their piers in the Hudson River on their way to European ports. As a child, I had seen the *S.S. United States* leaving on its maiden voyage from New York to Southampton. The ship broke the trans-Atlantic speed record by crossing from Ambrose Lightship to Bishop's Rock, Cornwall, in three days, ten hours, forty minutes.

never had one himself. He taught by example the important lesson of independence—independence of thought and of action.

Bob's father had owned a vast apple orchard in Dutchess County near Fishkill, and so apples were a seminal part of Bob's life. As his wife, writer Lucinda Franks, put it in a poignant 1980 *New York Times* piece, "He grows them—actually prunes the trees, and puts the bees out to pollinate the blossoms—cooks with them, eats them, collects paintings of them and even wears them on his lapel." When he was U.S. Attorney, he had in his office fridge a formidable collection of Rome Beauties, Ida Reds, and Macs. Visitors could have their pick.

On Bob's family property was a charming old farmhouse and a swimming pool. The musty study replicated the office of the secretary of the Treasury with an American flag and the flag of the Treasury Department on either side of the antique desk. To be there was to be an eyewitness to history. I often felt as if at any moment Henry Morgenthau would enter the room to take a call from Roosevelt.

One Saturday a year Bob would host the Assistants and their families to a picnic lunch at the orchard. On the bill of fare was freshly made unfiltered apple cider and always three or four kinds of apples. He delighted in taking the kids around the property. They would sit on a hay wagon drawn by a tractor with Bob at the wheel. It was always a grand occasion.

There was the famous story about Bob's father, and his role in opening the doors of the United States to Jewish refugees from the Nazi horror. In 1944, Secretary Morgenthau stood up to the State Department's callous indifference to the plight of the Jews of Europe. Assistant Secretary of State Breckinridge Long, in charge of refugee affairs, was notorious for his role as the official responsible for denying refugee visas to hundreds of thousands of European Jews fleeing the Nazis. When Long opposed a Treasury plan to bribe Rumanian officials with $170,000 to permit the evacuation of 70,000 Jews, mostly children, Morgenthau was quick to stare him down. "Well, Breck . . . we might be a little frank. The impression is [that] you, particularly, are anti-Semitic. . . . After all, Breck, the United States of America was created as a refuge for people who were persecuted the world over, starting with Plymouth . . . and as Secretary of the Treasury for 135 million people—I am carrying this out as Secretary of the Treasury, and not as a Jew."

In January 1944, Morgenthau and Treasury General Counsel Randolph Paul produced and delivered to Roosevelt a memorandum titled "Report to the Secretary on the Acquiescence of this Government in the Murder of the Jews." This missive amounted to an indictment of State Department policies, including both its active opposition to the release of funds for the rescue of European Jewry and its promotion of immigration policies closing America's doors to Jewish refugees.

The result was Executive Order 9417, which created the War Refugee Board, composed of the secretaries of State, Treasury, and War. Issued on January 22, 1944, the Executive Order declared, "[I]t is the policy of this Government to take all measures within its power to rescue the victims of enemy oppression who are in imminent danger of death, and otherwise to afford such victims all possible relief and assistance consistent with the successful prosecution of the war." It came late in the game, but the War Refugee Board succeeded in saving the lives of several hundred thousand Jews. The episode evokes Churchill's observation that "you can always count on Americans to do the right thing—after they've tried everything else."

Bob was a survivor, who spoke of the "importance of being lucky." He served four and one-half years in the Mediterranean and Pacific theaters in World War II. He was the executive officer of two destroyers, and fought at the battles of Okinawa and Iwo Jima in the South Pacific, where he actually saw the Marines raise the flag at

Mount Suribachi. Many of Bob's comrades were killed. He himself had a near death experience when his ship was cut in half, and he spent three hours in the water before being rescued. He spoke of his feelings at the time with his characteristically self-deprecating humor, "I made promises to the Almighty, but I didn't have much bargaining power."

Bob had a strong feeling for justice, perhaps tempered by his war experiences. He once said to me of anti-Semites, "You better know who you are, because *they* know who you are."[5]

Bob's dedication to public service was contagious, and he inspired excellence in an office of young lawyers. He loved the big investigations. He targeted the malefactors of great wealth, particularly the Swiss banks that provided a haven for tax evaders through a web of secret accounts. He seemed to be ubiquitous in the office. He attended sessions of the grand jury, popped into Assistants' offices to discuss their cases, interfaced with the federal agents on important cases, and met with defendants and persuaded them to cooperate with the government. "I can't help you," he would say to a defendant possessing valuable information, "unless you want to help yourself."

Bob knew how to work the press. He understood that the purpose of public prosecutions, particularly white-collar prosecutions, is to make examples of people in order to deter others from illegal conduct. To do this, it was necessary to give wide publicity to what he was doing—not to aggrandize himself, but to achieve the essential purpose of law enforcement.

And what a brilliant team of young lawyers he had handpicked to be around him! It was the All Star team and the Pro Bowl all rolled up into one large law office. There were the lawyers such as Pierre Leval, Steve Williams, Tony Sifton, John Sprizzo, Harold

---

5. Bob Morgenthau became chairman of the American Museum of Jewish Heritage, the magnificent Holocaust memorial on the southern tip of Manhattan Island. He said "you can't understand the Middle East and Israel unless you understand the Holocaust."

Baer, Sterling Johnson, Abe Sofaer, John Martin, and Peter Leisure, who all became federal judges, and there were scores of other lawyers who later achieved eminence at the Bar.

Bob was fiercely determined to maintain the independence of the office, even from the Department of Justice. Like Attorney General Robert Jackson, he recognized that a centralized bureaucracy in Washington ought not to assume the responsibilities of a U.S. Attorney. Accordingly, he skillfully deflected any attempt to intrude on his turf—even when it came from the highest levels of government. Carmen Basilio, who won the middleweight title from Sugar Ray Robinson in 1957, might have learned his amazing infighting skills from Bob.

Bob's insistence on independence from Washington pervaded the Office, and took on a religious fervor. When we were about to indict politically powerful Louis Wolfson for securities violations, perjury, and obstruction of justice, Bob received a call from Bobby Kennedy, then Attorney General, who urged that the prosecution occur in Wolfson's home state of Florida.

"I can't do that," said Morgenthau.

"Why not?" Kennedy asked.

"He wouldn't get a fair trial down there,"

"Why wouldn't he get a fair trial?"

"Because Wolfson has every judge in the state in his pocket."

The case against Wolfson went forward in the Southern District.

When Louis Oberdorfer, assistant attorney general in charge of the Tax Division of the Justice Department, wanted to take over an important argument in the Second Circuit of an appeal involving First National City Bank, Assistant U.S. Attorney Bob Arum, who had handled the case successfully in the Southern District, refused to knuckle under. Arum received a phone call from a *petit fonctionnaire* in Justice, who told him sternly that Assistant Attorney General Oberdorfer wanted to handle the case personally. What

Arum didn't know was that Oberdorfer was listening in on the conversation.

"Tell Oberdorfer he can go fuck himself," said Arum.

There was silence on the phone and then, "Mr. Arum, this is Assistant Attorney General Oberdorfer, and you are in a lot of hot water."

When Morgenthau heard about it, he laughed uproariously. The lawyers divided the argument. Arum argued, Oberdorfer argued, and the government eventually won the appeal in the Supreme Court.[6] Arum survived to become a fabulously successful boxing promoter.

Independence was not all Bob understood:

- He understood that what you did for other people is what counts in life and makes it all worthwhile.
- He understood that the government wins its point when justice is done—not the other way around.
- He understood that the law is the servant of the people, and that no one is above the law.
- He understood that the executive branch must err on the side of protecting our security, just as the judicial branch must err on the side of protecting essential human freedoms.
- He understood the supremacy of human rights everywhere. Like his father before him, he understood the unspeakable horror that can occur when organized criminals seize control of the state.
- He understood the imperative of excellence in government, and never compromised that standard. He bristled with an innate exhilaration about public service, which spread virus-like among his colleagues. He left an indelible impression on a whole generation of lawyers.

---

6. United States v. First National City Bank, 379 U.S. 378 (1965).

With these elements, he built into the Office a unity of purpose spawning an almost unimaginable level of loyalty, esprit, camaraderie, and fraternity, which abides to this day.

Bob was happiest chasing criminals, especially securities fraudsters, tax evaders, and their Swiss bankers who helped them use secrecy laws to evade American taxes.

On November 5, 1968, Richard Milhous Nixon was elected the 37th president of the United States, and for us in the U.S. Attorney's Office something precious was irretrievably lost. We in the office knew that Nixon would want to fire Bob and replace him with a Republican, but nothing happened immediately. The statute creating the Office of the U.S. Attorney states that the U.S. Attorney is appointed for a four-year term, and will serve until his successor is appointed and qualified. It also states that the U.S. Attorney is subject to removal by the president. Bob's term expired June 11, 1971, and he announced that he would serve out his term to complete a number of pending sensitive investigations involving organized crime and corruption involving prominent Republicans.

No one doubted that the president had the power to remove Bob, but we in the U.S. Attorney's Office, praying it wouldn't happen, put on blinders and continued with our official duties, like the family in *The Garden of the Finzi-Continis*, living in our little paradise and ignoring the gathering storm.

On December 17, 1969, the hammer fell. White House Press Secretary Ron Ziegler announced that Nixon would replace Morgenthau with Wall Street lawyer Whitney North Seymour Jr. I was devastated. There are cataclysmic moments in our lives when the world seems to stop spinning on its axis. For us in the Southern District U.S. Attorney's office, such was that December morning when we sadly gathered in the library outside Bob's office to say goodbye. It was the end of an era.

After a six-year hiatus, Bob returned to the prosecutor's office, this time as district attorney of New York County, where he served for 34 years, retiring at age 90.

Bob was the quintessential public servant. There was no lawyer I respected more highly for his single-mindedness and steadfastness of purpose. He was stubborn, he knew how to work the bureaucracy in Washington, he got it done, and he got it right.

No one more exemplified the culture of the Southern District than Bob Morgenthau. In my book, he ranks with Emory Buckner, John Cahill, and George Z. Medalie, the greatest U.S. attorneys ever to prosecute cases in the Mother Court.

# I, THE JURY

*Chorus of JURYMEN (advancing stealthily).*
*Oh, I was like that when a lad;*
*A shocking young scamp of a rover!*
*I behaved like a regular cad;*
*But that sort of thing is all over,*
*I'm now a respectable chap,*
*And shine with a virtue resplendent,*
*And therefore I haven't a scrap*
*Of sympathy with the defendant.*
    —**W.S. Gilbert,** *Trial by Jury*

It would be impossible to describe what goes on in the Mother Court without a word about the jury. The jury is the crown jewel of our legal system. We entrust jurors with such daunting questions as guilt or innocence, who will pay and how much, and, in some jurisdictions, even life and death. This responsibility goes not to bureaucrats, not to judges, not to elected officials, but to citizens drawn at random from the community.

Jurors are the sole triers of the fact. The word "jury" comes from the Latin *jurare*, meaning "to swear." At the outset of a trial of a criminal case, jurors in the Mother Court take the following oath:

> Do you and each of you solemnly swear that you will well and truly try and a true deliverance make between the United States and _____, the defendant at the bar, and a true verdict render according to the evidence, so help you God?

We ask jurors to decide who is telling the truth and what to make of the evidence on which they are instructed the verdict will turn. The word "verdict" comes from the Latin "to speak the truth." The judges don't tell them so, but juries are even entitled to ignore the evidence—and even the law—and reach a verdict based on their collective conscience. This is called "jury nullification." As my late great friend John Sprizzo, who later became a judge of the Mother Court, once said to me, "The jury is the last thing we have left in this country that can tell the government to go to hell."

After his appointment to the bench, John continued to pursue his obsession with jury nullification even in cases where he sat both as judge and jury. Presiding nonjury over a criminal contempt prosecution in 1995, he acquitted two Catholic prelates, an auxiliary bishop and a Franciscan friar, who had blocked the entrance to a Dobbs Ferry abortion clinic in violation of his own injunction. He partially based his decision on the ground of jury nullification, finding that the defendants' willful criminal conduct was motivated by "sincere objectively based religious conviction." The New York Civil Liberties Union called his ruling "an off-the-wall, scary decision."[1]

Who are these jurors that they deserve such power? They are ordinary citizens drawn at random from the community. What

---

1. Jan Hoffman, *Judge Acquits Abortion Protesters on Basis of Religious Beliefs*, N.Y. TIMES, Jan. 19, 1997.

special powers of judgment and discernment could they bring to the courtroom? Senatorial screening committees, bar association committees, the FBI, and of course, the press, carefully vet our federal judges. They are not chosen at random, but chosen after careful scrutiny, and everything from temperament, past writings, and political positions to their sexual peccadilloes is fair game.

But jurors take a different road to the courthouse. Ms. Jaundice and Mr. Prejudice populate the jury boxes. We know precious little about jurors' background, their education, or their walk of life. At best, we make educated guesses. Many think of them as juries of our peers. In fact, jurors are rarely the peers of those upon whom they sit in judgment.

Skepticism about the jury system abounds. We don't want jurors to read too much, lest they become biased by media commentary on their case. We don't want them to know too much either. A little learning is dangerous. The database for their decision must be found in the courtroom. Supreme Court Justice Hugo Black, who, as a former Alabama Senator, knew whereof he spoke, stated, "Legal trials are not like elections, to be won through the use of the meeting-hall, the radio, and the newspaper."[2] It now appears that Justice Black's fear that legal battles would be waged in the media was totally justified. The public's interest in high-profile cases is intense. In theory, this is a good thing. But, in reality, because media saturation infects potential jurors' independent judgment, the trier of fact may be influenced as to guilt or innocence before the trial even begins.

The jury system is as old as the dawn of the Republic. Article III, section 2 of the Constitution guarantees the right of trial by jury in criminal cases, and the Seventh Amendment to the Constitution guarantees the right of trial by jury in civil cases. Winston Churchill thought of the jury trial as one of the pillars of the "special relationship" between the United States and Great Britain.

---

2. Bridges v. California, 314 U.S. 252 (1941).

According to one of the Founding Fathers, Richard Henry Lee of Virginia, the primary purpose of the trial by jury in America was a check on the judiciary, a means to protect the public from corrupt or aristocratic judges:

> The impartial administration of justice, which secures both our persons and our properties, is the great end of civil society. But if that be entirely entrusted to the magistracy,—a select body of men, and those generally selected, by the prince, of such as enjoy the highest offices of the state,—these decisions, in spite of their own natural integrity, will have frequently an involuntary bias towards those of their own rank and dignity. It is not to be expected from human nature, that the few should always be attentive to the good of the many. . . . [E]very tribunal, selected for the decision of facts, is a step towards establishing aristocracy—the most oppressive of all governments.[3]

In the federal court, the judge may summarize the evidence and the contentions of each side. The judge's summation of the evidence is considered very carefully, as it is of great influence on the jury and may favor one side or the other.

The party having the burden of proof—the prosecutor in a criminal case, the plaintiff in a civil action—has the right to open first and close last in making arguments to the jury. In a criminal case this is particularly important because the jury retires to deliberate with the prosecutor's summation ringing in their ears.

I knew a tremendously effective prosecutor who believed the jury needed "a summation kick in the ass," and sometimes he overstepped his bounds. One such instance came during the trial of Christopher Hughes. Hughes was a hardened criminal who made his living

---

3. Letter from Richard Henry Lee to Edmond Randolph, Governor of Virginia (October 16, 1787), quoting Blackstone's Commentaries on the Jury Trial.

extorting money from homosexuals in the era when they hid in the closet. Hughes would go to the bar at Manhattan's Taft Hotel and meet a visiting businessman, preferably married and leading a secret life. Hughes, known as "the hawk," would go with the victim, known as "the chicken," to the victim's hotel room, get him in a compromising position, and steal his wallet. Hughes called the wallet the "poke," because he needed it to blackmail the victim. Weeks later, one of Hughes' confederates, usually a man named Rochford, would call on the victim at his home with the poke in hand, together with a phony New York state court warrant calling for the victim's arrest for the crime of sodomy. In those days oral and anal sex, known as acts of "deviate sexual intercourse," made out the crime of sodomy in New York—even if consummated between consenting adults. Rochford would offer to make the chicken's whole problem go away in exchange for a cash payment.

Hughes' co-conspirators testified for the government, as did the chicken, a married college professor from North Carolina. The evidence against Hughes was overwhelming. What was remarkable about the case was the prosecutor's astonishing summation:

> I said Mr. Hughes is doubly vicious because not only was he a part, and an important part of this, because his participation was needed for this play with . . . [the victim] and other plays like it that Mr. Rochford later on testified about, but he is *doubly vicious because he demanded his full constitutional rights here knowing full well he was guilty.* He demanded that we parade . . . [the victim] in here with all the embarrassment that would entail for . . . [him] for the rest of his life, perhaps.[4]

---

4. United States v. Hughes, *rev'd*, 389 F.2d 535 (2d Cir. 1968) (emphasis added).

The jury convicted Hughes, but the conviction was reversed on appeal because of the prosecutor's prejudicial summation. The appellate court reasoned correctly that there is no point in having a constitutional right to trial if the government could comment adversely about the assertion of that right:

> While the prosecutor's indignation was understandable, it was clearly improper to state that Hughes was "doubly vicious because he demanded his full constitutional rights." We cannot permit an argument that claiming any constitutional right is "vicious"; it is simply not an appropriate consideration for the jury, and yet—once called to their attention—could have great force. Moreover, allowing such comment on the exercise of a constitutional right tends to destroy it by "making its assertion costly."

The appellate judges were also critical of other aspects of the summation, in which the prosecutor referred to the members of the conspiracy as a "nasty bunch of animals":

> The courtroom reeked with the sordid nature of the scheme and the unsavory personal history of the conspirators. Resort to epithets, always undesirable, was hardly necessary for emphasis in this case.

The *Hughes* prosecutor sailed into choppy waters with his "kick in the ass" summation in another case, the federal prosecution of mobster John Gotti on racketeering charges.[5] The media dubbed Gotti the "Teflon Don" after he was acquitted three times in the state courts on various criminal charges where the proof was very

---

5. United States v. Locascio, 6 F.3d 924 (2d Cir. 1993), *cert. denied sub nom.* Gotti v. United States, 511 U.S. 1070 (1994).

strong. It later appeared that the acquittals resulted from jury tampering, or else embracery, an old English lawyer's term for bribery of a juror.

In Gotti's federal trial, the prosecutor made the following statement to the jury:

> Let me conclude with this. I want to talk about this briefly. I may be insulting some of you. I hope I'm not. If you accept the proof of what you are dealing with here, the boss of a murderous and treacherous crime family and his underboss, you would be less than human, if you didn't feel some personal concern[.]

The prosecutor was at that point interrupted by an objection, which was sustained by the trial judge. The appellate court sternly disapproved of the remarks in summation, particularly the "less than human" bit, but held it to be harmless error in the context of a lengthy trial. The Second Circuit was not about to let the "Teflon Don" get away with it again. The kick in the ass this time worked.

In civil law countries, such as Italy or France, a panel of nine lay jurors and three professional judges decides guilt or innocence. The jurors usually vote with the judges, and a majority is sufficient for a verdict.[6]

Picking a jury is said to be an art. In a federal criminal case the prosecution normally has six peremptory challenges; the defendant has ten. A peremptory challenge is defined as a challenge "exercised without a reason stated, without inquiry and without being subject to the court's control."[7] In the state courts, the lawyers question the jurors on their attitudes and qualifications, often outside the presence of the judge; in the Southern District and most federal

---

6. The recent Amanda Knox case in Perugia before such a jury has resulted in two trials, and may now involve a third. The reader will draw his own conclusion as to which system better serves the interests of justice.

7. Swain v. Alabama, 380 U.S. 202, 220 (1965).

courts, however, the judge examines the jurors based on questions submitted by counsel. The examination is called *voir dire*, from the old French "to speak the truth." The judge will probe for bias. He will normally cover the names of the parties and witnesses to see if anyone on the prospective jury has a relationship. He will then move on to attitudes about the facts in the case; attitudes about law enforcement, including whether the jurors will necessarily believe the police or the FBI; attitudes about the presumption of innocence; and whether there is any reason the person could not serve as a fair and impartial juror. The judge will also normally ask what the juror does for a living, whether he has been the victim of a crime, what his spouse, if he has one, does—all questions calculated to give the lawyers a superficial handle on who the jurors are, how intelligent they are, and how they might relate to the evidence and the witnesses who will appear at the trial. If a prospective juror gives an answer that demonstrates bias, he may be challenged for "cause." There are unlimited challenges for cause, and the judge will rule on whether the person so challenged remains on the jury. Edward Bennett Williams told me a war story about impaneling a jury in Washington. One prospective juror assured the court he could accept the presumption of innocence. "Look at him," said Williams pointing to his client, "Do you think he would be here if he were innocent?" "No sir," the juror answered. The man was excused.

Many lawyers I know are satisfied to take the first 12 individuals who are seated in the box. "Jury satisfactory to the defendant," they will proclaim with a grandiose sweep of the hand, believing that this will somehow ingratiate themselves to someone. Others are less cavalier. If the case warrants it, they will retain high-priced jury consultants to take demographics of the jury pool and impanel "focus groups" drawn from the pool to "deliberate" over the arguments while lawyers watch the "deliberations" through a one-way mirror. This is called "jury work."

When I tried a federal case in the small community of Catlettsburg, Kentucky, involving a requirements contract for blast furnace coke to be used in the manufacture of steel, we had no jury consultants. So we had to do our own form of jury work unknown in the megalopolis served by the Mother Court. My adroit friend and colleague Steve Isenberg, who had been chief of staff to Mayor John Lindsay, found out that a cross-section of the community gathered every evening at the Red Fox Lounge at the Holiday Inn in Ironton, across the Ohio River. The headliner at the Red Fox was an Elvis impersonator known as the "false Elvis." Our local lawyer assured us that women "would tear off their 'braazzeers' and throw them at the false Elvis." He wasn't far from wrong. The false Elvis, wearing a sequined leisure suit with a zipper low down the front revealing dyed blond chest hairs and a gold necklace from which hung a mystical amulet, turned out to be kind of hokey, but we did get to meet some unforgettable people and obtained valuable insights into the mentality of the people who might sit on our jury. We won the case.

Other lawyers seek clues from superficial characteristics. Observing a newspaper or magazine that the juror may have brought to court may tell a tale. A reader of the *Atlantic Monthly* is a horse of a different color from a reader of the *Daily Racing Form*. Polonius advised Laertes that the "apparel oft proclaims the man," so how someone is dressed is always a good clue.[8] An article of jewelry or a gold watch may indicate marital or economic status. Age, gender, race, religion, and ethnicity are always a factor. As the late Professor Irving Younger, a former Southern District prosecutor, said, "Why do I use these terrible social stereotypes in selecting a jury? Because there is some truth in them!"

Of course, there is always a risk in applying stereotypes. If I challenge too many women, will the remaining women be offended? If

---

8. *Hamlet*, act I, sc 3.

a prosecutor challenges too many African Americans or Asians or women, he will run afoul of the *Batson* case holding that such a pattern and practice is unconstitutional.[9] If I challenge someone who appears to be too smart or too stupid, am I losing a potential vote? Mostly, lawyers look for jurors whom they feel an empathy with or, more importantly, who seem to have empathy with their client's cause, someone they can sit down and reason with.

If my case is clear, I prefer a homogenous, compatible jury that is likely to reach agreement. If my case is weak, will I want a heterogeneous jury that is likely to disagree? As Professor Younger was fond of saying, "What's the right answer? There is no right answer. It's only important to think about the problem."

In a criminal case, a verdict must be unanimous, not just a consensus, not a majority, but guilt must be established to the satisfaction of each and every juror to a moral certainty beyond a reasonable doubt. Not established beyond all possible doubt, but beyond a reasonable doubt—the doubt that would make one hesitate before taking action. A verdict of acquittal must also be unanimous. If there are holdouts, even one holdout, there is no verdict, and the jury is "hung."

Fraudster John DeLorean had already been acquitted of drug charges in California when he stood trial in Detroit for criminal tax fraud. The Detroit case involved DeLorean's theft of some $12.5 million from an automobile project in Northern Ireland. After deliberating for some time, the jury sent back a note asking whether they must acquit if they couldn't agree on conviction. Instead of answering no, the newly appointed judge told them that he might have the reporter read back the portions of his boilerplate charge

---

9. In *Batson v. Kentucky*, 476 U.S. 79 (1986), the Supreme Court held unconstitutional the use of peremptory challenges to remove jurors based solely on their race. The *Batson* ruling may be extended to persons from other cognizable groups based on the group characteristic (e.g., ethnicity, gender, or religion).

relating to the verdict. The jury soon announced a verdict of acquittal. The judge then invited the jurors, the press, the lawyers, and DeLorean to his robing room for a reception celebrating the end of a long trial. One of the jurors inquired, "Your Honor, what's a hung jury?" The judge answered, "That's when the jury can't agree." The juror said, "Judge, we were a hung jury. Your Honor told us that if we were not unanimous for conviction, we had to acquit." The judge's jaw dropped. It was too late to do anything about it. DeLorean led a charmed life as far as criminal prosecutions were concerned.

In a criminal case, a jury disagreement may require a retrial. A hung jury frequently, but not always, benefits a defendant. The prosecutor may decide to drop the case after a jury disagreement, as in the recent trial of former presidential hopeful John Edwards. He may feel with some justification that the retrial is a waste of prosecutorial resources, or that it will have the appearance of a vendetta. If there is a retrial, the defendant has obtained additional ammunition—a preview of the government's case, and another iteration of the witnesses' testimony, all of which he can use for impeachment to contradict. This can be a matter of great advantage.

When jurors are deadlocked, the judge may decide to give them an *Allen* or "dynamite" charge.[10] This, in substance, instructs the jury not to yield their conscientiously held views, but to reexamine them in light of what other jurors have concluded, thus arguably inviting holdouts to yield to the view of the majority. The *Allen* charge is controversial, particularly in a criminal case where the majority of the jury may favor conviction.

In the corruption case of Keogh and Kahaner, which we will discuss at greater length in Chapter 9, Judge Weinfeld gave the jury a modified *Allen* charge.[11] After a month-long trial, the jury began

---

10. Allen v. United States, 164 U.S. 492, 501 (1896).
11. United States v. Kahaner, cited in 317 F.2d 459 (2d Cir. 1963).

their deliberations at 3:50 pm on Thursday, June 14, 1962. Late in the evening of Friday, June 15, the foreman sent a note to the court, which read: "We find it impossible to come to an agreement." Judge Weinfeld reconvened them and referred to the foreman's note as expressing a "desire to discontinue your efforts." He said, "It is desirable if a verdict can be reached that this be done both from the viewpoint of the defendants and the government," but that this was true only if the verdict "reflects the conscientious judgment of each juror and under no circumstance must any juror yield his conscientious judgment." He noted, "This Court has no purpose to ask and indeed does not have the right to inquire as to how you stand. But considering the length of the trial, the amount of testimony that was taken, the number of witnesses that have been heard, further consideration on your part is fully justified." The judge said in amplification that, considering the time devoted to the reading of testimony and to meals, "you really have not spent more than eight or nine hours in actual deliberations, and I do not consider that a sufficient time to have elapsed to permit you a full and fair opportunity not only to review the evidence but to discuss and consider amongst yourselves the various phases of the evidence." Judge Weinfeld then gave the *Allen* charge in the language of the Supreme Court case:

[A]lthough the verdict must be the verdict of each individual juror, and not a mere acquiescence in the conclusion of his fellows, yet they should examine the question submitted with candor, and with a proper regard and deference to the opinions of each other; that it was their duty to decide the case if they could conscientiously do so; that they should listen, with a disposition to be convinced, to each other's arguments; that, if much the larger number were for conviction, a dissenting juror should consider whether his doubt was a reasonable one which made no impression upon the minds of so many men, equally honest, equally intelligent with himself. If, on the other hand, the majority were for acquittal, the minority ought to ask themselves whether they might not reasonably doubt the correctness of a judgment which was not concurred in by the majority.

Weinfeld then concluded, "It has been a long trial and a trial, as I say, where I am satisfied each side prefers finality of judgment if it can be obtained on the basis of a conscientious reflection of each juror's final vote."

He again stressed that "if any individual juror still retains a conscientious view that differs from that of other jurors, . . . you are not to yield your judgment simply because you may be outnumbered or outweighed."

The next evening, 24 hours after they had announced they found it "impossible to come to an agreement," the jury returned a verdict of conviction against all defendants. Weinfeld's modified *Allen* charge was affirmed on appeal.[12]

I once had a long civil trial in the Southern District, an action seeking millions in damages for securities fraud. On the voir dire, the judge permitted the lawyers briefly to explain the issues to the panel. One prospective juror said to the judge, "Your Honor, I can't serve. I am a janitor in a school. I listen to these lawyers talking, and I don't understand half of what they are saying. They talk about a lot of reading heavy documents. I don't think I will understand them. I want to do my duty, but I don't think I can help." "Don't belittle yourself," the judge thundered. "You are a worthy citizen, what America is all about. You will make an excellent juror." The defense later exercised one of its peremptory challenges and excused him.

---

12. United States v. Kahaner, *supra*.

Defense lawyers worry that in a long trial with voluminous documentary evidence, intellectually challenged jurors may go for the plaintiff because they feel that there wouldn't be so many lawyers taking so much time over so many documents if there weren't something to the case. They also worry that the jury may hold it against the defense, which mounts its case second, for delaying the trial and keeping them there when they want to go home.

Trial by jury is a constitutional right in most federal civil cases, where the relief sought is money damages. The Seventh Amendment to the Constitution provides the following:

> In Suits at common law, where the value in controversy shall exceed twenty dollars, the right of trial by jury shall be preserved, and no fact tried by a jury, shall be otherwise re-examined in any Court of the United States, than according to the rules of the common law.

England, birthplace of the jury system, has effectively abolished the jury in almost all civil cases.[13] Defendants' lawyers frequently argue that in many civil commercial cases, the issues are too complex to be understood by the jury, so the issues should be tried to the bench.

They have had varying success. Some courts have perceived a "complexity exception" to the Seventh Amendment. District courts have stricken jury requests in civil cases, such as patent, antitrust, or complicated commercial cases, where the complexity and technical nature of the factual issues presented, and the massiveness of the case as a whole, have led them to doubt a jury's competence to render an

---

13. The first English jury trial took place in the court of Henry II in 1168. England does afford a jury trial in a civil action for fraud, slander, malicious prosecution, or false imprisonment unless the court is of the opinion that the trial requires any prolonged examination of documents or accounts or any scientific issue, which cannot conveniently be tried to a jury.

intelligent verdict.[14] The precedent established by these cases presents a tempting model to trial judges wishing to avoid supervising jury trials in protracted civil suits, and therefore threatens to carve out a dramatic departure from the Seventh Amendment's jury trial guarantee. Most courts, however, including the Southern District, have refused to go so far in sweeping aside such a basic constitutional right as trial by jury. Instead, judges try to address the problem by allowing jurors to keep trial notes, which are collected at the end of the court day. They reason that most judges and many lawyers keep contemporaneous trial notes, so why not the jury?

Jurors are expected to draw on their experience in their daily lives, their common sense, and their "subtle intuitions."[15] They are supposed to base their determinations on the evidence they hear in the courtroom, not on passion or prejudice. We have few means of measuring their common sense, and no way of telling whether they have left their common sense at the courtroom door. Yet, somehow, the system works.

I have great respect for jury verdicts. Churchill famously said: "Democracy is the worst form of government, except for all those other forms that have been tried from time to time." So let it be with the jury system.

---

14. *See, e.g.,* ILC Peripherals Leasing Corp. v. Int'l Bus. Machs. Corp., 458 F. Supp. 423 (N.D. Cal. 1978); Bernstein v. Universal Pictures, Inc., 79 F.R.D. 59 (S.D.N.Y. 1978); *In re* U.S. Fin. Sec. Litig., 75 F.R.D. 702 (S.D. Cal. 1977); *In re* Boise Cascade Sec. Litig., 420 F. Supp. 99 (W.D. Wash. 1976).

15. Holmes famously said of judicial decision making, "General propositions do not decide concrete cases. The decision will depend on a judgment or *intuition more subtle than any articulate major premise*." Lochner v. New York, 198 U.S. 45 (1905) (Holmes, J., dissenting) (emphasis added).

# 4

# THE LOST ART OF CROSS-EXAMINATION

*If you confront anyone who has lied with the truth, he will usually admit it—often out of sheer surprise. It is only necessary to guess right to produce your effect.*

—Agatha Christie, *Murder on the Orient Express*

To my mind, cross-examination is the crowning glory of our trial system. It is the climacteric of the proceeding. If the truth will out at all, it is through probing, pressing cross. Most of the cross-examinations I saw in the courthouse were quite mediocre. Counsel either led the witness to repeat what he had said on direct examination, thereby reinforcing the direct testimony, or produced some unexpectedly unfavorable answer that ruined his case. I was determined to conduct effective cross-examinations. For the most part, I succeeded.

One avenue of attack in cross-examination is to show bias. An example appears in Albert Osborn's classic work, *The Mind of the Juror*:

**Q:** Mrs. Smith, you are not an intimate friend of Mrs. Brown, against whose interest you have testified here, are you?

**A:** No. I am not.

**Q:** And you are a friend of Mrs. Robinson, for whom you have just testified here?

**A:** Mrs. Robinson is a very dear friend of mine.

**Q:** It gives you pleasure, does it not, to do a kindness for Mrs. Robinson?

**A:** It certainly does.

**Q:** And you are not restrained from doing a kindness for Mrs. Robinson when the act at the same time is unkindness to Mrs. Brown?

**A:** No, I am not.

**Q:** That's all, Mrs. Smith.

The manner and style of the cross-examination is key. If, eloquence is not misplaced in the courtroom, neither is drama. The lawyer must be a bit of a thespian, play-acting as though he is learning new facts for the first time that, in reality, he knew all along. Tempo and rhythm are essential ingredients in the mix. A soft and slow approach establishes a rapport with the witness so better to sink the harpoon. Regardless of whether slow or staccato, the questioning must command the jury's interest. Their thoughts provoked, the jury is intrigued and wants to learn along with the advocate who feigns ignorance until he plunges his forensic sword into the transparent breastplate of the falsity to expose the heart of the truth.

Peter Fleming was as fine a trial lawyer and cross-examiner as any I saw. He was amazing; he really knew how to do it; and there was no one better in our office. Peter gave me some great pointers on cross-examination. His basic advice was to read the transcripts of great cross-examinations. Lawyers live on precedent, and cross-examination is no exception. Rein in the witness tight; ask leading questions that you know the answers to, and insist on yes or no answers. "Just because it's called 'cross-examination,'" he counseled, "doesn't mean you have to cross-examine crossly." Read Wellman's classic *The Art of Cross-Examination*, originally published in 1903. Establish a rhythm with the witness so that the answer to a question leads you to the next question. Always hold back something for cross. "Try your case thin. Don't put everything you have into your case-in-chief, thereby showing your hand." Peter said, "the defendant will probably take the stand, and then you've got to hurt him." Great advice followed by prosecutors to this day.

Peter's cardinal rule, known to every trial lawyer, is *never* to ask a question of a witness, particularly a hostile witness, unless you either already know the answer or you don't care what the answer is. Know when to stop. If you get a favorable answer, quit while you're ahead; don't give him a chance to wiggle off the hook. As celebrated lawyer-turned-author Louis Nizer once said, "In cross examination, as in fishing, nothing is more ungainly than a fisherman pulled into the water by his catch."

Sometimes though, you have to fish. One example is when the examiner seeks to uncover some physical infirmity of the witness. There is the classic story of the old lady who testified she was an eyewitness to an accident. The defense lawyer didn't have much to go on, so he tread lightly:

Q: I see, Mrs. Kelly, that you are wearing glasses today, very becoming?

A: Yes. Thank you.

Q: Do you wear them for distance or for reading?

A: Both. Blind without them.

Q: Blind without them?

A: Yes.

Q: Of course, you were wearing them when you saw the accident?

A: I don't recall.

Q: Blind without them, and you don't recall? No further questions.

I prosecuted a state senator in the Southern District for lying to the grand jury about a bribe he received. He testified that he was given the money as a campaign contribution, but that he had returned it to the donor. Perjury, as Richard Nixon observed, is a hard crime to prove. One of my witnesses, an old coot of a man, testified that he had handed the senator $5,000 in cash in "fifties and hundreds" in behalf of a company seeking favorable legislation, and, to his knowledge, the money had not been returned. He testified that the senator asked him to lie to the grand jury about the payment, and say that the money had been returned. A bank teller who testified she recalled the senator depositing $5,000 in cash in his personal bank account two days after the money was paid corroborated the testimony. The denominations, she recalled, were "fifties and hundreds." The bank had dunned the senator over a personal loan, and he directed that the $5,000 be applied to pay down the debt.

Defense counsel's cross-examination of the elderly gentleman went something like this:

Q: You say you met with my client on September 25?

A: Yes sir.

Q: [In a loud voice] Didn't you hear him tell you he had given the money back?

A: No sir, I didn't hear him say that.

Q: [In a conversational tone, looking at the jury] Are you hard of hearing?

A: What did you say?

THE COURT: I think you made your point.

The cross didn't prove much, but managed to make the jury scratch their collective heads.

The rule about knowing the answer is often more honored in the breach than in the observance. Not every trial lawyer is mindful of this rule, and some get away with it. Maurice Edelbaum, who unsuccessfully defended Carmine DeSapio on conspiracy charges, was a big winner at the craps tables of Las Vegas. Edelbaum would often take a chance when he questioned a witness. Sometimes he won, and sometimes he crapped out. When he won, he would wave his clenched right fist as though he had rolled a big winner, something like a sixth-grade teacher shaking the chalk in his hand after writing on the blackboard. When he lost, he would look at the jury as if to say, "Just as I thought."

The rule is illustrated in Wellman's *Art of Cross-Examination* by what happened in an old British case where the plaintiff sued the defendant for biting off his ear—the type of very brutal assault committed in the ring many years later by the boxer Mike Tyson. The defense was, "I didn't do it."

A witness to the assault was on cross-examination:

Q: You testified on direct examination that you didn't see my client bite his ear off? [Good question! Always good to repeat on cross something favorable that came out on direct.]

A: Yes sir. [Now is the time to say "no further questions," and argue to the jury he really didn't see anything relevant. But the lawyer just had to ask a question that he didn't know the answer to.]

Q: What did you see?

A: I saw him spit it out.

Often, the rule is violated by a "why" question. A "why" question is most often objectionable because it argues with the witness.

Q: Did you go out of town?
A: Yes.
Q: Why did you do a thing like that?

But it is even more undesirable because it turns the witness on full throttle, allows him to say whatever is on his mind or whatever comes into his head. As illustrated by this old chestnut:

Q: What was the first thing your husband said to you that morning?
A: He said, 'Where am I, Cathy?'
Q: And why did that upset you?
A: My name is Susan!

When this happens, the only thing the unfortunate lawyer can do is take the advice of the old English barrister: "Go home, cut your throat, and when you meet your client in hell, beg his pardon."

Lawyers, even brilliant lawyers, often seem to forget this rule. Arthur Liman, a former Assistant U.S. Attorney for the Southern District of New York, was counsel for the Senate committee investigating the Iran-Contra affair. The witness was the villain of the piece, Colonel Oliver North, and millions closely followed the duel on national television.

Q: Colonel North, was the day Iran/Contra unraveled the worst day of your life? [What, conceivably, was the wily Colonel North going to say?]
A: No, Mr. Liman, the worst day was in Viet Nam when I was in a foxhole with my best friend, and the Viet Cong threw a grenade into the foxhole, and my friend threw himself on top of it and saved my life. My best friend died. That was the worst day of my life.

North turned the entire hearing around with that devastating answer. The senators' mail began to run heavily against Liman, and even more heavily in favor of North. He captured the sympathies of the nation. Liman was as smart a lawyer as I ever saw in a courtroom, but he had failed to control a hostile witness by asking a question he didn't know the answer to.

Another example of a derailed cross-examination occurred during the 1980 Southern District trial of Italian financier Michele Sidona on a host of bank fraud charges in the scandal involving Franklin National Bank in New York, the largest bank failure in U.S. history.

Sindona's lawyer was former Southern District judge Marvin Frankel, who had resigned from the bench only two years before the trial.

The star witness for the prosecution, led by John J. Kenney, a terrific trial lawyer, was a Sindona associate, Carlo Bordoni, who had testified for four days to Sindona's complicity in numerous instances of fraud. Frankel brought out on cross that Bordoni had publicly stated he "could have killed" Sindona. Frankel was here attempting to show bias and hatred on the part of the witness toward Sindona, and he should have stopped there. But, when Bordoni asked if he might elaborate the basis for his hatred, Frankel amazingly assented, and totally lost control of the witness.

"Michele Sindona tried to rape my wife," explained Bordoni. "It was a human reaction." There was stunned silence in the courtroom. The forelady on the jury burst into tears. Frankel's cross-examination of Bordoni had blown up in his face.

Sindona was convicted of 65 counts of conspiracy, fraud, false bank statements, and perjury, and Judge Thomas Griesa sentenced him to 25 years in jail.

Reed Brodsky is a fine young Southern District prosecutor who was trying Rajat Gupta on charges of insider trading conspiracy. Gupta, a former director of Goldman Sachs, was accused of tipping off his pal, Raj Rajaratnam, to confidential boardroom information so Rajaratnam could make profit on Goldman stock before the news hit the broad tape. On the defense case, Gupta called his daughter, a smart Harvard Law School lawyer, to testify that her father had had a falling out with Raj over a lost $10 million investment in a Raj fund and would have no reason to tip him off. She testified that after this episode, her father was "depressed, withdrawn and not himself." Juries understand that daughters want to help their fathers, so it would have been a good time for Brodsky to say "Your Honor, no cross."

Instead, moving close to the witness and melodramatically speaking in hushed tones, Brodsky went for the jugular:

Q: Do you love your father?" [Not a bad question, the answer is obvious.]

A: Yes. [Good time to stop, Reed, please, please sit down.]

Q: Would you do anything for your father? [Terrible question. Much better to ask, if you must, "You do not want to see him convicted by this jury, do you?]

A: I would do anything for my father, but I would not lie, though, on the stand. [A disaster.]

Disaster was not irretrievable, however. Brodsky went on to win the case.

Brodsky should have heeded the example of many great trial lawyers who choose not to cross-examine when they see they cannot score points.

Another approach to the dilemma is illustrated by the strange case of Alger Hiss, which I deal with in Chapter 5. Hiss's brother, Donald, flatly denied Whittaker Chambers's allegation that he, Donald, had been a member of a Communist apparatus. Prosecutor Thomas Murphy had nothing to contradict Donald with. So he asked a few well-chosen questions, shrugged his large shoulders, and sat down, as though to say, "I think you're lying, but I can't prove it."

Cross-examination is a terrific way of testing the assertions of a witness. Wellman has the classic story of the good doctor in Chicago who had given damaging testimony. The wonderfully imaginative opposing counsel had no ammunition to attack the doctor or his testimony, so the cross-examination went like this:

> Q: Doctor, you say you are a practicing physician. Have you practiced your profession in the City of Chicago for any length of time?
>
> A: Yes. I have been in practice here in Chicago for about 40 years.
>
> Q: Well, doctor, during that time you must have had occasion to treat some of our most prominent citizens, have you not?
>
> A: Yes. I think I have.
>
> Q: By any chance were you called as the family physician to the elder Marshall Field?
>
> A: Yes. I was his family physician for a number of years.
>
> Q: By the way, where is Mr. Field today?
>
> A: He is dead.
>
> Q: Terribly sorry. Were you the family physician of Colonel McCormick?
>
> A: Yes, also for many years.
>
> Q: Where is he, today?
>
> A: He is dead.

The lawyer went on to ask about eight or ten other prominent patients of the doctor who were now deceased. The jury smiled. The point was driven home.

One classic example of a great cross is the 1881 cross-examination of Charles J. Guiteau, the assassin of President James Garfield. Guiteau, a disgruntled office-seeker, admitted to the murder but claimed that he had been inspired by a divine command to commit the act. The defense was "moral insanity." Garfield was a Republican; Guiteau had written a speech that he thought was responsible for Garfield's election victory; Guiteau wanted to be appointed ambassador to France; and the Garfield administration had rejected his application.

Wellman argues that the cross-examination of Guiteau by John K. Porter "is often spoken of as one of the great masterpieces of forensic skill." Porter's cross bristled with sarcasm.

Q: You intended to kill him?

A: I thought the Deity and I had done it, sir.

Q: Who bought the pistol, the Deity or you?

A: I say the Deity inspired the act, and the Deity will take care of it.

Q: Who bought the pistol, the Deity or you?

A: The Deity furnished the money by which I bought it as the agent for the Deity.

. . .

Q: Did Mr. Maynard lend you the money?

A: He loaned me $15—yes sir, and I used $10 to buy the pistol.

Q: Were you inspired to borrow the $15 of Mr. Maynard?

A: It was of no consequence whether I got it from him or somebody else.

. . .

Q: Did you believe it was the will of God that you should murder him?

A: I believe it was the will of God that he should be removed, and that I was the approved agent to do it.

Q: Did he give you the commission in writing?

A: No sir.

Q: Did he give it in an audible tone of voice?

A: He gave it to me by his pressure on me.

Q: Did he give it to you in a vision in the night?

A: I don't get my inspirations that way.

. . .

**Q:** Did the Republican party ever give you an office?

**A:** I never held any kind of political office in my life and never drew one cent from the government.

**Q:** And you never desired an office, did you?

**A:** I had some thought about the Paris consulship. That is the only time I ever had any serious thought about it.

**Q:** That was the one which resulted in the inspiration, wasn't it?

**A:** No sir, most certainly not. My getting it or not getting it had no relation to my duty to God and the American people.

What a marvelous art form cross-examination is! You probe and press and pry and try to make points you can use in summation, all the while wary of the booby traps and mine fields in your path. If there's a better way to do it, no one has invented it. If there is any substitute for relentless cross-examination in bringing out the truth, I never heard of it.

# 5

# U.S. V. US: THE RED SCARE

*All this means . . . that freedom of speech and thought should reign; that courts of justice, independent of the executive, unbiased by any party, should administer laws which have received the broad assent of large majorities or are consecrated by time and custom. Here are the title deeds of freedom which should lie in every cottage home. Here is the message of the British and American peoples to mankind. Let us preach what we practice—let us practice what we preach.*
**—Winston Churchill, "Iron Curtain Speech," March 5, 1946**

The Mother Court was inevitably drawn into the epicenter of the "Red Scare," which engulfed the country in the decade or so following World War II. As the U.S. government knew in the 1940s and 1950s, there was a serious internal threat to our national security. The threat came from cells of Communist spies attempting to ferret out military and industrial secrets, even atomic secrets, and transmit them to the Soviet Union. Our obsession with the

Communist threat, and our efforts to deal with it, challenged our most basic constitutional right of free political expression.

As Justice Holmes most famously expressed it:

> [I]f there is any principle of the Constitution that more impera-
> tively calls for attachment than any other it is the principle of free
> thought—not free thought for those who agree with us but *freedom
> for the thought that we hate.*[1]

What the mood and temper of the public failed to understand in all the wartime hysteria was the crucial distinction between Soviet spies who truly threatened the country, and Americans who were sympathetic to the Communist ideology, including leaders of the open Communist Party, who presented no serious threat to the United States. Just as some failed to understand in the hysteria that followed 9/11 that not all Muslims were terrorists, even if all (or most) of the terrorists appeared to be Muslims, we failed to grasp that not all the Communists were spies even though the spies were dedicated Communist apparatchiks, working for the Soviet Union.[2] Communist Party members, present or past, became enemies of the people. Guilt by association is supposed to be alien to our laws, our freedoms, and our way of life. As a Mother Court judge charged the jury in a thoroughly litigated criminal case:

> Mere association without more, is not proof of participation in a con-
> spiracy. If a person associates himself with people who are not person-
> ally acceptable to you, you may not draw any adverse inference merely

---

1. United States v. Schwimmer, 279 U.S. 644 (1929) (emphasis added).
2. Some of those who spied for the Soviet Union were idealists who believed in the Soviet system and that the Soviets, who were wartime allies, should be on an equal footing with the United States. Others doubtless did it for money.

from that association. His guilt or innocence must be determined on the basis of his own acts.[3]

Nevertheless, "un-American activities" committees in Congress were quick to stigmatize Communist sympathizers, "pinkos," liberals, and those with Communist-leaning friends. Alleged spies were put on trial, as well they should have been. Some, however, were guilty of no more than harboring Communist beliefs or associating with others who did. Suspicion and hysteria reigned supreme and even infected the administration of justice.

Making the bright-line distinction between spies and political dissenters, the outstanding English jurist the Earl Jowitt, writing in 1953, cautioned against such hysteria:

> Let me admit that I have no sympathy whatever with the communist ideology so far as I understand it. Indeed, it seems to me that the "cold war" which is now being waged between the democratic way of life and Communism is in reality a contest between a wide idealism and a narrow materialism; between the concept of man as creature made in the image of God and the concept of man as a soulless creature destined merely to perform those tasks which are allotted to him. The due administration of justice is, I believe, the foundation on which our democratic system rests. We must take care if we are to be true to our ideals (and we shall not win the "cold war" unless we do remain true to our ideals), that no individual becomes a scapegoat for the sins of society. It is fitting that we should cleanse the Augean stable, but in so doing we must beware of inflicting injury on any innocent occupant of the stable.[4]

---

3. The Court of Appeals affirmed the district court's charge. United States v. Birnbaum, 373 F.2d 250, 261 (2d Cir. 1967).

4. THE STRANGE CASE OF ALGER HISS (1953).

The three cases I examine here, those of the Communist Party leaders, Alger Hiss, and the Rosenbergs, were all tried in the Mother Court at a time when it was popularly believed that Soviet Communism posed the most serious threat to the American Republic. The overwhelming majority of Americans detested Communists and Communist ideology. Thus, evidence of Communist Party membership or preference for the Soviet economic system was damning. It also could be terribly relevant as bearing on a motive to spy for the Soviets.

American civil liberties have never fared well in times of national emergency. Lincoln suspended the writ of habeas corpus during the Civil War. Roosevelt interned the Japanese during World War II, and the Supreme Court upheld his action 6–3.[5] George W. Bush evidently believed that his "war on terror" justified torture, secret surveillance of citizens, and imprisonment without hearing in Guantanamo.

The 1950s were a turbulent time for Americans. Hollywood studios blacklisted talented film writers, actors, and producers for their political beliefs. Those blacklisted could not find employment that had always been theirs. Publishers rejected books by prominent authors on ideological grounds. Investigators probed personal associations. People lost jobs. Those who refused to answer questions were jailed, even when the refusal was based on constitutional grounds. Some even committed suicide.

Friends betrayed friends who had done nothing more than been members of the Communist Party. In 1963, actor Sterling Hayden declared, "I was a rat, a stoolie, and the names I named of those close friends were blacklisted and deprived of their livelihood."

Playwright Clifford Odets occupies a special place in theatrical history. Critics have compared him to Eugene O'Neill, Tennessee

---

5. Korematsu v. United States, 323 U.S. 214 (1944).

Williams, and Arthur Miller as a luminary of the American theater. The author of such greats as *Waiting for Lefty* and *Golden Boy*, Odets created stage drama with a distinctively American idiom expressing an urban articulation. In this sense, he was a true pioneer, and his plays, which focused on the human cost of the harsh, exploitative economic conditions of the Great Depression, are a lasting legacy. Playwright Paddy Chayefsky, who vied with Odets for critical acclaim, said, "There isn't a writer of my generation, especially a New York writer, who doesn't owe his very breath—his entire attitude toward theater—to Odets."

In May 1952, Odets appeared before the House Committee on Un-American Activities (HUAC). He had been a member of the Communist Party for less than a year nearly 20 years before, between 1934 and 1935. He freely answered the committee's questions, repeating the names of Communist Party members he knew had been previously "outed" to the committee by his friend Elia Kazan.

Odets' cooperation prevented his blacklisting, but reactions to his testimony set him off course. He did not consider himself a stool pigeon, but the artistic community thought he was. Ostracized by his friends, he became a tormented man. His productivity disappeared after 1952. The HUAC episode had scarred his soul.

The politically charged prosecutions involved Communists, past and present. And it was the Communists, ironically enough, who limned the boundaries of our constitutional rights. Never before had there been a greater test of American values of free expression. The Mother Court was at the epicenter.

## THE SMITH ACT CASES

The Smith Act was the popular name for the Alien Registration Act of 1940, a measure intended to root out "fifth columnists" from a country at war. The statute was named after its sponsor,

Representative Howard W. Smith of Virginia, a Democrat, who led the antilabor bloc in Congress. The Smith Act criminalized the teaching or advocacy of the overthrow of the government "by force or violence." The prohibitions of the Smith Act extended to organizing "any society, group or assembly" devoted to revolution or being a member of such a group. Roughly 215 people, transcending the entire ideological spectrum, were indicted for violations of the Smith Act, including Communists, Trotskyites, Socialist Workers, Teamsters Union members, and Fascists. Most of the prosecutions violated basic First Amendment freedoms.

In the 1940s, the U.S. government, in conjunction with British intelligence, successfully decrypted Soviet cables confirming the existence of the World War II spy network. The decryption program, known as Venona, established that Soviet agents used certain American Communists to obtain and transmit classified information.

For reasons that remain unclear, the government chose to prosecute the Communist leaders not for instances of promoting espionage, but for violation of the Smith Act. Thus, the political prosecution was conceived and carried out. In his great book, *Freedom for the Thought That We Hate: A Biography of the First Amendment*, Anthony Lewis suggests that "the intended goal of FBI Director J. Edgar Hoover [was] to send the message to the country, 'Engage in unpopular political thought at your own risk.'" By today's standards, the Smith Act indictment smacks of Kafka in its ambiguity.

In 1949, 11 Communist Party leaders came to trial in the Southern District, indicted under the Smith Act for conspiring "to teach and advocate the overthrow and destruction of the Government of the United States by force and violence." The government did not charge the leaders with actually attempting the overthrow or conspiring to accomplish it, but only with conspiring to advocate it, to organize as the Communist Party, and willfully to advocate and teach the principles of Marxism-Leninism.

Justice Oliver Wendell Holmes famously set the essential legal test in the 1919 case of *Schenck v. United States* that political speech was protected by the First Amendment unless there was a "clear and present danger" that such action would lead to violence, a condition that Congress was empowered to legislate against. As Holmes put it,

> The most stringent protection of free speech would not protect a man in *falsely shouting fire in a theatre and causing a panic.* The question in every case is whether the words used are used in such circumstances and are of such a nature as to create a *clear and present danger* that they will bring about the substantive evils that Congress has a right to prevent. [6]

## THE TRIAL OF THE COMMUNIST LEADERS

The case of the 11 Communist leaders, known as *United States v. Dennis,* proceeded before Southern District Judge Harold Medina. The trial took almost a year to complete, making it the longest criminal trial in the history of the Mother Court until the "Pizza Connection" case set a new record in 1985.

Before taking the bench, Harold Medina enjoyed a lucrative career as a lawyer in private practice. A legal scholar, he was renowned as a teacher of law, and famously lectured a bar review course in which

---

6. 249 U.S. 47 (1919). All emphasis in quoted material is mine. Justice Douglas believed that Holmes's formulation presented only the narrowest exception to the rule that free speech may not be abridged. Douglas called the fire in the theater example one in which "speech is brigaded with action." In the view of Justices Douglas and Black, this was probably the only sort of case in which a person could be prosecuted for speech.

he had coached almost 40,000 students at $35 a pop. My father took Medina's course in the 1930s, and Medina was so colorful that my father took my mother to audit his lectures. Harold Medina loved young lawyers. His advice to them was succinct and sensible: "If you want to become a trial lawyer, apprentice yourself to a great trial lawyer, and carry his bag." After all, it is an art form.

When Medina went on the Southern District bench in 1947, he was making $100,000 a year in private practice; as a judge, he would earn $15,000. "I've made plenty of money," he said at the time of his appointment. "Now I'd like to do something for my country. I guess the best thing I have to contribute is law."

Advocating and teaching the principles of Marx and Lenin came within the criminalizing language of the Smith Act, namely, "overthrowing and destroying the government of the United States by force and violence." The Communist Party leaders were also accused of conspiring to "publish and circulate books, articles, magazines, and newspapers advocating the principles of Marxism-Leninism," including the *Communist Manifesto*, Lenin's *State and Revolution*, and Stalin's *Foundation of Leninism*, documents that were introduced as evidence for the prosecution.

The trial of the 11 defendants lasted ten months, consumed 16,000 pages of trial transcript, and was a donnybrook. The conduct of the defense lawyers was an abomination. The lawyers baited the judge and tried wherever they could to disrupt and delay the proceedings. They breached the most fundamental conceptions of courtroom decorum, but Medina had the patience of a saint, and never lost control.

"You scratched your head and pulled your ear," one of the lawyers said to Medina, trying to establish that Judge Medina was unduly dismissive of a defense argument. "You've called me corrupt and everything else you could think up," replied the judge. "I want you gentlemen to understand that when I scratch my head I'm just plain scratching my head."

Every day at 11:20 a.m. and 3:20 p.m., another defense lawyer accused the judge of lying. When the judge asked why the same time every day, the lawyer responded, "That is the deadline for the morning and afternoon editions [of the local papers]."

"You have a terrible mind to make an accusation of that kind," said the judge, "but you will not goad me into making any statements which will create errors in this courtroom." He ruled his courtroom with an iron hand.

At the trial's conclusion the jury returned a guilty verdict against all 11 defendants, and Judge Medina sentenced ten of them to five years' imprisonment and substantial fines. The 11th defendant, Robert G. Thompson, a distinguished hero of World War II, was sentenced to three years in consideration of his military record.

The Second Circuit affirmed the convictions, with Judge Learned Hand diluting Holmes'"clear and present danger" test. Hand interpreted the test to be "whether the gravity of the 'evil,' discounted by its improbability, justifies such invasion of free speech as is necessary to avoid the danger." Hand had first enunciated this standard as a Southern District trial judge in a case involving *The Masses*, an innovative magazine of socialist politics, which the Postmaster General sought to bar from the mails for obstructing conscription during World War I. His reformulation of "clear and present danger" at that time never caught on.

In *Dennis*, the Supreme Court, by a 6–2 vote, affirmed the conviction of the Communist leaders.[7] In so doing, the Court adopted the Hand standard first hatched in the Mother Court, stating that "it is as succinct and inclusive as any other we might devise at this time. It

---

7. Dennis v. United States, 341 U.S. 494 (1951).

takes into consideration those factors which we deem relevant, and relates their significances. More we cannot expect from words."

As a grace note to the trial, all of the five defense attorneys, including future Congressman George W. Crockett, were cited for contempt of court and given prison sentences. Their convictions were upheld on appeal.

As noted, the conduct of the defense lawyers in Judge Medina's courtroom was abominable. Judge Jerome Frank, an outspoken libertarian sitting in the Second Circuit, did not like to hold lawyers in contempt. He declared, however, in deploring their obstructive conduct, that he would affirm

> only because of the lawyers' outrageous conduct—conduct of a kind which no lawyer owes his client, which cannot ever be justified, and which was never employed by those advocates, for minorities or for the unpopular, whose courage has made lawyerdom proud.[8]

The case was an acid test for First Amendment liberties, and the courts sadly came down on the side of the government repressing the individual. *Dennis* watered down Holmes's "clear and present danger" test so the government could suppress political ideas that could not conceivably lead to its imminent overthrow.

In a blistering dissent, Justice Black referred to the hysteria of the times:

> Public opinion being what it is now, few will protest the conviction of these Communist petitioners. There is hope, however, that in calmer times, when present pressures, passions and fears subside, this or some later Court will restore the First Amendment liberties to the high preferred place where they belong in a free society.[9]

---

8. United States v. Sacher, 182 F.2d 416, 545 (2d Cir. 1950).
9. *Dennis*, 341 U.S. 494 (Black, J., dissenting).

Justice Black was right. Six years later, in 1957, the Court in *Yates v. United States*[10] restricted the holding in *Dennis*. Yates held that the Smith Act did not prohibit advocacy of forcible overthrow of the government without showing more. While *Yates* did not overrule *Dennis*, it rendered the broad conspiracy provisions of the Smith Act unenforceable. Finally, the 1969 landmark case *Brandenburg v. Ohio*[11] did away with *Dennis's* central holding, and struck down Ohio's criminal syndicalism law, positing that "mere advocacy" of any doctrine, including one that assumed the necessity of violence or law violation, was per se protected speech. The Court defined constitutionally unprotected speech to have a temporal element, namely incitement to "imminent lawless action." Under this test, the convictions of the Smith Act defendants would doubtless have been reversed.

The earlier views of Justice Brandeis were now vindicated. As he famously saw it, "Fear of serious injury alone cannot justify oppression of free speech. . . . Men feared witches and burnt women. It is the function of speech to free men from the bondage of irrational fears."[12]

As for the Smith Act case itself, Learned Hand said, "Personally, I would never have prosecuted those birds." The Communist 11 were plainly victims of the hysteria of the time.


## THE STRANGE CASE OF ALGER HISS

Another case from the 1950s that evoked a firestorm of controversy was that of Alger Hiss. The case focused not on Communist ideology, but on whether Hiss had been a member of a Communist network that spied for the Russians.

---

10. 354 U.S. 298 (1957).
11. 395 U.S. 444 (1969).
12. Whitney v. California, 274 U.S. 357, 453 (1927) (Brandeis, J., concurring).

President Truman called the Hiss trial a "red herring." It was a case of great human drama. Either Hiss or his accuser, Whittaker Chambers, was just plain lying. The question for the jury was a Cold War whodunit.

On January 21, 1950, at the conclusion of his second trial,[13] Hiss was convicted of two counts of perjury in denying to the Southern District grand jury in March 1948 both that he had handed over secret documents to Chambers, a Soviet agent, and that he had conversed with Chambers a decade earlier, in or about February and March 1938.

An honors graduate of Harvard Law School, Hiss had served as a law clerk to Oliver Wendell Holmes. After leaving Holmes, Hiss entered government service in 1933 in an entry-level position at the Agricultural Adjustment Administration, a New Deal agency designed to help farmers by reducing production of staple crops, thus raising farm prices and encouraging more diversified farming.

Hiss steadily rose in the ranks. In 1934, he became a legal assistant to the Nye Committee, investigating traffic in munitions. It was at about this time that he met Chambers. In 1936 Hiss joined the State Department as an assistant to Francis B. Sayre, head of the Trade Agreements section, where he remained through 1938.[14] Chambers alleged that during this period Hiss was regularly turning over to him confidential State Department documents. When Sayre transferred to the Philippines in 1939, Hiss became an assistant to the adviser on political relations at State, where he remained until 1944. Hiss was highly regarded. In 1944, Secretary of State Stettinius named him secretary to the American delegation at the

---

13. The first Hiss trial ended in a hung jury.

14. According to Malcolm Cowley, a writer and Communist sympathizer, Chambers alleged in 1940 that Sayre, who happened to be Woodrow Wilson's son-in-law, was the head of a Communist apparatus in the State Department. This was an "off the wall" allegation without any basis or justification. Chambers also accused Hiss's brother, Donald, of being a Communist and said he had collected Party dues from him. This allegation was not proved, and the government all but abandoned it at the trial of Alger Hiss.

Dumbarton Oaks conference, where delegations from China, the Soviet Union, Britain, and the United States discussed formation of an international peacekeeping organization, which eventually became the United Nations.

In early 1945, the State Department named Hiss Director of the Office of Special Political Affairs, and tapped him to accompany President Roosevelt to the Yalta Conference with Churchill and Stalin. After leaving the government in 1946, Hiss became president of the Carnegie Foundation of International Peace, a prestigious position he still held at the time of his trial. Until he was indicted, Hiss enjoyed an impeccable reputation for intelligence, industry, and honesty.

Chambers, an editor of *Time* magazine, did not have the same pristine reputation. He admittedly spied for the Russians in the 1930s.[15] In August 1948, a House Committee investigating "un-American activities" began to focus on Hiss and Chambers. The public hearings of the committee rocketed a little-known California congressman named Richard Nixon to national prominence. Before the committee and under oath, Chambers accused Hiss of being a member of the Communist apparatus at the time he was an employee of the State Department. Chambers even claimed that Hiss had collected Party dues from him. Before the Nixon Committee, Chambers testified that, though the set-up of the cell was "conspiratorial," the purpose "was not primarily espionage." Hiss's function, according to Chambers, was "messing up policy," presumably in a way favorable to the Soviets.

Hiss testified before the committee under oath and vehemently denied the charges. He swore that there was not a word of truth in Chambers's story; that he had never been a member of the Communist Party or apparatus; and that the name Whittaker Chambers

15. Chambers made his allegations about Communists in the government first in 1939 and again in 1945 and 1946. On those occasions, he denounced Hiss, among others.

meant nothing to him. Subsequently, the committee arranged a dramatic confrontation between Chambers and Hiss. After some hesitation, Hiss tentatively identified Chambers as a man he had known as "George Crosley,"[16] and said that he had difficulty remembering who Crosley was. Hiss's credibility crumbled, as he descended a slippery slope of acknowledging a much closer and longer relationship with Chambers that he could not conceivably have forgotten.

It appeared that in May 1935, after Hiss and his wife moved to another Washington apartment on P Street, Hiss sublet his 28th Street apartment in Washington to Chambers for a few months. Chambers had use of the furniture and the benefit of electricity for which Hiss continued to pay. When the time came for Chambers to take occupancy on 28th Street, there was some problem, and Hiss allowed Chambers and his wife and child to stay with the Hisses for several days on P Street.

When Hiss and Chambers both appeared before a HUAC subcommittee on August 17, 1948, they had the following dramatic exchange:

HISS: Did you ever go under the name of George Crosley?

CHAMBERS: Not to my knowledge.

HISS: Did you ever sublet an apartment on Twenty-Ninth Street [sic] from me?

CHAMBERS: No. I did not.

HISS: You did not?

CHAMBERS: No.

HISS: Did you ever spend any time with your wife and child in an apartment on Twenty-Ninth Street in Washington when I was not there because I and my family were living on P Street?

---

16. Hiss claimed that "Crosley's" appearance had changed because of dental work.

**CHAMBERS:** I most certainly did.

**HISS:** You did or did not?

**CHAMBERS:** I did.

**HISS:** Would you tell me how you reconcile your negative answers with this affirmative answer?

**CHAMBERS:** Very easily, Alger. I was a Communist and you were a Communist. [*Here's another example of why you should never ask an open-ended question of a hostile witness when you don't know the answer.*]

Hiss also testified that he allowed Chambers the use of a Model A Ford, which Hiss still owned but Chambers kept until July 1936, more than a year after Chambers vacated the 28th Street apartment. Some time later, Chambers, who could not afford rent, gave Hiss a rug worth $200 as part payment for rent and use of the car. Hiss disposed of the car in July 1936 in a questionable off-the-books transaction with the Communist employee of an automobile dealer, and the car ended up with a Communist. Everyone involved in the sordid affair seemed to be a Communist.

What was particularly odd about the Ford transaction was that, at the time, Chambers had a car of his own, so there was no demonstrable need for Hiss to do him such a favor. In November 1937, Chambers bought another car, this one a deluxe Ford four-door sedan. After trade-in, the net paid the dealer was $486.75. The source of finance was a mystery until Chambers alleged it was a $400 loan from Hiss. As it happened, there was a $400 withdrawal from the Hisses' bank account at a time just before Chambers made the $486 payment for the new car. If there was a financial transaction between them in late 1937, Hiss lied when he said there was a severance of the relationship at the end of 1936. Hiss, Chambers alleged, turned over the documents in February or March 1938.

Chambers, a man of many aliases, testified that he could not remember ever having used the name "George Crosley." Thomas Murphy, Hiss's salty-tongued prosecutor, of whom we will learn more later after he became a great judge of the Mother Court, ridiculed Hiss's story in his closing argument to the jury: "George Crosley, my aunt!"

Hiss challenged Chambers to repeat his allegations off the floor of Congress, where Chambers had immunity from a libel suit. Chambers obliged; and Hiss, disregarding all advice, threw caution to the winds and sued Chambers for libel in Maryland, seeking $75,000 in damages.

In the libel action, Hiss's lawyers served on Chambers a notice to produce, demanding "all documents relied on for [his] statement" that Hiss turned over secret State Department documents. Responding, Chambers furnished certain documents that he alleged Hiss handed over in early 1938. Four of these documents were in Hiss's handwriting, and were taken from confidential papers that Hiss worked on while in the State Department. Chambers also produced a series of documents dated early 1938, 43 of which had been typed on an old Woodstock typewriter belonging to Hiss's wife, Priscilla. She had used this typewriter to type some of her own letters, and experts said the fonts matched. At the trial, there was no serious dispute that Chambers had produced copies of confidential State Department documents to which Hiss had access that were typed on the Hiss typewriter. Indeed, in his closing argument, Murphy suggested to the jury that there were typing errors in the questioned documents that were identical to those in the personal letters typed by Priscilla Hiss on the old Woodstock.[17] Hiss's lawyers turned these documents over

---

17. Priscilla Hiss was at one time a committed Socialist. Alger Hiss's defenders theorized that it was Priscilla who inspired Hiss's career as a spy. The line goes that Hiss brought home State Department documents he was working on, and Priscilla, with or without his knowledge, typed copies and gave them to Chambers. Priscilla was a divorcée when she

to the FBI. Chambers said he had retained the documents as a "life preserver" when he was getting ready to leave the Communist Party. He also said he knew the documents would incriminate Hiss. In his fascinating book, *Witness*, Chambers said he contemplated suicide before he decided to produce the documents. He actually attempted suicide during the hearings before the grand jury.

The incriminating Woodstock typewriter became the key to the case. If Hiss had indeed used the typewriter to create copies of State Department documents, why didn't he destroy it? Instead, he gave the Woodstock to a servant who had performed odd jobs for him, thereby leaving a trail. In the run-up to the first trial, Hiss's attorney, Edward McLean, who later became a great judge of the Mother Court, located the Woodstock typewriter and purchased it for $40. Ignoring any Fifth Amendment issue of self-incrimination, McLean voluntarily turned the typewriter over to the government. Why he took this fateful step remains unclear.

Before the committee, Chambers had denied the existence of any such documents. As the libel case unfolded, however, Chambers switched positions, and claimed that documents in fact did exist, and disaster became irretrievable.

The revelation of the documents spurred the committee to fresh activity. Chambers took committee investigators to his Maryland farm, where he led them to a patch of pumpkins. From a hollowed-out pumpkin, Chambers produced various microfilms, some developed, some not. These 58 photographic frames represented confidential State Department documents. Two of them were introduced in evidence at the trial. The documents were all marked "Classified," but Hiss had access to them by reason of his official position. None of the "Pumpkin Papers" had been typed on the Hiss

---

married Alger Hiss. On the day of the wedding, his mother sent Hiss a telegram saying, "Do not take this fateful step."

typewriter. There was no direct evidence to connect Hiss with the "Pumpkin Papers" except the word of Whittaker Chambers.

In 1948, Hiss denied Chambers's charges under oath before a federal grand jury investigating the matter in the Southern District. A charge of perjury requires corroboration, and the corroboration existed in what the prosecutor, Thomas Murphy, called the "mute witnesses," the secret State Department documents, typed on the Hiss typewriter.[18]

Because the statute of limitations had run on the underlying crime, the grand jury indicted Hiss for perjury. Hiss might have saved himself before the grand jury. All he had to do was testify that many years before, he had flirted with Communism and had turned over a few government documents to Chambers, whom he knew to be a Soviet agent. On the assumption that Chambers's story was true, Hiss would have been home free as far as the criminal law was concerned, because the underlying offense was time barred. Of course, if such testimony ever leaked out, he would have become a pariah in the community and subject to indictment for perjury before the congressional committee or in the civil case.[19] Thus, Hiss was trapped in his own tangled testimony, and had every motive to continue to profess his innocence and lie his way out.[20]

Hiss's prosecutor, Thomas Murphy, was a brilliant advocate, full of charm and mordant wit. His crowning achievement as a lawyer was the Hiss prosecution. Hiss had two Southern District trials, the first of which resulted in a hung jury with eight jurors out of 12

---

18. There were also the State Department documents that Chambers produced from the pumpkin, some in Hiss's handwriting, that he claimed Hiss had given him. Since the Hiss defense was that he was framed, these documents proved nothing (unless, of course, Chambers was telling the truth), as they might have been stolen from Hiss.

19. Grand jury proceedings are secret. FED. R. CRIM. P. 6.

20. When Spiro Agnew pleaded "no contest" to tax evasion charges arising out of bribes he had taken when governor of Maryland, Roy Cohn, of whom we will hear more later, wrote him an open letter that appeared in *The New York Times*. The letter said in substance, "Why did you cop out, Spiro Agnew? Alger Hiss can still argue his innocence. You can't!"

favoring conviction. Hiss's counsel was the crafty criminal defense lawyer Lloyd Paul Stryker. The judge was Samuel H. Kaufman. Hiss's second trial was before Henry W. Goddard, a venerated judge of the Mother Court. This time, Hiss was convicted.

Hiss had called a psychiatrist, Dr. Carl A. Binger, to testify as an expert witness that he had read Whittaker Chambers's articles in *Time* magazine, and had observed him on the witness stand. His amazing opinion was that Chambers fit the profile of a "psychopathic personality" and a "pathological liar." Murphy conducted a withering cross-examination of Binger that is taught in the law schools to this day.

Noting, for example, Binger's conclusion that the tendency of Chambers to look up at the ceiling from the stand was a symptom of a psychopathic personality, Murphy asked what should be made of the fact that government lawyers had counted Binger eyeing the ceiling 50 times in less than an hour of his own testimony. Murphy followed with another alleged symptom of Chambers's psychopathic personality: his "untidiness" and lack of concern about his appearance. Murphy wondered whether other famous persons well known for untidiness or haphazard dress, such as Albert Einstein, Bing Crosby, and Thomas Edison, were, therefore, psychopaths too. Murphy also attacked Binger's conclusion that hiding microfilm in a pumpkin was indicative of a psychopathic personality. Murphy asked whether that meant other famous hidings, including "the mother of Moses hiding the little child in the bulrushes," was symptomatic of a serious personality disorder.

But it was Murphy's summation in the Hiss case that will go down as a classic. He spoke for almost three hours, scarcely glancing at his notes. Hiss's counsel had argued that this was not an ordinary case. But Murphy said that it *was* an ordinary case, and invoked the bedrock principle that is the watchword of the Mother Court: "This courtroom is the great leveler. Everyone in this courtroom is even."

Murphy based his closing argument on the State Department documents, the "immutable documents" proving Hiss's guilt.

Hiss had called a number of character witnesses to testify to his reputation in the State Department for honesty, integrity, truth, and veracity. Murphy dismissed this as "gossip," and argued that "character witnesses belong to another era" and that men may frequently conceal their true characters.

> I ask you what kind of reputation does a good spy have? A fox barks not when he goes to steal the lamb. [Couldn't Benedict Arnold] have called George Washington and all the members of the General's staff as character witnesses [before he was revealed as a traitor]? And Brutus before he stabbed Caesar could have stood before the Roman senate and called Caesar himself to say "What a great man." [And the devil] could have called on the Almighty himself before he was expelled from paradise. But we are here on a search for truth. We are not concerned with reputations. Poppycock.

Murphy's summation was dismissive of Hiss's claim that the FBI committed "forgery by typewriter." He argued that the typewritten State Department documents, the smoking gun, or, as Murphy put it, "the golden calf," were typed on the Hiss Woodstock typewriter and conclusively established Hiss's guilt.

> If you think, ladies and gentlemen, that any document, any shred of evidence, any testimony in this case was forged, manufactured or suborned by the FBI, acquit him.

Then, for the peroration:

> And now, ladies and gentlemen, consider again these proofs. Take them with you to the jury room, those photographs; take the machine,

the instruments. What do they prove? Ladies and gentlemen, it proves treason, and that [pointing to Hiss] is the traitor. And come back with the courage of your convictions and tell this world that our faith in the American jury system is well founded.

The verdict was guilty. The jury found that Hiss had perjured himself in denying that he "turned over" to Chambers secret State Department documents for transmittal to the Soviets, and Judge Goddard sentenced him to five years in jail. On his sentencing allocution, Hiss stated, "I am confident that in the future the full facts of how Whittaker Chambers was able to carry out forgery by typewriter will be disclosed. Time will show how the documents came to be typed." Time never did.

Although many clung to the myth that Hiss was the victim of some sort of elaborate frame-up, the evidence fairly shrieked his guilt. Hiss's wife, Priscilla, most probably typed the secret documents on the Hiss typewriter, and there was no way around it.

The controversy raged on. Two weeks after the conviction, Senator Joseph McCarthy made his famous Lincoln Day speech, in which he alleged that the State Department was infested with Communists. "I have here in my hand a list of 205 names made known to the Secretary of State as Communists, but who are still on the payroll." In fact, there were only 65 who had undergone further security tests. All passed. McCarthy himself said of McCarthyism, "McCarthyism is Americanism with its sleeves rolled." The verdict of history, however, is to the contrary.

After the fall of the Soviet Union, years after the trial, indications came out in Soviet archives and in Venona[21] documents that Hiss had indeed acted as a Soviet mole in the U.S. government. Senator

---

21. The Venona decryption project, a joint British/U.S. intelligence operation, informed the allies of traffic between the New York and Moscow stations of the Soviet spy services during World War II.

Daniel P. Moynihan of New York observed that "belief in the guilt or innocence of Alger Hiss became a defining issue in American intellectual life." Chairing a congressional commission that undertook a comprehensive review of the case in 1997, Moynihan concluded, based on Venona documents showing that a Soviet agent named ALES, indisputably Alger Hiss, had represented the United States at the Yalta conference, "The complicity of Alger Hiss of the State Department seems settled." Some later researchers, however, questioned the Venona findings as inconclusive or faulty. Hiss went to his grave still maintaining his innocence, and Chambers went to his also sticking to his story.[22]

Hiss's prosecutor, Thomas F. Murphy, went on to have a distinguished career as a New York City police commissioner, and a giant of a Southern District judge.[23]

## IRVING R. KAUFMAN AND THE ROSENBERGS

In 2003, on the 50th anniversary of the executions of Julius and Ethel Rosenberg, the *New York Times* observed, "The Rosenberg case still haunts American history, reminding us of the injustice that can be done when a nation gets caught up in hysteria." Not since the Sacco and Vanzetti case in 1927 has there been more controversy and intense reaction over a trial and the executions that followed.[24]

---

22. The importance of Alger Hiss in the U.S. government is perhaps overstated. Hiss held middle management posts in the State Department bureaucracy. The Right widely credits him with masterminding the 1945 Yalta conference, when all of Eastern Europe fell to the Communists. As unfortunate an outcome as Yalta was for the United States, this is surely an exaggeration. Hiss's activities at Yalta were limited to organization of the United Nations.

23. The NYPD is a very Irish police department. Of its 39 commissioners since 1901, four have been named Murphy, including its first commissioner, Michael C. Murphy. It does not appear that any of the Murphys are related.

24. Sacco and Vanzetti were anarchists convicted of a 1920 payroll robbery murder in Braintree, Massachusetts. Like the Rosenbergs, they died in the electric chair. Like the Rosenberg case, the integrity of the convictions and executions has been the source of endless debate around the world.

Writing about the Sacco and Vanzetti case in October 1927, H.G. Wells wrote in words that would apply with even greater force to the Rosenbergs that

> The guilt or innocence of these two Italians is not the issue. Possibly they were actual murderers, and still more possibly they knew more than they would admit about the crime. Executing political opponents as political opponents after the fashion of Mussolini and Moscow we can understand, or bandits as bandits; but this business of trying and executing murderers as Reds, or Reds as murderers, seems to be a new and very frightening line for the courts of a State in the most powerful and civilized Union on earth to pursue.[25]

## OF THE ROSENBERG CASE

So very much has already been written about the Rosenberg case that the pertinent facts are familiar to many. In 1950, the FBI arrested Julius and Ethel Rosenberg. Julius was an electrical engineer who from 1940 to 1945 had worked for the U.S. Army Signal Corps in Fort Monmouth, New Jersey. The grand jury indicted the couple in the Southern District for conspiracy to transmit classified military information to the Soviet Union in violation of the Espionage Act of 1917.[26]

The trial judge in the case was Irving R. Kaufman. The chief prosecutor was Irving Saypol, the U.S. attorney for the Southern District. Roy M. Cohn, later counsel to Senator Joseph McCarthy, assisted Saypol. Co-conspirator David Greenglass, the brother of Ethel Rosenberg, was the principal government witness against the

---

25. *Wells Speaks Some Plain Words to Us*, N.Y. Times, October 16, 1927.
26. 50 U.S.C. §§ 32(a), 34. The Espionage Act of 1917 is now found in 18 U.S.C. §§ 792 *et seq.*

Rosenbergs. Cohn was the lawyer who prepared Greenglass as a witness.

The fact that the trial judge and both prosecutors were Jews led some to question whether they had been handpicked by Attorney General Herbert Brownell's Justice Department to blunt any charge of anti-Semitism. Cohn, himself a twisted personality, wrote many years later that "The Communist press even argued that imposing the death sentence was a result of anti-Semitism, though the prosecutors and the judge themselves were Jewish."[27] The curious dramatis personae only added fuel to the fire as to whether the trial was political or, more importantly, whether it was fair.

It is interesting that the Rosenbergs were never charged with treason. Prosecutors knew that a treason charge couldn't conceivably stick. Article III, section 3 of the Constitution specifically defines treason as follows:

> Treason against the United States shall consist only in levying War against them, or in adhering to their Enemies, giving them Aid and Comfort. No Person shall be convicted of Treason unless on the Testimony of two Witnesses to the same overt Act, or on Confession in open Court.

At the time of the charged crimes (1944–1956), the United States was not at "War" with the Soviet Union. Indeed, the Soviet Union was thought of as an ally of the United States in its war against the Axis powers. The Espionage Act of 1917 made criminal the communication of the prohibited information "to the advantage of any foreign country" even if such communication does not injure the United States. And it makes no difference under the Espionage

---

27. COHN, A FOOL FOR A CLIENT 4 (1971).

Act that the United States was an ally or friend of the Soviet Union when the information was communicated.[28]

At trial, which began March 6, 1952, before Judge Kaufman, the government contended that in late 1944 the Rosenbergs had persuaded Ethel's brother, David Greenglass—an army private stationed at the Los Alamos atomic bomb project—to provide them with certain general information concerning the Los Alamos project for transmission to the Soviet Union. Greenglass complied, relating the names of important scientists working on the project, and giving information about both security measures and the nature of his work. Two months later, in January 1945 on the occasion of a trip to New York, Greenglass supplemented this information with a sketch of a high-explosive lens mold used in atomic experiments and a list of potential spy recruits. The principal evidence against the Rosenbergs came from Greenglass and his wife, Ruth. Greenglass testified that his sister, Ethel Rosenberg, had typed up notes he provided on the atomic bomb for transmittal to the Soviet Union.

According to Greenglass, Julius introduced him to a Soviet agent, Ann Sidorovich, who was supposed to visit New Mexico to receive further information. Because it was unclear that Sidorovich would be the courier, Rosenberg cut a Jell-O box top in two and gave one half to Greenglass. He said that the eventual courier would have the matching half. In June 1945, Harry Gold, a Soviet agent who had been in touch with Dr. Klaus Fuchs, a British atomic scientist and Soviet spy, met with Greenglass in New Mexico and presented him with the matching part of the Jell-O box top. Gold testified that he gave Greenglass the prearranged password, "I come from Julius."

---

28. Thus, Judge Kaufman correctly charged the jury, "I charge you that whether the Union of Soviet Socialist Republics was an ally or friendly nation during the period of the alleged conspiracy is immaterial, and you are not to consider that at all in your deliberations." Analogously, in 1987, Jonathan Pollard was convicted under the Espionage Act of 1917 of spying for Israel. He is currently serving a life sentence.

Greenglass then gave Gold a detailed sketch of the lens mold and a list of potential spy recruits. In December 1945, Greenglass, again in New York, prepared a cross-sectional sketch and 12-page explanation of the atom bomb based on conversations he overheard at Los Alamos. According to Greenglass, Ruth Greenglass and both Rosenbergs assisted in the preparation of the report. The trial lasted 14 days; the jury convicted; and Judge Kaufman imposed the ultimate penalty.

The Rosenbergs were the only two American civilians ever to be executed for espionage-related activity in the United States. In imposing the death penalty, Kaufman noted that he held them responsible not only for espionage but also for the American deaths in the Korean War:

> I consider your crime worse than murder. I believe your conduct in putting into the hands of the Russians the A-Bomb years before our best scientists predicted Russia would perfect the bomb has already caused, in my opinion, the Communist aggression in Korea, with the resultant casualties exceeding 50,000 and who knows but that millions more of innocent people may pay the price of your treason. Indeed, *by your betrayal you undoubtedly have altered the course of history to the disadvantage of our country.* No one can say that we do not live in a constant state of tension. We have evidence of your treachery all around us every day for the civilian defense activities throughout the Nation are aimed at preparing us for an atom bomb attack.

There is really no historical evidence to support any of these speculations. Historians accept that the purported atomic information passed on by Julius Rosenberg to the Soviets was essentially useless, and it is far-fetched indeed to argue that anything Julius Rosenberg turned over to the Russians emboldened Communist aggression in Korea. Nevertheless, the Second Circuit affirmed the convictions on appeal, and the Supreme Court denied review by a 6–3 vote. Legal issues riddled the case.

The Rosenbergs argued to no avail that the death sentence was an unconstitutional violation of the Eighth Amendment prohibition on cruel and unusual punishment. They contended that the sentence was disproportionate, and therefore "cruel," because they had acted not as traitors, but as foolish idealists who had sought to aid the Soviet Union during the war at a time that it was our ally. They contended that their sentence was "unusual" when compared with sentences given others who were at least equally guilty.[29] The Second Circuit never reached the constitutional issue, finding that the death penalty was well within the statutory discretion of the trial court.

The indictment charged a single conspiracy: that the Rosenbergs and Morton Sobell, their co-defendant, had conspired with others to transmit to the Soviet Union "documents, writings, sketches, notes and information relating to the National Defense of the United States." This would encompass both atomic and nonatomic secrets. Judge Kaufman's comments to the jury underscored that the indictment charged a conspiracy to obtain both atomic and nonatomic information for transmission to the Russians:

> Bear in mind—please listen to this, ladies and gentlemen—that the Government contends that the conspiracy was one to obtain *not only atomic bomb information, but other secret and classified information*; that the information including the report regarding fire control equipment requested of Elitcher by Sobell or Rosenberg was classified; that the atomic bomb information transmitted by the Rosenbergs was classified as top secret; that, based on Rosenberg's alleged statements to

---

29. The infamous British atom spy Klaus Fuchs, who really did help the Russians get the bomb, was sentenced to 14 years; the Rosenbergs' co-conspirator Harry Gold was sentenced to 30 years; David Greenglass was sentenced to 15 years; co-conspirator Morton Sobell, though not directly involved in transmitting A-bomb information, received 30 years. Ruth Greenglass got off scot-free.

Greenglass, other secret information such as mathematical data on atomic energy for airplanes, information relating to a "sky platform" project, and other information was obtained by Julius Rosenberg from scientist contacts in the country.

The proof, therefore, may have involved two conspiracies: one to steal atomic secrets, and another to steal nonatomic secrets. The participants in the first atomic conspiracy were the Rosenbergs, the Greenglasses, and Gold; the participants in the second non-atomic conspiracy were the Rosenbergs and Sobell. Sobell argued that this created prejudice at trial in that proof of the atomic con-spiracy spilled over to taint his conviction where he was unaware of the other group's atomic work. Kaufman did not charge separate conspiracies, and Sobell claimed that this was reversible error. The appellate court thought there was not much to the point, and that there was a basis for the district court's finding one all-encompassing conspiracy; namely, to provide Russia with all kinds of secret infor-mation, atomic and nonatomic. Were Sobell correct, he might have been granted a new trial, but the reversal as to him would not have helped the Rosenbergs.

The more interesting legal question was raised in the Supreme Court at the eleventh hour. In 1946, Congress enacted the Atomic Energy Act, which criminalized atomic spying but authorized the death penalty only on the jury's recommendation, which did not occur here. The Rosenbergs were indicted, tried, convicted, and sentenced in 1951 under the Espionage Act for a conspiracy last-ing from 1944 to 1950, but with all the overt acts committed prior to 1946, the date of enactment of the Atomic Energy Act.[30] Judge

---

30. The activities of the Rosenbergs and Sobell after 1945 all involved attempts to conceal their crime and possibly flee the country.

Kaufman also charged the jury in the language of the Atomic Energy Act.[31] Since there was a general verdict of guilty, it is not known under which statute the couple was convicted. The jury may well have convicted the Rosenbergs for stealing only atomic secrets. On this premise, the argument goes, Kaufman did not have a verdict on which the death penalty could be legally imposed. A "friend of the Court" argued in the Supreme Court that Congress impliedly repealed or superseded all or part of the Espionage Act with the Atomic Energy Act, which preempted the field with regard to atomic spying.[32] Thus, the argument ran, the Rosenbergs were sentenced illegally.

Justice Douglas found this repeal point to be "substantial" and on June 17, 1953, stayed the executions. In an unprecedented move, Chief Justice Vinson summoned the justices back from their vacations, and convened a special session. After only 12 hours of research and argument on both the power of a single justice to grant the stay and the substantiality of the question of implied repeal, the Court rushed to judgment, vacating Douglas' stay by a vote of 6–3.

In a curious footnote to history, one of the dissenters was Mr. Justice Frankfurter, who, as a Harvard Law School professor, wrote a 1927 article in the *Atlantic Monthly* criticizing the process in the Sacco and Vanzetti case. Clearly, Frankfurter did not take kindly to politically tinged prosecutions, particularly those ending with a death warrant. Frankfurter filed an opinion June 22, 1953, three days *after* the executions were carried out, in which he found the issues to be "complicated and novel," and decried the Court's rush

---

31. Judge Kaufman charged the jury in the language of section 10(b)(2) of the Atomic Energy Act that the Rosenbergs could be convicted if they intended or had reason to believe that the information was to be used "to secure an advantage to any foreign nation."

32. There is a canon of statutory construction that a specialized statute impliedly repeals a general statute.

to disposition that prevented "the deliberation necessary for a confident judgment."

Frankfurter flatly rejected the government's argument that the Rosenbergs' crime ended prior to the 1946 enactment of the Atomic Energy Act, since the overt acts in furtherance of the conspiracy were all pre-1946:

> The Government having tried the Rosenbergs for a conspiracy, continuing from 1944 to 1950, to reveal atomic secrets among other things, it flies in the face of the charge made, the evidence adduced and the basis on which the conviction was secured now to contend that the terminal date of the Rosenberg conspiracy preceded the effective date of the Atomic Energy Act.[33]

Frankfurter was also troubled that, under the statutory regime, discretion resided in the prosecutors, Saypol and Cohn, to charge under a statute that authorized the death penalty when there was a later statute that did not:

> These considerations—the fact that Congress and not the whim of the prosecutor fixes sentences, that the allegations of an indictment are to be judged by the relevant statute under which punishment may be meted out and not by the design of the prosecutor or the assumption of the trial court—cut across all the talk about repeal by implication and other empty generalities on statutory construction. Congress does not have to say in so many words that hereafter a judge cannot without jury recommendation impose a sentence of death on a charge of conspiracy that falls within the Atomic Energy Act. It is enough if

---

33. *Rosenberg*, 344 U.S. 838 (Frankfurter, J. dissenting).

in fact Congress has provided that hereafter such a death sentence is to depend on the will of the jury.[34]

He then made the following observation about the course of proceedings in the Rosenberg case:

> To be writing an opinion in a case affecting two lives after the curtain has been rung down upon them has the appearance of pathetic futility. But history also has its claims. This case is an incident in the long and unending effort to develop and enforce justice according to law. The progress in that struggle surely depends on searching analysis of the past, though the past cannot be recalled, as illumination for the future. Only by sturdy self-examination and self-criticism can the necessary habits for detached and wise judgment be established and fortified so as to become effective when the judicial process is again subjected to stress and strain. American criminal procedure has its defects, though its essentials have behind them the vindication of long history. But all systems of law, however wise, are administered through men, and therefore may occasionally disclose the frailties of men. Perfection may not be demanded of law, but the capacity to counteract inevitable, though rare, frailties is the mark of a civilized legal mechanism.[35]

Their doom sealed, the Rosenbergs were executed by electrocution in Sing Sing prison June 19, 1953.

## THE ROSENBERGS: WHAT HAPPENED LATER

Ethel Rosenberg was the second woman in history to be executed by the federal government. (The first, Mary Eugenia Surratt, a

34. *Id.*
35. *Id.*

boardinghouse owner, was hanged in 1865 for participation in the assassination of Abraham Lincoln.) The Rosenbergs' sentence evoked a firestorm. Rallies were held in their support in the United States and around the world.

Prominent Communists, such as Jean Paul Sartre, Diego Rivera, and Berthold Brecht, opposed the death penalty, condemning what they called "judicial murder." Non-Communists, such as Albert Einstein and Nobel Prize–winning nuclear physicist Harold Urey, also recorded their opposition to the death penalty. Even such stalwart anti-Communists as Pope Pius XII and J. Edgar Hoover registered their views against it. The case had created a cynosure of controversy.

Many years later in 2001 Greenglass admitted that his testimony, which sent his sister to the electric chair, was false. Ethel never had typed plans for the atom bomb, he said. Courts do not favor recantations of perjury. The New York Court of Appeals has observed,

> There is no form of proof so unreliable as recanting testimony. In the popular mind it is often regarded as of great importance. Those experienced in the administration of the criminal law know well its untrustworthy character.[36]

In the "popular mind," however, the recantation was highly significant, particularly in that the government had called a brother to testify against his own sister, and that his testimony sent her to the electric chair.

The recantation aside, there were serious questions about the guilt of Ethel Rosenberg. At trial, the evidence of a conspiracy to pass atomic secrets to the Soviets appeared to be overwhelming. Julius, a committed Communist, was head of an elaborate Soviet

---

36. People v. Shilitano, 218 N.Y. 161, 170 (1916).

spy ring and undoubtedly passed secret information to the Russians. Ethel's role, according to the prosecutors, was that she typed up notes describing the atomic bomb so that Julius could pass the information to the Russians. The 2008 release of scores of pages of grand jury minutes showed that prosecution witness Ruth Greenglass, Ethel Rosenberg's sister-in-law, had changed her testimony about Ethel. Before the grand jury Ruth was asked, "Didn't you write [the information] down on a piece of paper?" She replied, "Yes, I wrote [the information] down [on] a piece of paper and [Julius Rosenberg] took it with him."

At trial, Ruth Greenglass testified that Ethel Rosenberg personally "typed up notes about the atomic bomb." Which was it? There was a major discrepancy in the evidence, but if the defense knew about it, they never explored the inconsistency on cross-examination.

The discrepancy overlooked at trial is particularly telling when the prosecutor picked up on Ruth's trial testimony and ran with it during summation, telling the jury that Ethel "sat at that typewriter and struck the keys, blow by blow, against her country."

In what was to prove most damning to the Rosenbergs, Kaufman asked Julius on the stand if he had ever belonged to any group that discussed the Soviet system. What a question! The Soviet system was probably discussed at book clubs, coffee klatches, and universities across the nation. Julius answered, "Well, Your Honor, I feel at this time that I refuse to answer a question that might tend to incriminate me." Typically, such a situation would warrant a cautionary instruction from the trial judge to the jury to disregard the refusal to answer, or at least to draw no inference from it. Here, however, Judge Kaufman gave no such instruction.

Similarly, the prosecutor, Irving Saypol, cross-examined Ethel Rosenberg on her taking the Fifth before the grand jury on questions she freely answered at the trial wherein she asserted her innocence. In response to Saypol's questions, Ethel testified she couldn't remember why she had taken the Fifth in the grand jury. Kaufman failed to instruct the jury that they were to draw no inference against the Rosenbergs from their assertion of the privilege. Six years after the trial, the Supreme Court in *Grunewald v. United States*[37] held that it was reversible error for the prosecutor to bring out the assertion of the Fifth as bearing on credibility.

As Justice Black reasoned in his concurring opinion in *Grunewald*, joined in by Chief Justice Warren and Justices Douglas and Brennan:

> At the conclusion of the trial the judge instructed the jury that Halperin's claim of his constitutional privilege not to be a witness against himself could be considered in determining what weight should be given to his testimony—in other words, whether Halperin was a truthful and trustworthy witness. I agree with the Court that use of this claim of constitutional privilege to reflect upon Halperin's credibility was error, but I do not, like the Court, rest my conclusion on the special circumstances of this case. I can think of no special circumstances that would justify use of a constitutional privilege to discredit or convict a person who asserts it. *The value of constitutional privileges is largely destroyed if persons can be penalized for relying on them. It seems peculiarly incongruous and indefensible for courts which exist and act only under the Constitution to draw inferences of lack of honesty from invocation of a privilege deemed worthy of enshrinement in the Constitution.*[38]

Co-defendant Morton Sobell, a convicted member of the Rosenberg spy ring, brought on a habeas corpus petition in 1963 based on the *Grunewald* decision. Habeas is a procedure in the federal system whereby one convicted of a crime in either the state or federal court may collaterally attack his conviction based on a claimed denial of

---

37. 353 U.S. 391 (1957).
38. *Id.* (Black, J. concurring).

constitutional rights. The petition, which conjured the specter of a constitutionally flawed trial that resulted in two executions, raised the academic question of whether the Rosenbergs might have won a new trial were they alive. The petition came before Judge Friendly, who hardly ever met a habeas petition he liked. Friendly believed strongly that habeas should not be a vehicle for defendants to raise matters that could have been raised on direct appeal. Accordingly, he denied the petition. His voting memorandum, however, read, as follows: "[W]e must admit that on a direct appeal today we would reverse not only as to Ethel but almost certainly as to Julius and very likely as to Sobell as well."[39] Too little, too late.

The controversy raged on, particularly with regard to whether the supposed plans for the atom bomb that Julius passed to Ethel's brother, David Greenglass, were of any value to the Soviets. Much came out later with the fall of the Iron Curtain.

Senator Daniel Patrick Moynihan, vice chairman of the Senate Select Committee on Intelligence, looked into how much the Soviet spy ring helped the USSR to build their bomb. According to Moynihan, in 1945 physicist Hans Bethe estimated that the Soviets would be able to build their own bomb in five years. "Thanks to information provided by their agents," Moynihan concluded in his 1999 book *Secrecy*, "they did it in four. That was the edge that espionage gave them: one year."

The engineer who later became director of Chelyabinsk-40, the plutonium production reactor and extraction facility used by the Soviet Union to create its first bomb material, denied any involvement by the Rosenbergs. In 1989, Boris V. Brokhovich told the *New York Times* that development of the bomb had been a matter of trial

---

39. Friendly Voting Mem., Dec. 7, 1962, quoted in Dorsen, HENRY FRIENDLY, GREATEST JUDGE OF HIS ERA 498 (Harvard 2002).

and error. "You sat the Rosenbergs in the electric chair for nothing," he said. "We got nothing from the Rosenbergs."

According to Alexander Felsikov, the former Soviet agent who was Julius's control, Julius did not provide the Soviet Union with any useful material about the atomic bomb: "He didn't understand anything about the atomic bomb and he couldn't help us." However, in his book *The Man behind the Rosenbergs*, he claimed that Julius Rosenberg passed him a wealth of extremely useful information on U.S. electronic systems.

Venona added significant information to the case of Julius and Ethel Rosenberg, making it clear that Julius was guilty of espionage, but also showing that Ethel was probably innocent. Additionally, Venona and other information disclosed that although the content of Julius' atomic espionage was not as vital as alleged at the time of his trial, in other fields it was extensive. The information Rosenberg passed to the Soviets related to the proximity fuse for detonating explosives at desired distances from the target; design and production information on the Lockheed P-80, America's first jet fighter; and thousands of classified reports from Emerson Radio. The Venona evidence indicates that it was unidentified sources, codenamed "Quantum" and "Pers," who facilitated transfer of nuclear weapons technology to the Soviet Union from positions within the Manhattan Project, not the Rosenbergs. The government decided that it was inimical to "national security" to use the Venona information at the Rosenbergs' trial.[40]

Eliminating any lingering ambiguity about the facts in the case, Sobell admitted his guilt in 2008, stated that Julius Rosenberg also spied for the Soviets, and claimed that though Ethel was aware of Julius' espionage activities, she never actively participated.

---

40. As I describe later in Chapter 8, U.S. v. the Press, Americans who lived through the Pentagon Papers case learned to be highly skeptical of government claims of "national security."

The Rosenbergs' sons, Robert and Michael Meeropol, who for decades vehemently asserted their parents' innocence, accepted Sobell's account, but issues as to the propriety of the death sentences remain.

## OF JUDGE KAUFMAN

Playwright Eugene O'Neill was always critical of his father, James O'Neill. James was a fine actor, perhaps the John Barrymore of his day. Nevertheless, he was known primarily for one particular part, the title role of Edmond Dantès in *The Count of Monte Cristo*, which he played about 6,000 times. The role brought him wealth and fame; but quite paradoxically, it adversely affected his life and that life of his son.[41] He told Eugene that the play was his "curse," and Eugene saw his father as a one-trick pony who gave up artistic greatness to make money.

Much the same, the careers of Harold Medina, Thomas Murphy, and Irving Kaufman were largely defined in each instance by a single trial. For Medina it was the 11 Communist Party leaders; for Murphy it was the Hiss case, where he was the prosecutor; and for Irving Kaufman it was the Rosenbergs. These historic cases were their "15 minutes of fame." There is obviously nothing wrong with this, and all, with the exception of Kaufman, wore the mantle gracefully.

Diminutive in stature and imperious in nature, Kaufman was only 39 at the time of his appointment to the Southern District bench. He was a startlingly ambitious man who seemed to believe that there could never be enough recognition for his putatively prodigious accomplishments.[42]

His Wikipedia biography begins:

41. James O'Neill was the prototype for the character James Tyrone in Eugene O'Neill's masterpiece, *Long Day's Journey into Night*.
42. President Kennedy elevated Kaufman to the Second Circuit in 1961.

**Irving Robert Kaufman** (June 24, 1910—February 1, 1992) was a federal judge in the United States. He is best remembered for imposing the controversial death sentences on Julius and Ethel Rosenberg.

Kaufman would have abhorred this description. He didn't want to be "best remembered" for the Rosenberg case. Indeed, he spent the rest of his life after the executions trying to resurrect his tarnished reputation, all to no avail.

Kaufman and his family sought and received FBI protection for many years after the Rosenberg trial. The doormen in the apartment building at 1185 Park Avenue where they lived were re-outfitted in blue uniforms with caps and silver badges to create the impression that they were police officers. Nodding to his doorman in the morning, he could not conceivably have left his home without thinking of the Rosenbergs.

Judges Friendly and Kaufman never enjoyed a good relationship—to put it mildly. Their differences appeared to be personal, not intellectual or philosophical. Part of it undoubtedly had to do with the Rosenberg case. The wife of one of my law partners was fond of giving dinner parties, and often she invited me to dinner. Frequently present were the Friendlys, Henry and Sophie, or the Kaufmans, Irving and Helen—but never at the same time. Once, our hostess asked Kaufman how he could justify the Rosenberg death penalty. There was stunned silence in the room. "I consulted with Learned Hand and other judges in the courthouse before I did it," he said in a tone of solemnity. "They all agreed it was the right thing to do."

Learned Hand was not the only one Kaufman "consulted" with before imposing sentence. David Dorsen, Judge Friendly's biographer, writes that Friendly was "outraged" when Kaufman announced that he had gone to a synagogue to pray over whether to impose the death penalty on Julius and Ethel Rosenberg.

Kaufman coveted a promotion to the Supreme Court, but Justice Felix Frankfurter, infuriated with Judge Kaufman's performance at the Rosenberg trial, was determined not to let that happen. Frankfurter, who as noted had filed a dissenting opinion in the case, considered Kaufman's comment that he went to the synagogue before imposing sentence "unjudicial conduct," and a blatant effort to obtain publicity in his drive to win the "Jewish seat" on the Court. Frankfurter wrote to Learned Hand: "I despise a judge who feels God told him to impose a death sentence. I am mean enough to try to stay here long enough so that K will be too old to succeed me."[43]

The issue that dogged Kaufman's footsteps for his entire life was not whether the Rosenbergs were innocent of the charge of espionage (they were not) or even whether they had received a fair trial (they did not); rather, it was whether the death penalty should have been their punishment.

When death penalty lawyer Anthony Amsterdam unsuccessfully argued a capital case in the Supreme Court, one of the justices asked him how he would feel about the death penalty if he were the judge sentencing Adolf Eichmann, murderer of millions of Jews. Amsterdam, himself a Jew, paused for a minute, swallowed hard and answered, "Death is different."[44]

The execution of the Rosenbergs indelibly stained Kaufman's reputation. Kaufman was fond of Le Cirque, an elegant restaurant on Manhattan's Upper East Side and a favorite of presidents and kings, movie moguls and rock stars. It was a place to see and be seen. Along the wall at the right as you entered was a row of tables in

---

43. He got his wish. Frankfurter retired from the Supreme Court in 1962 after suffering a stroke. He was succeeded by Arthur Goldberg.

44. Gregg v. Georgia, 428 U.S. 153 (1976) (oral argument). As Amsterdam argued to the Court in two cases argued with *Gregg*, "Death is final. Death is irremediable. Death is unnullable; it goes beyond the world. Death is different because even if exactly the same discretionary procedures are used to decide issues of five years versus ten years, or life versus death, the result will be more arbitrary on the life or death choice."

front of a banquette where, one evening in the 1980s, some 30 years after the trial, I sat dining with a client. Kaufman and his wife happened to pass by my table on their way in to dinner. I overheard the man next to me whispering to his attractive companion, "That's Irving Kaufman, the judge who fried the Rosenbergs."

Kaufman, an able and energetic judge, courted the press in later years and invariably ruled for the newspapers in press freedom cases. He didn't want his obituary to identify him for condemning the Rosenbergs, as he thought he had accomplished so much more as a judge in so many fields. Nevertheless, the verdict of history is there. The front-page headline in the *New York Times* of February 3, 1992, read, "Judge Irving Kaufman, of Rosenberg Spy Trial and Free-Press Rulings, Dies at 81."

"He sentenced the Rosenbergs" was to be his epitaph.

The death sentence was unquestionably what Emile Zola termed in his exposé "*J'accuse*" about the Dreyfus case, "*une erreur judiciare*"—a miscarriage of justice. An intelligent man, Kaufman must have gone to his grave at age 81 with the dawning realization that Amsterdam was right when he said, "Death is different."

# U.S. V. SEX

*All hopes, benefactions, bestowals,*
*All the passions, loves, beauties, delights of the earth,*
*All the governments, judges, gods, follow'd persons of the earth,*
*These are contain'd in sex, as parts of itself,*
*and justifications of itself.*
—**Walt Whitman, "A Woman Waits for Me,"** *Leaves of Grass*

*Sex, a great and mysterious motive force in human life, has*
*indisputably been a subject of absorbing interest to mankind through*
*the ages.*
—**Justice William J. Brennan, writing for the Court in**
*Roth v. United States***, 354 U.S. 476 (1957)**

Justice Brennan had it right. Sex is undoubtedly a "mysterious motive force in human life." Jefferson thought it the "strongest of human passions." Benjamin Franklin considered it essential to health. Sex caused Henry VIII to renounce Catholicism and Edward VIII to renounce the throne,[1] sullied the reputations of John F. Kennedy and Bill Clinton, and paused the promising careers of Eliot Spitzer and David Petraeus.

Let's face it. Americans are obsessed with sex, and our obsession is not restricted to our own intimate relationships. We hunger to know what astonishing sex acts others, particularly our public officials, may perform, and with whom, in what position.

Erotic ideas find expression in books, movies, television, tabloid newspapers, and supermarket magazines and on Internet videos. Sex abides in museums, and is not necessarily limited to painting and sculpture. The Museum of Modern Art in New York recently featured a show by performance artist Marina Abramovic where the viewer could enter the exhibit by squeezing between two facing nude models (usually, but not always, a man and a woman—take your pick). Sex sells. It is a multimillion-dollar business. Ask any of the Mad Men.

Interest in erotica pervades the ages. The 2,000-year-old Indian temples at Khajuraho, which have been called the "apogee of erotic art," are festooned with pornographic carvings showing tantric sex in all the permutations of the *Kama Sutra*. In the ancient cities of Pompeii and Herculaneum, one can visit secret cabinets and see on the walls every kind of sexual coupling, including a statue of a satyr copulating with a goat.

Yet Americans are totally ambivalent about our urges. Many think of this "absorbing interest" in the prurient, perceived by Justice Brennan, as a bad thing—degrading or even a sin against God, who gave us our libidinal urges in the first place. Thus, we have viewed erotic expression as something immoral or even illegal, an

---

1. Edward's affair with Wallis Simpson caused his mother, Queen Mary, to remark, "[T]o think he gave up all *this* for that." SARAH BRADFORD, KING GEORGE VI 198 (1989).

appropriate matter for courts and judges. Cole Porter's haunting "Love for Sale," written from the point of view of a streetwalker, was considered shameful and scandalous when first published in 1930, and was even banned from the airwaves as being too raw for radio audiences. In spite of the ban, or perhaps because of it, "Love for Sale" became a timeless hit.

Clerics denounced Whitman's *Leaves of Grass* from the pulpit as pornographic and obscene. One critic pounced on Whitman's supposed homosexuality, saying that the great poet was guilty of "that horrible sin not to be mentioned among Christians."

Governments have historically outlawed "obscenity," suppressed it, and driven it underground. In 1819, when King Francis I of Naples visited the Pompeii exhibition at the National Museum with his wife and daughter, he was so disturbed by the erotic illustrations that he had them locked away, accessible only to scholars, where they remained until the year 2000. No less an autocratic figure than King Francis was my platoon sergeant in the U.S. Army, who, in 1964, periodically searched the barracks of Fort Leonard Wood, Missouri, for "screw books," which he dutifully confiscated.

Americans, in particular, are in sharp disagreement as to what books belong on open library shelves and what movies should be shown. Since much erotica came from Europe, where attitudes tend to be less prudish, we made laws proscribing the importation of obscene books. James Joyce's *Ulysses*, Henry Miller's *Tropic of Cancer*, and Anais Nin's *Delta of Venus*—novels that are tame by today's standards—were deemed contraband, like opium, to be confiscated by the authorities. When I returned to New York from Paris on a Dutch student ship in the fall of 1960, I had in my suitcase a well-thumbed copy of *Tropic of Cancer*, which I had purchased in a *librairie* near the Place Vendome. Customs officers seized the book at the dock.

Under section 305(a) of the Tariff Act of 1930:

> All persons are prohibited from importing into the United States from any foreign country . . . any obscene book, pamphlet, paper, writing, advertisement, circular, print, picture, drawing, or other representation, figure, or image on or of paper or other material, . . . .

The law requires that upon the appearance of any such book or matter at any customs office, the collector shall seize it and inform the U.S. Attorney, who is to institute forfeiture proceedings.

If Americans were ambivalent about sex, preferring to deal in private with what Justice Brennan saw as a "great and mysterious motive force in human life," the federal courts were even more dodgy as they groped for workable definitions as to what constituted obscenity and what was protected by constitutional values of free expression.

Supreme Court justices particularly were all over the lot, formulating such unworkable tests as "whether to the average person, applying contemporary community standards, the dominant theme as a whole appeals to the prurient interest."[2] Some judges thought that material couldn't be obscene if it had "redeeming social value," as though a line from the Bible might redeem a book of hard-core erotica.[3] This test soon morphed into the much more persuasive "utterly without" standard adopted by other judges. This iteration was, leaving prurience and community offensiveness aside, whether the publication is "found to be *utterly without* redeeming social value."[4]

One justice, Potter Stewart, would have outlawed only hard-core pornography, which he could only define this way:

---

2. Roth v. United States, 354 U.S. 476, 489 (1957).
3. A Book Named "John Cleland's Memoirs of a Woman of Pleasure" v. Massachusetts, 383 U.S. 413 (1966).
4. *Id.* at 418–420.

I shall not today attempt further to define the kinds of material I understand to be embraced within that shorthand description [hard-core pornography]; and perhaps I could never succeed in intelligibly doing so. *But I know it when I see it,* and the motion picture involved in this case is not that.[5]

Stewart was astonished that he became better known for this statement than any other he had written in his 23 years on the Supreme Court.

Justice Harlan allowed the federal government to outlaw only hard-core pornography, but gave greater leeway to the states. At the margins, Justices Black and Douglas made it easy, declaring that all putatively obscene matter is constitutionally protected "except where it can be shown to be so brigaded with illegal action that it constitutes a clear and present danger to significant social interests." Go figure that one out; you can't make this up. In 1966 a commentator observed that the Supreme Court had elaborated at least five separate and contradictory tests for what was obscene.[6]

Second Circuit Judge Henry Friendly, whom his biographer David Dorsen calls "the greatest judge of his era," in the only pornography case he ever considered, *United States v. A Motion Picture Called I Am Curious (Yellow),*[7] appeared annoyed that such matters even came before the courts. With advances in entertainment technology, erotica was now on the silver screen.

The Supreme Court, perhaps overlooking the point, never suggested in its elaborate and diverging definitions of obscenity that a different standard would apply to a movie or a visual representation than to a book, perhaps failing to anticipate that in another

---

5. Jacobellis v. Ohio, 378 U.S. 184 (1964).
6. Magrath, *The Obscenity Cases: Grapes of* Roth, 1966 Sup. Court Rev. 7, 56–57.1.
7. 404 F.2d 196 (2d Cir. 1968).

generation most of us would get our information from a screen of some sort.

The landmark obscenity cases in the United States originated in the Mother Court. Perhaps most notable involved a book. The case was styled *United States v. One Book Called Ulysses*, and it was the granddaddy of all obscenity cases.

## *ULYSSES*

In 1922, James Joyce first published in Paris his magnum opus, *Ulysses*. The book, set in Dublin, is 265,000 words long and is divided into 18 episodes. It was recently ranked first on the Modern Library list of the 100 best English-language novels of the 20th century. The title alludes to Odysseus, hero of Homer's *Odyssey*, and the episodes tie in to characters and events in Homer. In one of Joyce's episodes, "Nausicaa," the protagonist, Leopold Bloom, surreptitiously watches Gerty, a young woman on the street, and contemplates love, marriage, and sexuality. As she exposes her legs and underwear to him, Bloom's sexual fantasies escalate and reach a masturbatory climax heightened by the fireworks at the nearby bazaar. Never let it be said that it was Philip Roth's Alexander Portnoy who first brought masturbation out of the closet and into the library.

The *Little Review* serialized the novel in America over a three-year period. In 1920, after the *Little Review* got to "Nausicaa," the New York Society for the Suppression of Vice was successful in getting the state court to ban the book in the United States.[8] The basis

---

8. Prior to its lawsuit against *Ulysses*, the NSSV, among other actions, encouraged authorities to arrest Olga Nethersole and others for "violating public decency" in Clyde Fitch's Broadway play *Sappho*. All were found innocent. It forced off the market Stanisław Przybyszewski's *Homo Sapiens* and Theodore Dreiser's *The Genius*. It opposed Margaret Sanger and publishers of birth control books. In 1919, NSSV failed in its effort to suppress the fantasy novel *Jurgen, A Comedy of Justice* by James Branch Cabell, and only succeeded in giving the work considerable publicity and boosting its sales.

of the action was the masturbation scene, and the court declared the work obscene.

In 1933, publisher Bennett Cerf of Random House, represented by renowned literary property lawyer Morris Ernst, decided to launch a test case about *Ulysses*. One copy of the book would be imported and then seized by customs at the pier. The issue was joined in the Mother Court. The case came before district judge John Woolsey, who didn't have at hand—and didn't need—the divergent definitions of obscenity that perplexed Supreme Court justices in later years. What Woolsey added to the fledgling obscenity jurisprudence was that a work must be taken as a whole, and not just judged on the dirty parts taken in isolation.

Woolsey was a gentleman of the old school, noted for his well-crafted and scholarly opinions. Hailing from Aiken, South Carolina, he attended Philips Academy, Yale College, and Columbia Law School. Calvin Coolidge first nominated Woolsey to the federal bench; when the nomination failed, Herbert Hoover renominated him. The second time he got through.

Prior to his *Ulysses* decision, Woolsey had a number of important decisions on freedom of expression. In *United States v. One Obscene Book Entitled "Married Love,"* he found that a work by a physician on enhancing marital sexual relations was not obscene. In a similar case, *United States v. One Book Entitled "Contraception,"* he held that a book containing information on birth control was not obscene or immoral, and therefore not subject to confiscation.[9]

Judge Woolsey took a lighthearted and whimsical view of *Ulysses*:

> The words which are criticized as dirty are old Saxon words known to almost all men and, I venture, to many women, and are such words as

---

9. The form that obscenity cases took in those days was an action in rem against the book itself rather than against its publishers or importers. This was accomplished by government seizure of the offensive property. The publisher would then lay claim to the book, and the issue would be joined.

would be naturally and habitually used, I believe, by the types of folk whose life, physical and mental, Joyce is seeking to describe. In respect of the recurrent emergence of the theme of sex in the minds of his characters, it must always be remembered that his locale was Celtic and his season spring.[10]

He then dismissed the case and vacated the seizure. The Second Circuit by a 2–1 vote affirmed Judge Woolsey.[11] The appellate reasoning, like Judge Woolsey's, was that the offending book must be taken as a whole in order to scrutinize the allegedly obscene passages in context.

Writing for the appellate court, Judge Augustus Hand stated the following:

That numerous long passages in Ulysses contain matter that is obscene under any fair definition of the word cannot be gainsaid; yet they are relevant to the purpose of depicting the thoughts of the characters and are introduced to give meaning to the whole, rather than to promote lust or portray filth for its own sake. The net effect even of portions most open to attack, such as the closing monologue of the wife of Leopold Bloom, is pitiful and tragic, rather than lustful. The book depicts the souls of men and women that are by turns bewildered and keenly apprehensive, sordid and aspiring, ugly and beautiful, hateful and loving. In the end one feels, more than anything else, pity and sorrow for the confusion, misery, and degradation of humanity. Page after page of the book is, or seems to be, incomprehensible. But many passages show the trained hand of an artist, who can at one moment adapt to perfection the style of an ancient chronicler, and at another become a veritable personification of Thomas Carlyle. In numerous places there

---

10. United States v. One Book Called "Ulysses," 5 F. Supp. 182 (S.D.N.Y. 1933), aff'd sub nom. United States v. One Book Entitled Ulysses by James Joyce, 72 F.2d 705 (2d Cir. 1934).

11. In the majority were the iconic cousins, Judges Augustus and Learned Hand. Dissenting was the corrupt Chief Judge Martin Manton, the subject of a later discussion.

are found originality, beauty, and distinction. The book as a whole is not pornographic, and, while in not a few spots it is coarse, blasphemous, and obscene, it does not, in our opinion, tend to promote lust. The erotic passages are submerged in the book as a whole and have little resultant effect. If these are to make the book subject to confiscation, by the same test Venus and Adonis, Hamlet, Romeo and Juliet, and the story told in the Eighth Book of the Odyssey by the bard Demodo-cus of how Ares and Aphrodite were entrapped in a net spread by the outraged Hephaestus amid the laughter of the immortal gods, as well as many other classics, would have to be suppressed. Indeed, it may be questioned whether the obscene passages in Romeo and Juliet were as necessary to the development of the play as those in the monologue of Mrs. Bloom are to the depiction of the latter's tortured soul.[12]

Cerf reprinted Woolsey's landmark decision in the Random House edition of *Ulysses*, making the opinion perhaps the most widely circulated judicial pronouncement in history. But the story doesn't end there.

## THE CURIOUS CASE OF *I AM CURIOUS (YELLOW)*

By any standard in 1968, the Swedish film *I Am Curious (Yellow)* was a dirty movie, and was certainly far more explicit than anything shown before in the United States. As Chief Judge Lumbard put it in his dissenting opinion in the Second Circuit:

> While the sex is heterosexual, the participants indulge in acts of fel-latio and cunnilingus. Needless to say these acts bear no conceivable relevance to any social value, except that of box office appeal.[13]

---

12. 72 F.2d 705.
13. 404 F.2d 196 (2d Cir. 1968) (Lumbard, J., dissenting).

We need not speculate over what Lumbard would have said less than two decades later about the fake orgasm in the Katz's Delicatessen scene in *When Harry Met Sally*, not to mention the family of hard-core films that emerged in the period known as the "Golden Age of Porn."

*I Am Curious (Yellow)* is about a young Swedish girl named Lena and her search for identity. Lena wants to know all she can about life and reality. She collects information on everyone and everything, storing her findings in an enormous archive. She experiments with relationships, political activism, and meditation. The film turns to Lena's interpersonal relationships, including those with her lover.

Judge Murphy, after a jury trial in the Southern District, backed the government in its confiscation of the film under the Tariff Act of 1930, on the ground that it was "obscene or immoral." The court of appeals reversed and found error in Judge Murphy's putting the issue of obscenity to the jury: "[T]he question whether a particular work is [obscene] involves not really an issue of fact but a question of constitutional judgment of the most delicate and sensitive kind."

The majority rejected Chief Judge Lumbard's argument that "[T]he verdict of a jury of twelve men and women is a far better and more accurate reflection of community and social value."

Judge Friendly, in the only opinion he ever wrote on pornography, concurred in the result. He noted that as an inferior court judge, he was not writing on a blank slate and was bound by the Supreme Court precedents, which were difficult to harmonize. He concluded:

> When all this has been said, I am no happier than Chief Judge Lumbard about allowing Grove Press to bring this film into the United States. But our individual happiness or unhappiness is unimportant, and that result is dictated by Supreme Court decisions. . . . What we ought to make plain, however, and not at all in a "tongue-in-cheek" fashion, is that our ruling is limited in two respects: [minors will be

excluded from the audience; and that] the importer, distributors and exhibitors . . . [may not] advertise the film in a manner calculated to capitalize on its extensive portrayals of nudity and sexual activity rather than its supposed serious message. . . . With these reservations and with no little distaste, I concur for reversal.[14]

Friendly's distaste may have been exaggerated, merely reflecting a desire to soothe the sensibilities of his colleague, Chief Judge Lumbard. David Dorsen, who wrote a brilliant biography of Friendly, uncovered in the course of his research the voting memorandum in the case in which Friendly states:

Somewhat to my surprise I vote to reverse . . . I did not find the film so offensive as I expected. . . . I cannot believe any catastrophic result will ensue from the film being seen by anyone foolish enough to go.[15]

Dorsen further reveals that Friendly harbored great skepticism and reservation that pornography leads to antisocial conduct. In a 1963 letter to Professor Louis Henkin, Friendly wrote:

It should have been completely obvious that among the motivations behind legislation against obscenity the idea of preventing action considered to be anti-social is almost the least important, and that in consequence the Supreme Court is way off the beam when it applies to dreary pornography the same test that it does to Communist propaganda.[16]

---

14. *Id.* (Friendly, J., concurring).
15. Friendly, Voting Mem., July 24, 1968, quoted in DORSEN, HENRY FRIENDLY, GREATEST JUDGE OF HIS ERA 151 (Harvard 2012).
16. Friendly Letter to Prof. Louis Henkin, Apr. 15, 1963, quoted in DORSEN, *supra* note 15.

*I Am Curious (Yellow)* is probably the seminal case permitting the kind of hard-core pornography that saturates the Internet today. As the Romans put it, and Chief Judge Lumbard knew, *obsta princi-piis*—beware the opening wedge.

## *DEEP THROAT,* OR HOW FAR DOES A GIRL HAVE TO GO TO UNTANGLE HER TINGLE?

The Second Circuit opinion on *I Am Curious (Yellow)* spawned a succession of hard-core films as though spat out of a pornographic cornucopia. We had arrived at the "Golden Age of Porn." The origins of the Golden Age are typically associated with the 1970 film *Mona the Virgin Nymph*, the first adult film to obtain a wide theatrical release in America. Following this was the massive success of the 1971 gay film *Boys in the Sand* and the notorious *Deep Throat* and *Behind the Green Door*, which were both released in 1972. These three were the first hard-core films to reach a mass mixed-sex audience, and all received positive reviews in mainstream media. Other key films from the period include *The Devil in Miss Jones* and *Score*, the first pornographic films to appear in mainstream movie houses.

*Deep Throat*, the 1972 American pornographic film written and directed by Gerard Damiano and starring Linda Lovelace, offered a cascading continuum of streaming fellatio on a scale never before seen on the screen. What *I Am Curious (Yellow)* was for the literati and the art film crowd, *Deep Throat* was for lowbrow moviegoers seeking sheer titillation.

Judicial acceptance of *Deep Throat* was long in coming. There was a criminal trial in the New York state Supreme Court, Manhattan, just across the street from the U.S. court house. Despite expert testimony that the practices depicted in the film were well within the bounds of "normal" sexual behavior, state court Judge Joel Tyler reacted with righteous indignation against the film. On March 1,

1973, he wrote of *Deep Throat* with overblown judicial invective, calling it "this feast of carrion and squalor," "a nadir of decadence," and "a Sodom and Gomorrah gone wild before the fire."

Continuing, Judge Tyler wrote:

> Oh, yes! There is a gossamer of a story line—the heroine's all-engrossing search for sexual gratification, and when all sexual endeavors fail to gratify, her unique problem is successfully diagnosed to exist in her throat.... The alleged story lines are the facade, the sheer negligee through which clearly shines the producer's and the defendant's true and only purpose, that is, the presentation of unmistakably hard-core pornography.[17]

Tyler fined the producers $100,000, later reduced on appeal. But the ruling gave the film must-see cachet in many quarters. It was not long before *Deep Throat* was widely shown, although with some scenes cut in some states. It became the most popular X-rated film of all time. Silent partners in the film were Anthony Peraino Sr. and his son Louis, members of the Colombo crime family, who raked in millions from the venture. The mob had found a new line of business.

In 1983, *Deep Throat* reached the Mother Court. In *United States v. Various Articles of Obscene Merchandise,* Judge Sweet held that various "hard-core" pornographic articles of merchandise (videocassettes and magazines), including *Deep Throat*, were not "patently offensive" under contemporary community standards in the Southern District, and hence not "obscene."

Interestingly, in the *I Am Curious (Yellow)* case, Judge Friendly was worried that the film would be advertised "in a manner calculated to capitalize on its extensive portrayals of nudity and sexual

---

17. People v. Mature Enters, 73 Misc. 2d 749, 751–52 (1973).

activity rather than its supposed serious message." He was apparently appreciative of the blunt commercial truth that "sex sells." Just a few years later, *Deep Throat* acquired the teaser subtitle, *How Far Does a Girl Have to Go to Untangle Her Tingle?*

The court of appeals affirmed paying deference to Judge Sweet, who had been deputy mayor in the Lindsay administration, and his knowledge of New Yorkers' acceptance of sexually explicit materials. The Second Circuit opinion included a tongue-in-cheek concurrence by Judge Thomas Meskill, the former governor of Connecticut.[18]

After noting that the seized material portrayed "nudity, sexual intercourse between consenting participants, apparently adults, as well as oral and anal sex, including explicit and detailed pictures of genitalia," Judge Meskill made the following observation, which paid great deference to a judge of the Mother Court:

> The question is whether the average person in the community would find the articles patently offensive. New York City may be the most sophisticated and cosmopolitan community in the Nation, but I cannot imagine its residents to be indifferent to what I witnessed in the screening room. If these articles are acceptable to and tolerated by the average member of the community, I wonder if any form of pornography can be lawfully seized ... in the Southern District of New York. Measured against the community standards with which I am familiar, these articles are obscene; they offend my sense of decency and insult the standards of the community that I know. However, I am not a resident of nor as well acquainted with New York City as is Judge Sweet, and I am not well versed in the varieties and types of pornography which circulate there. Consequently, I am ill equipped to question

---

18. 709 F.2d 132 (2d Cir. 1983). Meskill, a Connecticut Yankee, successfully reminded himself that he was sitting in a neighboring court.

Judge Sweet's assessment. Moreover, the government failed to introduce any evidence pertaining to community standards to facilitate our
review. Had this case originated in the District of Connecticut, in a
community whose standards are familiar to me, I would not hesitate
to reverse; but it did not. I reluctantly concur.[19]

*Deep Throat* was good to go.

## THE OFILI CASE—SEX IN THE MUSEUM

In 1999, Mayor Rudy Giuliani failed in his effort to close down the
Brooklyn Museum for showing Chris Ofili's work *The Holy Virgin Mary*. The work, a paper collage, was rendered on linen in the
medium of oil paint, glitter polyester, resin, and elephant dung. The
painting depicted a Black Madonna (Ofili is Nigerian) surrounded
by close-ups of female genitalia cut from pornographic magazines,
and elephant dung. These were formed into shapes reminiscent
of the cherubim and seraphim, which are commonly depicted in
images of the Immaculate Conception and the Assumption of
Mary. Giuliani deemed the exhibit to be "sick stuff."[20] He declared
that the First Amendment does not confer the right to "desecrate
religion" or "do things that are disgusting with regard to animals."
A lawyer, Giuliani apparently never understood Holmes's statement
that the First Amendment guarantees "freedom for the thought that
we hate."

Nina Gershon is an outstanding federal district judge who, prior
to her appointment to the Eastern District federal bench, was a U.S.
magistrate judge in the Mother Court. In a landmark decision, she

---

19. *Id.* at 138.
20. Brooklyn Inst. of Arts and Scis. v. City of N.Y. & Rudolph W. Giuliani, 64 F. Supp. 2d 185
(E.D.N.Y. 1999).

courageously enjoined Giuliani from withholding funding from the Brooklyn Museum for its exhibition of *The Holy Virgin Mary*. Judge Gershon refused to distinguish between books and the visual arts, stressing that

> The relative power of books and visual art is of course immaterial. The communicative power of visual art is not a basis for restricting it but rather the very reason the First Amendment protects it. As recently stated by the Court of Appeals for the Second Circuit, "[v]isual art is as wide ranging in its depiction of ideas, concepts and emotions as any book, treatise, pamphlet or other writing, and is similarly entitled to full First Amendment protection.[21]

*New York Times* art critic Michael Kimmelman wrote of the work:

> The dung in Mr. Ofili's work has a second function. Mr. Ofili has said that "the paintings themselves are very delicate abstractions and I wanted to bring their beauty and decorativeness together with the ugliness" of the dung, so that people "can't ever really feel comfortable with it."[22]

What the whole Ofili flap proved is what attempts at censorship have always proved. Labels such as "Banned in Boston," "X-Rated," or "Sued by Giuliani" only attract curious viewers. Lines formed outside the Brooklyn Museum, with people eager to see what the Ofili/Giuliani fuss was all about.

As Kimmelman wrote at the time:

---

21. *Id.* at 202.
22. Kimmelman, *Of Dung and Its Many Meanings in the Art World*, N.Y. TIMES, Oct. 5, 1999.

The only good thing to come out of the Brooklyn Museum of Art debacle may be that it forces everyone to think again about how art communicates. Had Mayor Rudolph W. Giuliani not singled it out, Chris Ofili's "Holy Virgin Mary" would certainly have gone almost unnoticed in the current "Sensation" exhibition, being a work that, under normal circumstances and in the context of all the really outlandish art in the show, doesn't deserve much attention.[23]

Face it. Times have changed. Outside of child pornography, which is properly viewed as criminal, there is now little legal activity in the field of art censorship. We just don't see the cases we used to see. The New York Society for the Suppression of Vice dissolved in 1950. The Catholic Legion of Decency and its rating system for books and movies have all but disappeared. Contemporary community standards of what is obscene have become porous, perhaps because of the Internet. Indeed, the Internet, where pornography is freely available with epithetic descriptions and explicitly graphic videos, has made censorship virtually impossible. Only its dull repetitiveness and superfluous specificity differentiates pornography from the irrelevant sex scene of the modern cinema. What once was X has become R; R has become PG-13; the really dirty films have become NR—not even rated at all. We now have a new normal.

Indeed, sex in the courtrooms of the Mother Court nowadays has taken on a new—and totally unforeseen—dimension. Pornography has been displaced by same-sex marriage. An 84-year-old gay woman, widowed by the death of her same-sex marital partner, recently sued the United States, claiming that the government's rejection of her right to the spousal estate tax deduction denied her equal protection under the Constitution. The plaintiff,

---

23. *Id.*

Edie Windsor, whom I interviewed on my talk show program, prevailed in the Southern District and in the Supreme Court.[24]

*O tempora, o mores!* We know them when we see them.

---

24. Windsor was quite charming, and her lawyer Robbie Kaplan launched a brilliant equal protection attack on section three of the 1996 Defense of Marriage Act, which, among other things, defines marriage for all purposes under all federal statutes and regulations as "a legal union between a one man and one woman as husband and wife." It seemed like an obvious definition in 1996.

# 7

# U.S. V. THE PRESS AND THE REMARKABLE CAREER OF JUDGE MURRAY I. GURFEIN

*Some newspapers are fit only to line the bottom of birdcages.*
—Spiro Agnew

Judges often surprise us with how they react on the bench as contrasted with our perception of their preappointment dispositions. Hugo Black, a Dixiecrat Senator from Alabama and member of the Ku Klux Klan, turned out to be one of the most libertarian justices of the Supreme Court. Black was a textualist. He used to carry a paperback printed copy of the Constitution with him and read to people from the First Amendment. When the framers said:

Congress shall make no law respecting an establishment of religion, or prohibiting the free exercise thereof; or abridging the freedom of speech, or of the press; or the right of the people peaceably to assemble, and to petition the Government for a redress of grievances.

Black insisted that "no law" meant *no* law.

Earl Warren was a Republican California prosecutor who administered a Court unwavering in its protection of the rights of the accused. Harry Blackmun, a Nixon appointee, wrote the *Roe v. Wade* decision. Chief Justice Roberts, a dyed-in-the wool conservative, voted with the majority to uphold the Patient Protection and Affordable Care Act. Roberts plainly disliked Obamacare, but stated:

Members of this Court are vested with the authority to interpret the law; we possess neither the expertise nor the prerogative to make policy judgments. Those decisions are entrusted to our Nation's elected leaders, who can be thrown out of office if the people disagree with them. It is not our job to protect the people from the consequences of their political choices.[1]

It is not? New one on me. Roberts surprised everyone with his vote. Some even claimed that he first decided the other way, but changed his mind at the last minute.

Many were surprised by the courageously independent performance of Murray Gurfein, the judge of the Mother Court in the *Pentagon Papers* case, when he ruled against President Nixon's attempt to enjoin the *New York Times* from publishing a leaked Defense Department study of the Vietnam War. I was not. I knew Murray Gurfein well when I was in the U.S. Attorney's Office. In

---

1. Nat'l Fed. of Indep. Bus. v. Sebelius, 567 U.S. 1 (2012).

his day, he was a brilliantly successful criminal lawyer who seemed to settle most of his cases. But there was more to Murray Gurfein than met the eye.

A roly-poly kind of guy with an abbreviated walrus mustache, Gurfein wore his dazzling intellect on his sleeve. Second in his class at Harvard Law, and frequently sporting his Phi Beta Kappa key at his navel, he was possessed of a certain intellectual arrogance, but I found him delightful. He had enjoyed a stellar career both as a prosecutor and defense counsel. Before ascending the Mother Court bench, Gurfein served as an Assistant U.S. Attorney, and a star Assistant District Attorney under Thomas E. Dewey. Dewey said that had he won the presidential election of 1948, he would have appointed Gurfein to the Supreme Court. Gurfein enjoyed a distinguished service in the O.S.S. during World War II, serving under the legendary "Wild Bill" Donovan, who had created the agency. He headed up an intelligence operation that utilized convicted Italian-American mobsters to help plan the invasion of Italy. Later, he served as an aide to Justice Robert H. Jackson in prosecuting the Nazi war criminals at Nuremberg.

Gurfein was a staunch Republican and a great patriot. He was outspokenly anticommunist. As a lawyer, he was eloquent in his defense of Judge Kaufman when some at the Bar Association criticized Kaufman over the Rosenberg death sentence. Gurfein was a name partner in the redoubtable firm of Goldstein, Gurfein, Shames & Hyde, along with Republican Nathaniel Goldstein, who served as Attorney General of New York State for over a decade. The Hyde in the firm was Henry B. Hyde, fabled spymaster under Donovan, who helped pave the way for the Allied landings in France. Gurfein had known Hyde since O.S.S. days.

Murray Gurfein's life experiences inevitably informed his judicial character. As an appellate judge later on, he applied the lessons he had learned in the war and at Nuremberg to his judicial thinking.

For example, in *United States v. Natelli*, which we consider later, Gurfein sensitively weighed the situation of Joseph Scansaroli, an audit manager employed by Peat, Marwick Mitchell & Co. The manager contended that he lacked criminal intent because he was only carrying out the orders of the partner, Anthony Natelli. This is what Gurfein had to say:

> There is some merit to Scansaroli's point that he was simply carrying out the judgments of his superior Natelli. The defense of obedience to higher authority has always been troublesome. *There is no sure yardstick to measure criminal responsibility except by measurement of the degree of awareness on the part of a defendant that he is participating in a criminal act, in the absence of physical coercion such as a soldier might face.* Here the motivation to conceal undermines Scansaroli's argument that he was merely implementing Natelli's instructions, at least with respect to concealment of matters that were within his own ken.[2]

The "I was only following orders" defense didn't work for the defendants at Nuremberg with Gurfein the prosecutor, and it wasn't going to work before Gurfein the judge.

At the Bar, Murray Gurfein's career occasionally featured some high-profile cases, but none with the scope and dimension of *Pentagon Papers*. One of Gurfein's cases was the Woodward case in Nassau County. Known as the "shooting of the century," the case involved racehorse owner William Woodward, heir to the Hanover National Bank fortune. Woodward's wife, Ann, allegedly shot and killed her husband, who, as it happened, was cheating on her. After a dinner party for the Duchess of Windsor, the Woodwards returned to their Oyster Bay estate on the North Shore of Long Island and retired to

---

2. 527 F.2d 311 (2d Cir. 1975).

their separate bedrooms. It seems Bill Woodward was coming out of the bathroom late at night, and Ann said she thought he was a prowler. Gurfein helped Ann Woodward prepare her testimony for the grand jury, which refused to indict. He sure knew how to spin a story. Afterwards, Ann Woodward moved to Europe, hoping to escape her past, but she stood indicted in the court of public opinion. At a fancy party in Venice, she found herself talking to a titled Italian in a gondola. The nobleman's wife appeared and said loudly, "It's one thing to flirt, darling, but must you flirt with a murderess?"[3]

Gurfein defended Larry Knohl, an underworld figure and large-scale fencer of stolen securities, on obstruction of justice charges. Knohl had endeavored to persuade one Mrs. Fuller, a witness before the grand jury, to testify falsely about the source of several hundred thousand dollars in stolen treasury bills, which Mrs. Fuller allegedly laundered for Knohl at various banks. When the FBI intercepted Mrs. Fuller at one of the banks, she learned of the illicit source of the bills. She thereupon went back to Knohl, who told her what he wanted her to tell the grand jury. Knohl told her to say that the source was a recently deceased individual named O'Neil, when in fact the source was Knohl himself. There was a tape-recorded meeting with Knohl, Mrs. Fuller, and her lawyer at Mrs. Fuller's apartment, in which the attempted subornation occurred. Knohl told her, "Don't worry about ... [the subpoena]. You stick to the O'Neil story and nothing will happen." Knohl had previously said to her, "Stick to your story, the O'Neil story . . . because a dead man can tell no tales." The jury returned a guilty verdict against Larry Knohl.

I first met Murray Gurfein when I was a federal prosecutor. Gurfein represented Knohl, who was seeking a lenient sentence before Judge Murphy based on purported cooperation with the

---

3. Recounted in the enthralling chronicle of the Woodward case by Susan Braudy, *This Crazy Thing Called Love.*

government in making a number of new criminal cases. Gurfein tried valiantly to persuade me that Knohl had "gotten religion," but I could find no evidence of this in the files. Murray Gurfein always made me smile.

In another case, Gurfein brought me two witnesses, businessmen from the North Shore of Long Island, who had been defrauded out of millions of dollars. The case was, as Judge Friendly put it, "another of those sickening financial frauds which so sadly memorialize the rapacity of the perpetrators and the gullibility, and perhaps also the cupidity, of the victims."[4]

A flamboyant fraudster named Salvatore Marino, who was in the habit of flashing large wads of currency, had led Gurfein's clients to believe that there was an "eccentric millionaire" who was dying of cancer and loved to lose at the racetrack. The millionaire liked to make exotic bets, such as "fifth for second." This meant that the millionaire was betting that the fifth horse to go off in the odds at every racetrack everywhere in the country would finish second. Under this scenario, the millionaire invariably lost his improbable bet, and Marino, the grand ringmaster and *metteur en scene* of the conspiracy, always won; hence the wads of cash. The victims were only too eager to participate. Marino said it would be difficult, but they could do it if they deposited $500,000 in escrow with a lawyer Marino knew, who according to Marino was a cousin of Senator Javits. The crooked lawyer, of course, immediately allowed Marino to loot the escrowed funds. After the victims had been allowed to win a little, they were told that the millionaire's bet for the week was "last for last," an obvious sucker bet. The last horse to go off in the odds would probably finish last; it is probably still running. Not satisfied to have drawn the victims into a bet that they could not

---

4. United States v. Benjamin, 328 F.2d 854 (2d Cir. 1964).

conceivably win, Marino and his confederates bribed the typesetter at the *Morning Telegraph* racing paper to change the odds on the last horse from, say, 70 to one to 700 to one. It would take a sharp-eyed editor indeed to catch this one, since no one cared about the odds on the last horse to finish the race.

Then, Marino moved in for the kill. He told his victims that they had lost millions of dollars, and that they better pay up before the millionaire brought in a team of enforcers from the Mafia. The money in escrow, he said, was payment on account. To underscore the threat, Marino had a henchman named Donnie Alfano, a hefty individual who looked something like the Luca Brasi character in *The Godfather*, come to his table at a restaurant near Lincoln Center, where he was dining with the two victims. Alfano had his hand in his pocket and looked at the victims menacingly. Marino informed them that if they didn't come up with the money, they were both dead men. They promised to get the money, but instead ran out of town as fast as they could. Then, they called Murray Gurfein, who called me. I alerted the FBI.

After the victims gave me statements and testified before the grand jury, I indicted Marino, Alfano, the corrupt lawyer, and some other bit players in the sting, including a tall willowy blonde from Belmar, New Jersey, named Marie McGinley, and tried them before Judge John Cannella and a jury. McGinley, who was actually Marino's girlfriend, had been introduced to the victims as the girlfriend of the nonexistent "eccentric millionaire." This was supposed to lend credibility and substance to the millionaire's existence. In my summation, I called McGinley the "spoonful of sugar who made the medicine go down" in Marino's scheme to defraud.

Judge Cannella was a primitive man, a star football lineman at Fordham. A seasoned trial judge who had come up through Democratic politics and the state court system, Cannella was a master of metaphor, often the mixed metaphor. If a lawyer overtried a case, instead of admonishing him that he was gilding the lily, Cannella would accuse the miscreant of "gelding the cake."

In the Marino case, Cannella gave a jury instruction that tyrannized all analogy. A conspiracy, he explained, is like "a symphony":

> There is the conductor (Marino), the violinists, the flutists and players of other instruments (the minor players in the conspiracy). Then, there is a heavy-set musician who crashes two cymbals together (Alfano), and there may be a tall blonde lady (McGinley) who holds a small triangle. Mr. Zirin would call her the "spoonful of sugar." At just the right moment in the symphony, the conductor points to her, and she strikes the triangle. Maybe you hear her, and maybe you don't. But, they are all part of the same symphony.

During the trial, Jimmy Breslin called me. He said he had been talking to Judge Cannella, because he wanted to write a column for the *Daily News* on the case. "What was Marie McGinley doing there?" Jimmy asked, "Giving blowjobs to everybody?" I laughed, "Jimmy, I can't answer a fucking shitty question like that." It was the Morgenthau office's version of "no comment," since in those days, decency prevented the press from printing expletives, and professional ethics prevented prosecutors from trying their cases in the press. The jury returned a guilty verdict against all defendants. It made Murray Gurfein very happy.

Some years later, when I was in private practice, I had a civil case in Los Angeles involving airplane seats for the new wide-bodied jets. I flew out to the Coast with my client, who said he had heard about a great Italian restaurant in Westwood. The restaurant was packed to the rafters. We were tired, but my client was willing to wait at the bar. To my trained sensibilities, the place smelled of a mob hangout.

I went to the men's room. Over the urinal were some autographed photos. Some of the pictured subjects I recognized, including Vito Genovese, Carlo Gambino, Meyer Lansky, and Bugsy Siegel. I returned to the bar. A heavyset bartender approached us, and we ordered drinks. The bartender looked uncomfortably familiar. It was Alfano, recently out of prison. I wondered whether there might not be ground glass in the scotch.

"Are you from New York?" he inquired.

"Yes."

"Your last name don't begin with a Z, does it?"

"Yes."

"Do you remember Sal Marino? I'm Donnie Alfano. You sent me away for two years."

"Oh yes, hi Donnie, happy to see you."

"Are you here on business?" he asked.

His face darkened when I said yes. "But I'm not a prosecutor any more," I was quick to add. "I'm a defense lawyer."

"Great to see you, DA" said Donnie, his face lighting up. "You know anything you want in the place is yours."

"How about a table for two?"

Alfano looked out over the restaurant and caught the eye of two heavies in the middle of a spaghetti dinner, bright red tomato stains bespattered on the large cloth napkins they had tucked under their prominent chins. He snapped his fingers and motioned for them to leave. My client and I sat down at the table and enjoyed a late Italian dinner. I owed the success of the evening, quite indirectly, to Murray Gurfein.

Back to Murray Gurfein, United States judge. It was Richard Nixon himself who appointed Gurfein to the bench of the Mother Court to succeed Judge Murphy in 1971. Age 65 at the time of his appointment, Gurfein had always very much desired judicial office.

Gurfein presided over the *Pentagon Papers* case, a knock-down drag-out fight in the all-out war between Nixon and the press.[5] It was his first case as a judge. He drew the case in a random assignment system. Nixon was surely overjoyed to be before Gurfein because of his Republican leanings, but the new judge was not to bend to the will even of the president and administration that had put him in office.

The government is unquestionably entitled to its secrets, but once those secrets are revealed, the press is entitled to publish them, unless publication poses a clear and present danger to national security. The press protection afforded by the First Amendment is therefore not exactly absolute, but the qualification ought to apply only in the narrowest of circumstances.

Chief Justice Hughes gave two examples in *Near v. Minnesota*:

> No one would question but that a government might prevent actual obstruction to its recruiting service or the publication of the *sailing dates of transports or the number and location of troops*. On similar grounds, the primary requirements of decency may be enforced against obscene publications. The security of the community life may be protected against incitements to acts of violence and the overthrow by force of orderly government. The constitutional guaranty of free speech does not "protect a man from an injunction against uttering words that may have all the effect of force."[6]

Sometimes, these two values assume a collision course.

In the 1970s Nixon seethed with hatred of the media. His ill will verged on paranoia, and bashing the press became the favorite pastime of the administration. The *New York Times* and the *Washington*

---

5. United States v. N.Y. Times Co., 328 F. Supp. 324 (S.D.N.Y. 1971).
6. 283 U.S. 697, 716 (1931).

*Post* were his favorite piñatas. They were among the "nattering nabobs of negativism," and the "hopeless, hysterical hypochondriacs of history," the alliterative phrases his vice president, Spiro Agnew, used to describe them.[7] When Nixon learned he had to invite *Washington Post* publisher Katharine Graham to a White House Medal of Freedom dinner, he ordered her to be seated as far away as possible, and with no VIPs at her table. At one time, he even wanted to indict the *New York Times*.

It was hard to know which Nixon hated more: the leakers in his administration or the press that published the leaked information. In 1969, responding to suspected news leaks about Vietnam, he had Kissinger, acting without court approval, order FBI wiretaps on the telephones of 17 journalists and White House aides. Many news stories based on the purported leaks questioned progress in the American war effort, further fueling the antiwar movement. In a tape from the Oval Office on February 22, 1971, Nixon said, "In the short run, it would be so much easier, wouldn't it, to run this war in a dictatorial way, kill all the reporters and carry on the war." The "first thing" Shakespeare's Dick the Butcher wanted to do was "kill all the lawyers."[8] Nixon evidently differed, believing that it was the press that should come first.

"The press is your enemy," Nixon explained five days later in a meeting with Admiral Thomas H. Moorer, chairman of the Joint Chiefs of Staff, according to another tape.

---

7. White House speechwriter Bill Safire, later a *New York Times* columnist, wrote these for Agnew. Nixon bugged Safire's phone when he was at the White House to see if he was leaking information to the press.

8. *Henry IV, Part 2*, act IV, sc. 2. This oft-repeated quote is almost universally misconceived as lawyer bashing. Actually, it was a compliment to lawyers. In plotting a revolution, Shakespeare's character saw the lawyers as an independent group who would protect free institutions and get in the way. Nixon intended no such compliment to the press.

Enemies. Understand that? . . . Now, never act that way . . . give them a drink, you know, treat them nice, you just love it, you're trying to be helpful. But don't help the bastards. Ever. Because they're trying to stick the knife right in our groin.[9]

Unfortunately for Nixon and his place in history, the press won; Nixon's groin lost.

The Pentagon Papers were an analytical history of American decision making in Vietnam from 1945 to 1967, commissioned in 1967 by Secretary of Defense Robert McNamara, one of the "best and the brightest."[10] Until 1971, the existence of the Papers and their contents were a closely guarded secret—even within the government.[11] Morton Halperin and Les Gelb were in charge of the project. They tasked 36 government researchers, including Richard Holbrooke, who had served the State Department in Saigon, and Daniel Ellsberg to write portions of the study. The study revealed how wrong-headed the war was, how it was plagued with a host of disastrous decisions, and how the government covered up its mistakes and misjudgments. Understandably, the Pentagon Papers carried a "Top Secret" classification.

Ellsberg, a consultant with the think tank Rand Corporation, had access to the Papers. Originally a hawk, he later became an opponent of the war, and sought to leak the Papers because they demonstrated that President Johnson consistently lied to the American people and the Congress about his intentions. Ellsberg copied the Papers in late 1969, and in March 1971 gave them to Neil Sheehan,

---

9. Woodward & Bernstein, *40 Years after Watergate, Nixon Was Far Worse Than We Thought*, WASH. POST, June 8, 2012.

10. In his chilling account of the men in power who led us to the Vietnam War, titled not without some sarcasm *The Best and the Brightest* (1972), David Halberstam called McNamara "a fool."

11. Even President Johnson, Secretary of State Dean Rusk, and National Security Adviser Walt Whitman Rostow were unaware of the report.

a reporter for the *Times*. After the *Times* published excerpts from the Papers on June 13, 1971, Attorney General John Mitchell sent a telegram to *Times* publisher Arthur Sulzberger at the behest of President Nixon demanding that the paper stop further publication of the excerpts. Mitchell stated that disclosing the information would cause "irreparable injury to the defense interests of the United States," and claimed that the publication was in violation of laws against espionage. Sulzberger refused to cease publication, and the government sued the *Times* for an injunction. The case came before the newly appointed judge Murray Gurfein in the Southern District of New York.[12]

It appeared anomalous that Nixon was so hell-bent on suppressing the study, as it reflected badly on prior Democratic administrations. Starting with Johnson's 1964 Gulf of Tonkin Resolution, by 1971 the country had been at war in Vietnam for seven years, with 59,000 American soldiers dead and many more wounded. Nixon's first instinct when he heard about the leak was to do nothing. But Secretary of State Henry Kissinger convinced the president that it would be a bad precedent for protecting future secrets. The overarching reason was that Nixon wanted to teach the press a lesson about its boundaries, and perhaps destroy his archenemy, the *New York Times*.

Many books have been written about the *Pentagon Papers* case, a case for the ages in the history of constitutional law.[13] It is far beyond my power to add or detract. I will not attempt to describe

---

12. Ellsberg also gave copies to the *Washington Post*, which commenced publication June 18. The government sued the *Washington Post* in the District of Columbia, and the district judge, Gerhard Gesell, a reporter before he became a lawyer, denied the injunction. Gesell was affirmed on appeal.

13. The best blow-by blow account I have seen is in Jim Goodale's fine book, *Fighting for the Press* (2013). Goodale argues that governmental claims of "national security," used to scotch press freedoms, are usually "hot air."

the twists and turns that the litigation took or the views of the various judges who grappled with the issue.

My focus here is Murray Gurfein, who, with the courage and characteristic independence of a Mother Court judge, vindicated the basic right of free expression and the public's right to know something other than what the government wants it to know. An old warrior and a great patriot, Gurfein guarded many secrets during his career. He was the ideal judge, in light of his O.S.S. background, to sense that the information in the Pentagon Papers really didn't implicate national security. He understood that the case arose because the Papers were embarrassing to the government. In this respect, he was the quintessence of judicial independence. Transports were not about to sail; troop locations and the identities of spies were not imperiled. On the contrary, four years after the Papers were commissioned, much of the material in question was already in the public domain.

The Papers did show, however, that the government made colossal and unforgivable mistakes in its conduct of the Vietnam War, and this suit was the government's attempt to cover that up. The claim that publication would be disastrous was necessarily spurious.[14] At the hearing before Gurfein, the government offered evidence it claimed would support the "Top Secret" classification. Pressed by Gurfein to identify what parts of the Papers damaged national security and how, the witnesses were short on answers. All the government came back to was that the Papers were stolen.

Gurfein denied the injunction and ruled for the *Times*. The superb decision immediately won him eminence as a judge. The *Pentagon Papers* case became a landmark limiting the government's

---

14. Shortly after publication by the *New York Times* and the *Washington Post*, the government itself published the papers. The documents had been over-classified to cover up the mistakes of government officials in the conduct of the war during the Kennedy and Johnson administrations.

right to impose censorship on a newspaper's publication of material allegedly affecting national security.

In ringing words dealing with press freedom issues that still resonate today, Gurfein said:

> *The security of the Nation is not at the ramparts alone.* Security also lies in the value of our free institutions. A cantankerous press, an obstinate press, an ubiquitous press must be suffered by those in authority in order to preserve the even greater values of freedom of expression and the right of the people to know.
>
> These are troubled times. There is no greater safety valve for discontent and cynicism about the affairs of the government than freedom of expression in any form.[15]

Gurfein's "not at the ramparts alone" opinion ranks with Holmes's "freedom for the thought that we hate" as most often quoted by constitutional lawyers in the field of government attempts to censor free expression. A judge of the Mother Court had held that the right to publish of a free press trumped a conclusory, unsubstantiated governmental claim of national security.

In the *Pentagon Papers* case, the Second Circuit, its eight active judges sitting en banc, reversed Gurfein with three judges dissenting. The Supreme Court, however, reversed the Second Circuit and affirmed Gurfein, 6–3, stressing that in order to exercise prior restraint on the press, the government assumed a heavy burden of showing that the publication could cause "grave and irreparable danger." And so it was Gurfein who had called it correctly from the very beginning. The opportunity to seize history and shape it presented itself. Five judges

---

15. United States v. N.Y. Times Co., 328 F. Supp. 324, 331 (S.D.N.Y. 1971) (emphasis added).

of the Second Circuit and three justices of the U.S. Supreme Court missed the boat. Murray Gurfein got it, and got it right.[16]

In our digital age, where ideas and pornography run riot on the Internet, the cases of the fugitives Julian Assange for publishing classified State Department cables on his Internet dump, WikiLeaks, and of Edward Snowden for leaking details of top-secret surveillance programs to the *Manchester Guardian* have yet to reach the U.S. courts, but the principles of the *Pentagon Papers* case apply. They should, in my view, protect Assange but not Snowden from criminal prosecution in the United States.[17] The facts are only distinguishable because the publication occurred before an injunction could be issued.[18]

In the age of the Internet, volumes of leaked materials can be readily published before there is a chance for the government to challenge the publication in court. So the government must shift its tactics to indicting the publisher in order to deter future misconduct. Such an indictment, to the extent it imposes a "chilling effect" on future publications by Assange or by others, is tantamount to the "prior restraint" on speech outlawed in the *Pentagon Papers* case. It is more worthy of Turkey or China, where dissidents are arrested for their posts, Tweets, and blogs, than of a country ruled by law with political freedoms among its core values.

---

16. Nixon elevated Gurfein to the Second Circuit three years later on July 11, 1974, the month before he resigned the presidency.

17. Army Pfc Bradley Manning, who stole the documents and gave them to Assange, in a general court martial pleaded guilty to 10 out of 22 charges of communicating national defense information to an unauthorized source. He has said he acted alone. Manning also stood trial on the remaining charges, including the most serious charge, "aiding the enemy." The military judge acquitted Manning of "aiding the enemy." Manning was sentenced to 35 years in prison. Assange, who may be the subject of a sealed indictment in the United States, has holed up in the Ecuadorian embassy in London, and has thus far avoided extradition to Sweden.

18. Much has been made by former *Times* Executive Editor Bill Keller that Assange is not a true journalist entitled to First Amendment protections, but a "rock star leaker," who exercised no journalistic discretion. To my mind, this is a distinction without a difference. Both are publishers of leaked information.

Unlike England, we have no Official Secrets Act to criminalize the media's possession or publication of stolen documents.[19] There is the 1917 Espionage Act, which former Southern District Judge Michael Mukasey calls an "oldie but goodie." Mukasey argues that the Espionage Act should apply to Assange. Mukasey, an arch conservative, said he would like to see Assange prosecuted under two clauses of the 1917 Espionage Act, "one of which criminalizes the publication of defense-related information, and the other of which criminalizes the publication of classified information."

But there has never been a criminal prosecution under the 1917 Espionage Act against a publisher of stolen classified information; and, were there to be, there are serious constitutional questions about such a prosecution. Mukasey is gleefully confident that the Supreme Court would uphold the prosecution as a reasonable limitation on press freedoms. Others, champions of a free press, are not so cocksure.

Murray Gurfein, the "voice of one crying in the wilderness"[20] in the *Pentagon Papers* case, served an illustrious three-year career on the Mother Court, and later for four years as a judge on the Second Circuit—his career sadly cut short when he died of cancer in 1979. A man could not wish for a richer legacy. He had quite a run.

---

19. In the Second Circuit argument of the Pentagon Papers case, when lawyers for the *Times* resisted the term "stolen," the judges referred to the papers as "received from someone who had no authority to give it to them," although Judge Friendly said, "Let's say they received the goods in the process of embezzlement."

20. Isaiah 40:3; John 1:23.

# U.S. V. THE MOB

*Conspiracy is the "darling of the modern prosecutor's nursery."*
—Judge Learned Hand in *Harrison v. United States*[1]

The Mother Court played a major role in the degradation and destruction of the American Mafia, and the government charged most of the mobsters who came before the court with conspiracy.

The federal conspiracy statute provides as follows:

> If two or more persons conspire either to commit any offense against the United States, or to defraud the United States, or any agency thereof in any manner or for any purpose, and one or more of such persons do any act to effect the object of the conspiracy, [each shall be fined or imprisoned].[2]

A conspiracy is a partnership in crime. When two or more people agree to commit an illegal act, the crime of conspiracy is complete

---

1. 7 F.2d 259, 263 (2d Cir. 1925) (L. Hand, J.).
2. 18 U.S.C. § 371.

once there is an overt act in furtherance of the conspiracy. The agreed-upon crime need not be accomplished. The object of the conspiracy need not be achieved. Two people may agree it might be a good idea to rob a bank; but if it is nothing more than an idea, there is no crime. If one of them, however, rents a getaway car to be used in the robbery, the conspiracy is made out even if the robbery is never even attempted. The essence of the conspiracy is the agreement, which may be inferred circumstantially from the acts, declarations, or conduct of the conspirators. The agreement need not be reduced to writing. It rarely is. It may be evidenced by a handshake, a nod, or a wink. A conspiracy is relatively easy to establish. No wonder it is, as Hand said, "the "darling of the modern prosecutor's nursery."

The unique feature of the conspiracy doctrine is how it is proved. The Federal Rules of Evidence define hearsay as an out-of-court "Statement [defined in the Rules as "a person's oral assertion, written assertion, or nonverbal conduct"] that . . . a party offers in evidence to prove the truth of the matter asserted in the statement."[3] It's simple if you think long enough about it.

There is, however, an exception to the hearsay rule in conspiracy cases. There, the out-of-court declarations of a co-conspirator in furtherance of the conspiracy constitute evidence against the other conspirators, *even if introduced to prove the truth of the matter asserted*.[4] This is because each co-conspirator is considered an agent of the others in carrying out the agreed-upon plan. So that if Butch Cassidy goes alone to a clothing store and says to the store clerk witness, "Two ski masks, please, and by the way is there a gun shop nearby, as I am also shopping for my friend Sundance who is looking for a

3. FED. R. EVID. 801(a)–(c).
4. Federal Rule of Evidence 801(d)(2)(E) sets out the traditional elements of the co-conspirator's declaration exception. The rule states, in material part, that such statements are admissible if they are made "by a co-conspirator of a party during the course and in furtherance of the conspiracy."

Winchester," but for the conspiracy exception to the hearsay rule, the testimony of the store clerk that Cassidy asserted Sundance wants to buy a gun would be inadmissible as it is being introduced as proof of the truth of the matter asserted, namely that Sundance in fact needs a gun. But the hearsay exception makes the out-of-court declaration admissible evidence against Sundance, and so we have a great movie.

The evidence in the Rosenberg case was that one of the spies went to New Mexico and introduced himself to Greenglass with the prearranged password, "I come from Julius." This out-of-court declaration, offered in evidence to prove the truth of the matter asserted, namely that the spy in fact came from Julius Rosenberg, would similarly be evidence against both Julius and Ethel Rosenberg since the declaration was in furtherance of the conspiracy. Normally, someone can be convicted only on the basis of his own acts, declarations, or conduct. But if there is a conspiracy, and a defendant is established to be a member, his guilt can be proved by acts and declarations of the other co-conspirators to which he was not a party. Hence, the conspiracy dragnet, catching multiple people in its web, is anathema to libertarians.

When I joined the U.S. Attorney's office, everyone was still talking about the conspiracy case *United States v. Bufalino*, known as the "Apalachin affair," a 1960 Southern District trial before Judge Irving Kaufman. This was perhaps because my friend John Sprizzo, who was then assistant chief of the criminal division and later became a federal judge, had represented the government in this high-profile case that prosecutors won before a jury and then lost on appeal. The case involved 20 of the more than 60 mobsters who attended a summit meeting of the American Mafia on November 14, 1957, at the 130-acre estate of boss "Joe the Barber" Barbera in Apalachin, New York. Before the meeting could get off the ground, state police and federal agents raided Barbera's home.

The government charged the Apalachin 20 with conspiracy to obstruct justice by giving similarly false and evasive answers before the grand jury as to the nature of the meeting. The defendants, many of whom were festooned in Italian tailor-made suits, drove expensive cars, and had come long distances to attend the meeting, were apprehended as they tried to escape the house into the nearby woods, which police found strewn with $100 bills.

Apalachin is a small town along the south shore of the Susquehanna River, about 200 miles northwest of the Foley Square Courthouse. The jury must have wondered why anyone would go there. There was no evidence at trial of the purpose of the meeting or that there was anything improper or illegal about it. There was no evidence, moreover, that any violation of state or federal law took place at the gathering or that any criminal acts were being planned. No one at the trial was permitted to say the word "Mafia," as it was deemed too prejudicial.[5] Still, the jury must have known that sitting in the well of the courtroom before them was a rogues' gallery of the American underworld. The guest list at the Barberas' that evening read like a who's who of mobsters. Mario Puzo and Francis Ford Coppola could not have done any better. Among those were notorious gangsters were mob kingpin Don Vito Genovese, Carlo Gambino, Joe Profaci, and Joseph "Joe Bananas" Bonanno. Questioned by police, virtually all of them claimed that they had visited the house from such far-flung locations as Buffalo, Rochester, Dallas, Denver, and Los Angeles because they heard that Barbera was not feeling well. Anther claimed he had visited the house to deliver fish.

The lawyers were the very cream of the criminal defense bar. These included prominent out-of-town lawyers Percy Foreman of

---

5. The trial occurred about a decade before Congress enacted the Racketeer Influenced and Corrupt Organizations Act (RICO), which made the organized criminal conspiracy a crime in and of itself. After 1970 in RICO prosecutions, the word "Mafia" found its way into the courtroom lexicon.

Dallas for defendant Joseph Civello, and Frank Raichle of Buffalo for John Montana. The New York lawyers were Abe Brodsky for Michele Miranda, Henry Singer for Joseph Profaci, and Osmond Fraenkel for the troika John Scalish, Paul Castellano, and Carmine Lombardozzi.

Radical lawyer Leonard Boudin eventually joined these luminaries in the court of appeals, and Nanette Dembitz of the New York Civil Liberties Union piled on with an amicus brief.[6]

Although at least 50 men managed to escape into the woods outside Barbera's house, state troopers and federal agents successfully arrested another 58. State Trooper Edgar Croswell, a real-life Inspector Javert who had been channeling Barbera for about a year, headed the raiding party.

The government contended that the conspiracy was hatched in the 40-minute period between the time that Barbera's wife saw unmarked police cars parked outside the house and the time when the mass exodus began, arguing that the similarity of the implausible statements insofar as "they all deny planning and seek to concoct a picture of accidental and coincidental presence at Barbera's [house]" could only be accounted for by an illegal agreement. The defendants were convicted before Judge Kaufman, who imposed sentences ranging from three to five years.

The Second Circuit reversed Judge Kaufman, holding that there was no evidence of a conspiracy, namely, that the defendants had agreed to lie about the gathering or that they had reason to anticipate that any of them would be called to testify under oath about the events of that day.

---

6. An amicus brief, usually authored by a lawyer, is filed only with leave of court. The lawyer submitting the brief does not represent a party to the controversy, but seeks to assist the court with his take on the legal issues before it.

As Second Circuit Judge Lumbard, a former Southern District U.S. Attorney, put it,

> The fact that none of those present admitted that he was asked to attend a meeting for other than social purposes and that at least some of those present must have lied, does not warrant a jury's conclusion that any or all lies were told pursuant to an agreement made on November 14. There is nothing in the record or in common experience to suggest that it is not just as likely that each one present decided for himself that it would be wiser not to discuss all that he knew.[7]

Is the law an ass, Mr. Bumble?

And as to the law of conspiracy, the appellate court sounded a warning in a stinging rebuke to Judge Kaufman:

> We doubt the advisability of requiring that the government meet any absolute standards in conspiracy cases. At the same time we cannot state too strongly our view that it is incumbent on trial judges, in deciding whether the government has made out a sufficient case to go to the jury, to analyze with meticulous care the evidence *as to each defendant*. When this is not done, it is the duty of the appellate courts to act. Cases such as this prove all too well the need for the caution, which from time to time has been articulated by the Supreme Court with respect to the indiscriminate indictment of numerous defendants in conspiracy cases.[8]

The takeaway from the Apalachin case was that it confirmed for the public the existence of the American Mafia. The FBI had

---

7. 576 F.2d 446.
8. *Id.* (emphasis added).

refused to acknowledge the existence of a national crime syndicate, as J. Edgar Hoover preferred to concentrate his agency's efforts on the Communist threat rather than organized crime.[9] Now things would be different.

The background and purpose of the meeting all came out in due course. Vito Genovese and Frank Costello had been rivals in seeking control over the Luciano crime family in New York. Costello, known as "Prime Minister of the Underworld," did not attend the Apalachin meeting. He was under intense police surveillance after an attempt on his life. Genovese had allied with notorious mobsters Tommy Lucchese and Carlo Gambino. Costello's allies were Joe Bonanno, Joe Profaci, and Nino Magaddino, who had secretly switched sides. This created a war within Cosa Nostra. Hungry for power, Genovese schemed with Lucchese and Gambino to assassinate Costello and his henchman Albert Anastasia.

Costello had a long and studied history as a mob boss. After starting his career in the early 1900s as a petty criminal, he rose to become a powerful and highly respected underworld luminary. Strangely, he wanted to enter high society, and even engaged a psychiatrist to help him—a scenario since emulated in both the film *Analyze This* and the TV serial *The Sopranos*.

During the early 1950s Costello agreed to testify before the televised Kefauver Senate Committee hearings into organized crime. He was front stage center. Asked by Committee Counsel Rudolph Halley,[10] "What have you done for your country, Mr. Costello?" he famously evoked uproarious laughter with the answer, "I paid my

---

9. The book *Official and Confidential: The Secret Life of J. Edgar Hoover* (1993) claimed that Meyer Lansky and Frank Costello, who both missed the Apalachin meeting, had blackmailed Hoover into laying off the mob with compromising photos of Hoover and long-time aide Clyde Tolson engaged in sexual congress.

10. With the hearings, Halley achieved eminence. He went on to become the announcer for the CBS radio thriller *Gang Busters*, became president of the New York City Council, and even launched an unsuccessful bid for mayor.

tax." Costello then walked out of the hearings and went to jail for 18 months. This was followed by a conviction for tax evasion that was overturned on appeal, and another trial and conviction. By 1957 Costello was out of jail, but seriously weakened in prestige.

Hit man Vincent "Chin" Gigante, a protégé of Genovese and a rising star in the mob, made the attempt on Costello's life. He took his shot at Costello on May 2, 1957, in the lobby of the Majestic, an Art Deco apartment building on Central Park West and 72nd Street. The Majestic, one of New York's most famous luxury cooperatives, was home to a number of members of the Genovese crime family, including Lucky Luciano and Meyer Lansky as well as Costello. Gigante, who had been stopped by police leaving Barbera's house the previous year, was unable to attend the Apalachin meeting, as he had another engagement. He was in prison.

Gigante botched the assassination attempt. Before shooting, he shouted, "This is for you, Frank." Startled, Costello turned his head sufficiently to dodge the bullet, which left him nicked with a minor head wound.[11]

Costello's number two, Albert Anastasia, was not so lucky. On the morning of October 25, 1957, Anastasia entered the barbershop of the Park Sheraton Hotel in Midtown Manhattan for his regular trim and shave. As he relaxed in the barber chair, a hot towel over his face, two masked gunmen rushed in, shoved the barber out of the way, and fired. After the first volley of bullets, Anastasia lunged at his killers. However, the stunned Anastasia had actually attacked the gunmen's reflections in the wall mirror of the barbershop. The gunmen continued firing and Anastasia finally fell to the floor, dead in a pool of blood. The *Daily News* featured front-page photos of the body draped in a barber's cloth. Although Genovese doubtless

---

11. The case against Gigante collapsed when Costello failed to identify his assailant.

ordered the hit, no one was ever charged in the case. The barber's chair in which Anastasia was reclining fetched $7,000 at auction, and is now in the Mob Museum in Las Vegas.

Prior to the Apalachin meeting, Genovese made Costello "an offer he couldn't refuse." Costello abdicated as boss in favor of Genovese, but kept certain gambling operations in the South. Genovese had made the peace. The purpose of the Apalachin meeting was to solidify Genovese's power as supreme boss of the mob and to divide the Mafia gambling and narcotics operations controlled by Anastasia. Because of the raid, the meeting was a complete fiasco.

The subsequent trial in the Southern District, though the verdict was ultimately reversed on appeal, had many unfortunate ramifications for Genovese. First, the existence of La Cosa Nostra became so clear that even Hoover had to acknowledge it. Second, a number of top Mafia figures, including Genovese, were soon indicted. And the FBI for the first time gave the organized criminal syndicate prioritized attention.

Genovese took the Fifth in June 1958 before the Senate McClellan committees investigating organized crime. The next month he and Gigante were indicted in the Southern District on a narcotics conspiracy charge. Genovese was sentenced to 15 years and later died in prison of natural causes, but not before he ordered hits on at least three infamous mobsters. One of these, Joe Valachi, escaped an assassination attempt in prison. Displeased with the mob's intention to whack him, he became a government witness and revealed what he knew of La Cosa Nostra. As a result of Apalachin, the Mafia as it had existed went into a period of decline.

UN British Ambassador Sir John Sawers, who later became head of MI6, Britain's CIA, reminded me once that it is for the executive branch to protect our safety, and for the judiciary to protect our liberties. In the Apalachin case we saw both interests served.

Put another way, General Michael C. Hayden, director of Central Intelligence under George W. Bush, said that when it came to terror suspects, he would play in fair territory, but with "chalk dust on [his] cleats." Going as close to the line as you possibly can was the Justice Department's thinking in prosecuting in the Apalachin case.

One can't write about mobster conspiracy trials without mention of the "Pizza Connection" case of the 1980s, which stands as the longest trial in U.S. history. The narcotics conspiracy trial, before Judge Pierre Leval in the Mother Court, was against 22 defendants and took 17 months to complete. The jury convicted 18 of the original defendants; one was acquitted, two pleaded guilty during the trial, and one was shot and killed as he walked on a Greenwich Village street.

The then U.S. Attorney Rudy Giuliani prosecuted the case. A lead lawyer for the government in Giuliani's office was Louis J. Freeh, who later became a judge of the Mother Court, and then FBI director in the Clinton administration.

The evidence proved that a mobster-run enterprise, directed by Bonanno crime family *caporegime* Salvatore ("The Baker") Catalano, distributed large amounts of heroin and cocaine, and then laundered the cash proceeds before sending them back to suppliers in Sicily.[12] The street value of the narcotics came to $1.6 billion over a nine-year period. The evidence, largely obtained from informants and wiretaps, as is standard in such cases, was that the defendants used a number of independently owned pizza shops as fronts for their illegal operations.

Mario Puzo could not have written a better trial scenario. The defendants and their lawyers, seated in rows, filled the well of the courtroom and overflowed into the spectators' section. Witnesses

---

12. A *caporegime* or "capo" is a high-ranking Mafia boss.

for the government included an FBI agent named Joe Pistone, better known by his undercover name, "Donnie Brasco,"[13] and Tomasso Buscetta of the Sicilian Mafia, who testified against his former criminal cohorts as to the Sicilians' dominance of the U.S. drug trade during the early 1970s.

Then there was Salvatore Contorno, who turned state's evidence after learning that he was the target of a foiled Mafia hit. He testified to a 1980 meeting in Sicily attended by five of the defendants on trial. The mobsters exhibited packages containing a white powder in clear plastic envelopes, "each bearing different tiny scissor cuts or pen or pencil marks to identify the original owner."

Conspiracy cases are often proved by circumstantial evidence showing connections and relationships that together become a mosaic clarifying the factual picture. Learned Hand called this type of proof a "cumulation of instances."[14] Two weeks after the meeting, federal narcotics agents in Milan seized 40 kilograms of 85 percent pure heroin worth $80 million on the street. It was not until Contorno decided to cooperate four years later that the authorities removed the seized heroin from a safe, and noticed that the contraband was contained in plastic bags with small scissor cuts in the tops.

Defendant Gaetano Badalamenti strangely decided to testify on his own behalf. Badalamenti was by trade the Mafia boss of Palermo, Sicily, a dubious distinction that he did not deny. His story was that the cryptic wiretapped conversations he had with other defendants did not relate to narcotics, but he refused to explain on cross-examination what those conversations were about, and further

---

13. Pistone later wrote a book about his exploits titled *Donnie Brasco: My Undercover Life in the Mafia*. When the book made the movies, Johnny Depp played the role of Pistone.

14. "The cumulation of instances, each explicable only by extreme credulity or professional inexpertness, may have a probative force immensely greater than any one of them alone." United States v. White, 124 F.2d 181, 185 (2d Cir. 1941).

declined to discuss other transactions revealed by the wiretaps that he said would incriminate him in Italy. The jury didn't buy it, and Judge Leval sentenced him to 45 years in jail. Badalamenti died in a federal prison.

After the verdicts were announced, Rudy Giuliani claimed victory, but said, "I was worried. . . . We'd invested a great deal of time into this case." Unlike Apalachin, the trial outcome stuck. All but one of the Pizza Connection convictions, against a low-level defendant, were affirmed on appeal.

When Will Wilson of Texas, Assistant Attorney General in charge of the Justice Department's Criminal Division in the Nixon administration, visited Foley Square in 1969, ten years after Apalachin and two decades before Pizza Connection, he obtusely inquired of Morgenthau and Mollo how many "Italians" were under indictment. As Shakespeare's Antonio said to his co-conspirator Sebastian, "What's past is prologue."[15]

---

15. *The Tempest*, act II, sc. 1. Proving the tyranny of stereotypes, today's gangsters and murderers often have Arabic or Russian or Chechen ethnicities.

# U.S. V. OFFICIAL CORRUPTION

*Corrupt actions of public officials "cast a shadow upon the administration of justice [and] gives comfort to the cynic and weakens the faith of the believer."*
—Judge Edward Weinfeld in sentencing Justice J. Vincent Keogh and Elliott Kahaner

No too long ago, I was in Shanghai, China, lecturing a group of law students at Fudan University. When it came time for the Q&A, the first question out of the box was:

How do you bribe the judges in the United States? It is a secret, but you know it goes on.

My answer produced smiles of disbelief from the audience:

Actually, we don't. Because we have something in our country called the First Amendment, which doesn't exist here in China. The First

Amendment guarantees, among other things, press freedoms. And our free press has ways of finding out about these things. And if it existed, it would involve a serious abuse of a public trust. We would come down very hard on those involved.

## THE MANTON CASE

Actually, we have had, here and there, cases of judicial corruption, and the corrupt judges have been convicted and removed from the bench. The mother of these scandalous cases came before the Mother Court. It involved the chief judge of the U.S. Court of Appeals for the Second Circuit, Martin Manton. Manton came to the bench after a stellar career as a criminal defense lawyer. He had represented Charles Becker, a corrupt New York City police lieutenant who, in 1912, orchestrated the Times Square execution of Herman Rosenthal, a small-time bookmaker. Becker ordered the hit because Rosenthal had decided to cooperate with the authorities and testify about Becker's extorting money for police protection. Rosenthal's executioners were members of the Lenox Hill gang. The Lenox Hill gang had names out of Damon Runyan: Harry Horowitz, alias "Gyp the Blood,"[1] "Lefty" Louis Rosenberg, "Dago Frank" Cirofici, and "Whitey" Louis. All, including Becker, were convicted of murder and died in the electric chair, which made Becker the first American police officer ever to receive the death penalty.

For his role in representing Becker in a highly profiled case, or perhaps for political reasons,[2] President Woodrow Wilson appointed

---

1. Gyp the Blood was a vicious Manhattan gangster of the period. Standing only 5' 4¾' and weighing 140 pounds, he would on a small bet from one of his colleagues grab passersbys and break their backs over his knee.

2. Manton's law partner was one W. Bourke Cockran, a power in Democratic politics.

Robert M. Morgenthau, left, U.S. Attorney for the Southern District of New York, and Attorney General Robert Kennedy pose on the steps of the U.S. Courthouse on June 14, 1961. *(AP Photo)*

Alger Hiss prosecutor and giant of a federal judge Thomas F. Murphy, January 1, 1951. *(© Michael Rougier/Getty Images)*

Edward Weinfeld: the Dean of American trial judges. A seasoned trial lawyer said: "When you're in his court, you know you're before the bar of justice." *(Stanley Seligson/Courtesy of New York University Archives)*

Lawyers of the period taking a break, with the Foley Square Courthouse of the Mother Court in the background. This is one of the mementos I lost on September 11, 2001. *(Henri Cartier-Bresson/Getty Images)*

Federal Judge Irving Ben Cooper in his chambers at The Mother Court, March 4, 1970. He said to a lawyer once, "The trouble with you is you think the judge is a schmuck." *(AP Photo/Marty Lederhandler)*

Roy M. Cohn. The crown prince of rogues, he cheated justice four times. *(© Hank Walker/Getty Images)*

A-spies Julius and Ethel Rosenberg. Their execution on June 19, 1953, haunts the American conscience to this day. *(© AFP/Getty Images)*

August 23 1969. Lines stretched for half a block in each direction at Vogue Theater an hour before the doors opened for *I Am Curious (Yellow)*. The curious queued up. *(Photo By Barry Staver/The Denver Post via Getty Images.)*

Alger Hiss, December 15, 1948. "What kind of reputation does a good spy have?" *(© Thomas D. McAvoy/Getty Images)*

Harold R. Medina. He presided over the Communist leaders trial and then held their lawyers in contempt. *(© Werner Wolff/Getty Images)*

Irving R. Kaufman. The Rosenberg case followed him to his grave. *(© Al Fenn/Getty Images)*

The mighty stone columns that grace the exterior of The Mother Court. *(Museum of the City of New York)*

Pierre Leval presided over the "Pizza Connection" case, the longest federal criminal trial in history, and the Westmoreland libel suit sifting the conduct of the Vietnam War, which ended in a stalemate. *(Rick Kopstein/New York Law Journal)*

John Martin. The federal sentencing guidelines drove him off the bench. *(Rick Kopstein/New York Law Journal)*

Mobster Frank Costello. On May 2, 1957, the hitman who tried to whack him shouted, "This is for you, Frank," before he fired. Startled, Costello turned his head and dodged the bullet. *(© New York Daily News Archive/Getty Images)*

UNITED STATES ATTORNEY'S OFFICE, NOVEMBER 2, 1967

The 1967 "class photo" of the Morgenthau United States Attorney's office. Silvio Mollo is to the right of Bob Morgenthau in second row center. Stephen Kaufman is to Morgenthau's left. Peter Fleming is fourth from the left in the second row. I am the tall Assistant wearing glasses third from the right in the top row.

Six of the pictured Assistants became distinguished federal judges. They are Sterling Johnson (fourth row, second from left); Pierre Leval (second row, second from left); Tony Sifton (fourth row, third from left); Abraham Sofaer (first row, third from right); John Sprizzo (second row, third from left); and Stephen Williams (fourth row, second from right). *(Courtesy of Benjamin Naftalis)*

Manton to the Southern District bench in 1916. At age 36 Manton was the youngest federal judge in the country, and he served in the Mother Court for two years before his elevation to the court of appeals. He narrowly missed elevation to the Supreme Court of the United States. President Warren G. Harding was set to appoint him to fill a "Catholic seat"[3] created by the retirement of William R. Day. Chief Justice William Howard Taft, who knew a "hawk from a handsaw,"[4] interceded, and Harding appointed Justice Pierce Butler instead.

So Manton remained on the court of appeals, where he sat in panels with Augustus Hand, Learned Hand, and Thomas Swan, the greatest judges of their era. As chief judge, Manton was in charge of assigning pending cases to particular colleagues on the court for disposition. Frequently, he assigned cases in which he had a personal interest to none other than himself.

Unfortunately, Manton was influenced in his decision-making by factors other than God and conscience. He became, as his prosecutor John P. Cahill, U.S. Attorney for the Southern District, painted him at trial, a "merchant of justice."

As a successful lawyer, Manton was rumored to be worth over $1 million before taking the bench. He had suffered, however, major financial reverses after the great crash of 1929. He had a bagman named Fallon with whom he enjoyed an extraordinarily close relationship. The *New York Times* called Fallon a "salesman of judicial favoritism." The evidence showed that Manton owned stock in companies that were litigants before him and in whose favor he decided. It also showed that at least six litigants paid Fallon more than $175,000, exclusive of purported loans, with the understanding

---

3. Today, there are six Catholics on the Supreme Court and three Jews. There is no longer thought to be a Catholic or a Jewish seat. The imbalance, however, may suggest to the president, when the opportunity arises, that he appoint someone to fill the "Protestant seat."

4. *Hamlet*, act II, sc. 2.

that the funds would be paid or loaned to Manton to procure Manton's judicial favor.

There was no showing that any of the decisions Manton made favoring his financial benefactors were other than correct, but the court held this was beside the point.[5] The conspiracy contemplated the payment of money to a judge to exercise judicial power in favor of the bribe givers without regard to the merits.

As the appellate court put it,

> Judicial action, whether just or unjust, right or wrong is not for sale; and if the rule shall ever be accepted that the correctness of judicial action taken for a price removes the stain of corruption and exonerated the judge, the event will mark the first step toward the abandonment of that imperative requisite of even-handed justice.

The Manton case of course created a sensation. Burton Heath of the *New York World-Telegram* won a Pulitzer in 1940 for his coverage of the trial.

Manton stood convicted of conspiracy to obstruct justice and to defraud the United States. The trial judge sentenced him to two years in a federal penitentiary, a remarkably lenient sentence by today's standards, particularly in light of the seriousness of the offence. The Mother Court, however, had risen to the challenge and purged "corruption in the palace of justice."

As an aside, one of the lawyers for the government, working under Cahill on the Manton trial and appeal, was Silvio J. Mollo, who, as I have related, was Chief Assistant U.S. Attorney when I served in the Morgenthau office.

---

5. Manton famously dissented in one case that had not been fixed, *United States v. One Book Entitled Ulysses*, 72 F.2d 705 (2d Cir. 1934).

Sil was an iconic figure who profoundly influenced an entire generation of lawyers. He was not a deep thinker, but a correct one. Lacing his judgments with salty language, Sil had an unerring instinct, leavened by decades of experience, as to what went into a criminal prosecution, and the tactics that would make a prosecution a success. He backed up his Assistants even when they were wrong. He was hard as nails about the whining of criminal defense lawyers that something was unfair or some Assistant was high-handed. His characteristic response was "Fuckum!" He once told me that I had to remember that the government lawyer held all the cards in a criminal case, and we were to waive nothing except the flag. When Bronx District Attorney Burt Roberts called Sil to tell him I was a "cocksucker" for bringing a cooperating informant Burt thought he "owned" from state custody in the Bronx to the Federal House of Detention, Sil's reply was, "Burt, if he were on your side, you would love him." When Sil died, it was a sad day for me and for the Office. Along with so many of Sil's Assistants, I mourned his passing. He was a great minister of justice for many reasons other than his role in the Manton prosecution.

The U.S. Attorney's Office for the Southern District of New York is at One Saint Andrew's Plaza next to the church. It has been named the "Silvio J. Mollo Federal Building" in Sil's name and honor. The building is in the shadow of the Mother Court.

## THE KEOGH CASE

The government tried J. Vincent Keogh, a prominent and highly respected justice of the State Supreme Court in Brooklyn, on charges of corruptly endeavoring to obstruct the due administration of justice.[6] A judge with 37 years of public service, Keogh

---

6. Various acts in furtherance of the conspiracy occurred in Manhattan; hence the indictment was filed in the Mother Court.

enjoyed great influence. His brother, powerful Brooklyn Congressman Eugene Keogh, was a close friend and early supporter of John F. Kennedy.[7] One of Keogh's co-defendants was Elliott Kahaner, acting U.S. Attorney in the Eastern District of New York. The case stemmed from a criminal matter in Brooklyn federal court where three individuals were awaiting sentence. The outcome of the case turned on whether Keogh and Kahaner had received money for trying to fix the federal sentencing.

The case had everything: powerful but corrupt public officials; a bagman named Robert Erdman, a Manhattan physician, who happened to be doctor and friend to both Keogh and Kahaner; a co-defendant named Anthony "Tony Ducks" Corallo, who was a New York City mobster and boss of the Lucchese crime family; a battery of skilled defense lawyers; and the greatest American trial judge, Edward Weinfeld.

The facts were fairly straightforward, with Erdman the star witness for the prosecution. On January 5, 1961, the FBI arrested six men in Brooklyn on charges of criminally concealing assets in the Eastern District bankruptcy proceeding of Gibraltor Amusements, Ltd., a Long Island jukebox enterprise. The government's evidence showed that Dr. Erdman hatched a scheme with Kahaner, then Chief Assistant U.S. Attorney in the Eastern District, whereby only two, or at most three, of the six arrested would be indicted.

One individual to be omitted from the indictment was one Jacob Cohen, a minor employee of Gibraltor. Cohen's cousin, Seymour Deutsch, was Erdman's accountant. When Kahaner found out that Cohen would not be indicted, the plan broadened to seek lenient treatment for the three, who were indicted and pleaded guilty, by

---

7. There was testimony from two of the government witnesses that Congressman Keogh, the defendant's brother, was enlisted to talk to federal Judge Rayfiel about the sentencing. It was never alleged that the Congressman received any of the payoff money.

having the case assigned for sentencing before a specific judge, Judge Leo Rayfiel, whom the conspirators thought might be favorably disposed towards the three defendants. For this Kahaner wanted $35,000, with $15,000 paid before sentencing and the balance held by Corallo, who was apparently a silent partner in Gibraltor.

Kahaner initially met in Erdman's office with Sanford Moore, a principal of Gibraltor and one of the three indicted co-defendants. Moore also would become a witness for the prosecution. Moore paid Kahaner $5,000 on account. Ka-ching! Thereafter, Kahaner told Erdman that "pressures" were being applied because of Moore's unsavory background, and that Keogh would have to be involved. At the end of February, Erdman met with Keogh in his chambers. Keogh undertook to help for a price. He even set out his financial needs on two index cards that he handed to Erdman. In March Moore gave $10,000 to Erdman, $5,000 of which Erdman gave to Kahaner, and $5,000 to Keogh. Ka-ching, ka-ching!

There was testimony about a meeting of Kahaner, Moore, and Corallo on March 15, at which Corallo stressed the importance of Moore's not being sent to prison. There was a demand by Kahaner for the rest of the money. At a coffee shop meeting on March 29, the day before the scheduled sentencing before Judge Rayfiel, Moore paid Kahaner an additional $2,500. Later that day, Erdman paid Keogh $17,500 and reminded him of the impending sentencing. Another ka-ching! The agreed sum of $35,000 had now changed hands, with $22,500 going to Keogh and $12,500 going to Kahaner. The money paid, Keogh, in Erdman's presence, called Judge Rayfiel and invited him to lunch that very day, asking him to bring a copy of Moore's presentencing report.[8]

---

8. Keogh's plea for leniency fell on deaf ears. Rayfiel sentenced all three defendants to jail for bankruptcy fraud, including Moore, who received a three-year sentence.

One of the hotly contested issues was the admissibility of previous gifts and loans by Erdman to Keogh that had nothing to do with the conspiracy.

Judge Weinfeld received the gifts and loans evidence "solely for the purpose of showing the relationship and association between the two." Of course there was the inescapable inference that the so-called "gifts and loans" had a corrupt purpose. The judge ruled that these transactions were relevant to show an "attitude of mind" in Keogh, in which he knew he might obtain a financial reward for his intercession with Judge Rayfiel. Evidence relevant to proving one crime is not incompetent because it discloses the commission of another unless the "minute peg of relevancy will be entirely obscured by the dirty linen hung upon it."[9]

Eloquence and drama are never misplaced in a courtroom. A student at the time, I sat in the courtroom and attentively listened to much of the testimony and all of the summations. Although the defendants sharply disputed most of the testimony of the government witnesses, I concluded that the evidence fairly shrieked their corruption.

Bill Hundley, a seasoned prosecutor, who was born in Brooklyn and educated in Catholic schools before ascending to head of the Organized Crime and Racketeering Section of the Justice Department in Washington, represented the government. Hundley served as a special assistant to Attorney General Robert F. Kennedy. Tall, forceful, and persuasive, he easily won the jury's confidence.

Bill Kleinman represented Kahaner. Quite a contrast to Hundley, he was short and barrel-chested. Impeccably dressed in a bowler hat, white-gold wire glasses, and a double-breasted pinstriped suit, he was the very picture of a criminal defense lawyer. Kleinman had a

---

9. United States v. Kahaner, 317 F.2d 459 (2d Cir. 1963). As it happens, this is a quotation from a Washington State case that Judge Friendly often cited.

low sonorous voice, a *basso profundo*. He addressed the jury in measured stentorian tones.

Henry Singer represented Keogh. Taller than Kleinman, he stood in sharp contrast to his colleague, a man seemingly in perpetual motion. Singer, a bit of a charlatan, was dramatic, and at times histrionic. He chewed up the scenery. Singer timed the coda of his peroration for noon, when he knew the steeple bells would peal in nearby St. Andrews Roman Catholic Church. BONG, BONG, BONG. "Listen to them, ladies and gentlemen." BONG, BONG, BONG. "Listen to the bells." BONG, BONG, BONG. "The bells are saying it: 'Innocent, Judge Keogh. Innocent!'" BONG, BONG, BONG. With the last "Innocent" the final bell tolled 12 and the tintinnabulation slowly subsided.[10] You could have heard a pin drop in the hushed courtroom.

Three days later the jury convicted the defendants of conspiracy to obstruct justice. Later, members of the jury told reporters they believed the government witnesses. The jury announced the verdict on Saturday, June 16, 1962. According to the *New York Times*, as Judge Weinfeld entered the courtroom at 6:58 p.m. to receive the verdict, the bells of St. Andrew's again began to toll the hour.

In sentencing Keogh and Kahaner, Judge Weinfeld made a ringing statement that no one, however highly placed, is above the law:[11]

> I have received scores of letters … [that] say these defendants because they have been humbled from their former high public positions of trust and respect have already suffered and been punished sufficiently, that no useful purpose will be served by jail terms. It is true that defendants Keogh and Kahaner … have brought disgrace upon themselves.

---

10. On the façade of the Church is inscribed, in Latin, *Beati Qui Ambulant in Lege Domini* ("Happy are they who walk in the law of the Lord").

11. Judge Weinfeld sentenced both Keogh and Kahaner to two years in jail. They were both released after serving eight months in Danbury, Connecticut, federal prison.

They have brought sorrow to their innocent families. . They have dishonored their professions. . . . However, there still remains the factor of the community interests. The community has a right to expect that those trusted with high public office will scrupulously and religiously live up to their oath of office . . . The crimes of which these defendants have been convicted struck at the very heart of the administration of justice. A civilized society is strong only as long as its laws are fairly administered honestly, fairly and impartially by those who are sworn to do so, and none are under a more positive duty of scrupulous allegiance to law and order than the judge, the prosecutor and the lawyer. The defendants here . . . violated that duty. . . . The law does not seek retribution. It does require that the public interest be vindicated and that when a public servant has violated his trust, he shall not escape just punishment merely because his own wrongdoing has condemned him publicly. . . . *These defendants . . . have no right to expect they will be treated differently than any other defendant.* The crime was calculated; it was deliberate. The motive for the corrupt effort to interfere with justice was venality and greed.[12]

The conviction stuck. In affirming Judge Keogh's obstruction of justice conviction, Judge Friendly wrote:

Every criminal case imposes special responsibilities on judges. These are enhanced when there is a sharp conflict in the evidence and the Government's case depends in large part on the testimony of persons who admit guilt of the crime with which the other defendants are charged. The responsibilities become greater still when the case threatens the deprivation of life or, as here, imperils much that makes life worth while—in one instance a reputation built over 37 years

12. Italics mine. Stenographer's Minutes of Sentencing Proceedings. United States v. Kahaner, 61 Cr. 113, Aug. 2, 1962.

of public service and culminating in judicial office, and in another a young lawyer's promising career. Yet we must say also that the offense here charged—an attempt to interfere with the administration of justice—strikes at the very foundation of government, and that the high position in the community held by one of the defendants, and the role of another as a federal prosecutor, would aggravate the offense—if it occurred.[13]

And, in an extraordinary tribute to Judge Weinfeld, Judge Friendly declared:

Absolute perfection in trials will not be attained so long as human beings conduct them; few trials of this length and difficulty can have been so nearly free of error as this one.

In the Southern District, guilt or innocence turned on the evidence—not what any lawyer said.

---

13. Affirming the conviction in *Kahaner*, 317 F.2d 459.

# 10

# U.S. V. THE
# ACCOUNTANTS

*In our complex society the accountant's certificate and the lawyer's
opinion can be instruments for inflicting pecuniary loss more potent
than the chisel or the crowbar.*

—Judge Henry Friendly[1]

An accountant's "clean" certificate proclaims that his audit was
conducted in accordance with "generally accepted auditing
standards," and that the financial statements it covers are "fairly
presented" in accordance with "generally accepted accounting principles." This is the accountant's independent assurance to the public
of the enterprise's financial health.

But over the years, the accountant's certificate of "generally
accepted" quality in the audit took on a kind of guildsmanship, an
anchor to windward to fend off those who would hold him accountable for financial statement falsity. The accounting profession took

---

1. United States v. Benjamin, 328 F.2d 854 (2d Cir. 1964).

the position that if a "generally accepted" audit did not detect some collusive management fraud, and the financial statements were presented in accordance with "generally accepted" accounting principles, the auditor was blameless for failing to expose the fraud even though the statements were false and misleading. Who was it that made the standards and principles "generally accepted"? Of course, it was the accountants themselves.

I remember arguing in the court of appeals against the magnificent plaintiff's attorney Abe Pomerantz, who represented some shareholders in actions against accountants. I urged that my clients were protected by generally accepted accounting principles, and should be held to no higher standard than those of their profession. "Who sets these standards?" thundered Pomerantz. "Who are these professionals? Other accountants! They, like all of us, are subject to the sins of the flesh."

No area better exemplifies the character of the Mother Court than its cases subjecting partners of nationally known accounting firms to criminal liability for knowingly certifying false financial statements. The Southern District was at the vanguard elaborating the auditors' responsibility, and concluding that dishonest profession of opinion, not adherence to professional standards, sets the essential legal test.

When I left the U.S. Attorney's Office in 1970, there were eight nationally known accounting firms whose certificate was the gold standard of the profession.[2] Today, by reason of merger and the outrageous indictment of Arthur Andersen in the Enron case, which the Supreme Court threw out shortly after Andersen went out of business, there are only four: PricewaterhouseCoopers, Deloitte & Touche, Ernst &Young, and KPMG.

---

2. These were Price Waterhouse, Arthur Andersen, Peat Marwick & Mitchell, Haskins & Sells, Lybrand Ross Bros. & Montgomery, Touche Ross, Ernst & Ernst, and Arthur Young.

The Morgenthau U.S. Attorney's Office pioneered the field of accountants' criminal responsibility with the prosecution of two partners and a senior associate of Lybrand Ross Bros. & Montgomery for issuing a dishonest certificate.[3] In this case, the auditors turned a blind eye to Harold Roth, the guiding spirit of their client, a company known as Continental Vending Machine Corporation, who was systematically stealing money from the corporate till. The form the looting took was that Valley Commercial Corp., a shell company owned or controlled by Roth, borrowed money from Continental, and Roth in turn immediately borrowed money from Valley to be used for his own personal purposes. These so-called "loans" were uncollectible, and Continental went bankrupt. It was the first criminal case brought against accountants where there was no evidence of venality on the part of the accountant.

Judge David Peck, then a senior litigation partner in the venerable firm of Sullivan & Cromwell and formerly presiding justice of the appellate division in Manhattan, represented Lybrand partner Carl Simon, who led the Lybrand team on the Continental audit. Peck had a sense of outrage like no lawyer I have ever known. He publicly accused the U.S. Attorney's Office of lacking a sense of noblesse oblige in pressing as a criminal case something that Peck regarded as a civil matter. This caused the street-smart Sil Mollo to run around the office saying, "I've lost my *nobleese oblike*"—which caused gales of laughter among the Assistants. Two troublesome issues in criminal accounting cases are always motive and criminal intent. Why would a highly trained professional, one who has reached the pinnacle of success in a nationally known accounting firm, willfully certify a false financial statement? The fee goes to the firm, not the accountant, so there is little if any impact on his

---

3. The Lybrand firm eventually merged with the firm known today as PricewaterhouseCoopers.

compensation. The accounting firm has many clients, and so is not ordinarily dependent on any one of them in terms of sustaining its business.

As Judge Gurfein put it:[4]

> It is hard to probe the intent of a defendant. Circumstantial evidence, particularly with proof of motive, where available, is often sufficient to convince a reasonable man of criminal intent beyond a reasonable doubt. When we deal with a defendant who is a professional accountant, it is even harder, at times, to distinguish between simple errors of judgment and errors made with sufficient criminal intent to support a conviction, especially when there is no financial gain to the accountant other than his legitimate fee.

Motive and criminal intent may be inferred from a finding of willful falsity in the financial statements. More often than not, accountants falsify to cover up a prior mistake.

In the *Simon* case, the government's evidence mainly revolved around asset items totaling $3.54 million, the "Valley receivable."

With respect to this receivable, Footnote 2 of Continental's 1962 audited financial statements read as follows:

### Notes to Consolidated Financial Statements

2.    The amount receivable from Valley Commercial Corp. (an affiliated company of which Mr. Harold Roth is an officer, director and stockholder) bears interest at 12% a year. Such amount, less the balance of the notes payable to that company, is secured by the assignment to the Company of Valley's equity in certain marketable securities.

---

4. United States v. Natelli, 527 F.2d 311 (2d Cir. 1975).

As of February 15, 1963, the amount of such equity at current market quotations exceeded the net amount receivable.

This information contrasted starkly with the facts, as defendants knew them, namely that Roth's "borrowings" from Continental through the Valley conduit were in fact systematic stealing of corporate funds, which Roth appropriated to his own use. Additionally, the Valley receivable is what is referred to as a "bootstrap asset." The "certain marketable securities" that purportedly secured the loan consisted largely of stock and convertible debentures of Continental itself, which had a market value far less than the amount of the Valley receivable.

The first trial was before Judge Frederick van Pelt Bryan of the Southern District, who enjoyed an uncomfortably close relationship with the lead defense counsel, Judge Peck. This spelled trouble for the government. Under the Federal Rules of Criminal Procedure, a defendant may waive trial by jury with the consent of the government and try his case to the court, making the judge the trier of both the law and the facts.[5] If a defendant chooses to waive his right to trial by jury, the government withholds its consent only in the rarest of circumstances. Peck, confident that his clients' future was assured before Bryan, sought to waive his clients' constitutional right to a jury trial. The government had less faith in Judge Bryan. In an extraordinarily unprecedented action, it withheld its consent, and the *Simon* case had to be tried to a jury.

Usually at a criminal trial, the defense dreams up theories to keep incriminating evidence away from the jury. Before Judge Bryan, the government team, led by the excellent Peter Fleming, had to

---

5. Rule 23(a) of the Federal Rules of Criminal Procedure provides as follows:

**Jury Trial.** If the defendant is entitled to a jury trial, the trial must be by jury unless: (1) the defendant waives a jury trial in writing; (2) the government consents; and (3) the court approves.

scrounge for theories to get incriminating evidence in. There was a pattern and practice of rulings against the government. This caused Fleming to employ another extraordinary procedure in a criminal case, and petition to the Second Circuit for a writ of mandamus ordering Bryan to change his rulings.[6]

On the appellate oral argument, Judge Peck accused Fleming of being a crybaby, to which Fleming rejoined, "We have lost our share of cases, but we don't want to lose this one because of the trial court's rulings. We are entitled to get our proof to the jury."

Judge Kaufman of the Second Circuit then asked Fleming: "You don't think, Mr. Fleming, that Judge Bryan is biased against the government?"

To which Fleming replied: "We are saying, your Honor, that there is a pattern and practice of rulings against the government." (A direct question does not necessarily require a direct answer.)

Then, Fleming reached the coda of his argument: "It is said that this Court is all that stands between a defendant and an unjust conviction; it is also all that stands between the government and an unjust acquittal."

The Second Circuit denied the petition for mandamus. Peck won; the government lost. But Fleming had sown the seed. The trial resumed and resulted in a hung jury. When Judge Bryan announced that he would retry the case before himself, this was too much for Fleming, as it was for the Second Circuit. He brought another mandamus proceeding, and the appellate court ordered that the second trial be conducted before another judge. The retrial, before Judge Walter Mansfield, resulted in the conviction of all three defendants.

---

6. A writ of mandamus is a rarely used procedure where a party may ask the court of appeals to order the district judge to change his rulings before the case is over.

Mansfield fined all three, but sentenced none of the defendants to prison.

As might be expected, a key issue in the case was what motive men who had led blameless lives and were respected members of a learned profession might have had to falsify their certificate. The government found motive in Simon's desire to preserve Lybrand's reputation and conceal derelictions in the Continental audit in prior years. The Second Circuit, in analyzing the sufficiency of the evidence, did not completely buy the government's argument, but said it didn't have to:

> Even if there were no satisfactory showing of motive, we think the Government produced sufficient evidence of criminal intent. *Its burden was not to show that defendants were wicked men with designs on anyone's purse, which they obviously were not, but rather that they had certified a statement knowing it to be false.* As Judge Hough said for us long ago, "while there is no allowable inference of knowledge from the mere fact of falsity, there are many cases where from the actor's special situation and continuity of conduct an inference that he did know the untruth of what he said or wrote may legitimately be drawn."... Moreover, so far as criminal intent is concerned, the various deficiencies in the footnote should not be considered in isolation. Evidence that defendants knowingly suppressed one fact permitted, although it surely did not compel, an inference that their suppression of another was likewise knowing and willful.[7]

And as for the defense of reliance on generally accepted accounting principles:

---

7. Italics mine. United States v. Simon, 425 F2d 796, 809 (2d Cir. 1969).

Generally accepted accounting principles instruct an accountant what to do in the usual case where he has no reason to doubt that the affairs of the corporation are being honestly conducted. Once he has reason to believe that this basic assumption is false, an entirely different situation confronts him. Then, as the Lybrand firm stated in its letter accepting the Continental engagement, he must "extend his procedures to determine whether or not such suspicions are justified." If as a result of such an extension or, as here, without it, he finds his suspicions to be confirmed, full disclosure must be the rule, unless he has made sure the wrong has been righted and procedures to avoid a repetition have been established. At least this must be true when the dishonesty he has discovered is not some minor peccadillo but a diversion so large as to imperil if not destroy the very solvency of the enterprise.[8]

Peck had said that the U.S. Attorney's Office had lacked noblesse oblige in bringing the case. Noblesse oblige, my aunt!

Another criminal accounting case that resulted in convictions was *United States v. Natelli*, prosecuted in the Southern District in 1974, which involved the national accounting firm of Peat Marwick Mitchell & Co.[9] Peat's audit client was National Student Marketing Corporation (NSMC). NSMC's business was to obtain clients who wished to reach the college marketplace. There was a fixed-fee program where NSMC would develop for its clients overall marketing programs, including mailings, posters, and other forms of advertisement. NSMC's management believed it was appropriate to recognize revenues based on its fixed-fee contracts even though no cash was ever received.

---

8. *Id.* At 806, 807.
9. United States v. Natelli, 527 F2d 311 (2d Cir. 1975).

The guiding spirit and CEO of NSMC was one Cortes Randall, who later confessed to being a fraudster. Anthony Natelli was the Peat Marwick engagement partner, and his co-defendant Joseph Scansaroli was the manager on the NSMC audit.

Unlike *Simon*, which involved *audited* financial statements, *Natelli* involved the auditors' responsibility for *unaudited* statements of their client with which they were associated that they knew or suspected to be false. The case was a four-week jury trial before Judge Harold Tyler, one of his last before he resigned from the bench to become deputy attorney general.

Peat did the audit for the fiscal year ending August 31, 1968. Natelli agreed with NSMC's management to recognize income on the fixed-fee commitments, using the generally accepted "percentage of completion method."[10] A weakness in NSMC's financial picture was that the "contracts" NSMC relied on were largely oral. As Samuel Goldwyn said, "An oral contract is as good as the paper it's written on." Had the company not booked the oral commitments as contracts, the result would have transformed NSMC's profit of $388,031 at year-end August 31, 1968, into a loss of $232,000. Scansaroli in a random way attempted to confirm the oral "commitments" by telephone, but even these telephonic contacts failed to disclose little more than a mere intention by prospective clients to use NSMC's services.

At NSMC's urging, Scansaroli did not seek written confirmations. Instead of extending his procedures, he accepted a "schedule" prepared by the corporate controller showing roughly $1.7 million in sales commitments. With the post balance sheet adjustment of

10. NSMC calculated a "percentage of completion" by dividing the time and related costs an account executive had incurred on an NSMC client's project at the balance sheet date of August 31, 1968, by the total time and related costs the work was *estimated* to take. The resulting percentage was applied to the total fee set forth in the contract, with the resulting amount taken into revenue. Thus, the lower the *estimated* cost and the more inflated the actual cost of performing the contract, the greater the revenue.

$1.7 million in sales based on unbilled accounts receivable, together with NSMC cost and time estimates, Natelli agreed to recognize year-end profit of $388,031, an apparent doubling of profits from the prior year. The footnote describing the post balance sheet adjustment made no mention of the dubious nature of the "commitments," although Natelli advised NSMC management that in the future income would only be recorded based on written commitments supported by contemporaneous documentation. Mark Twain said famously, "Figures don't lie, but liars figure."

Within five months of release of the audited financial statements, NSMC wrote off more than $1 million of the $1.7 million in bogus sales. NSMC, however, buried the write-off in the books of account. Scansaroli "netted" an extraordinary item, a deferred tax credit, against the million-dollar write-off.

On September 27, 1969, NSMC filed a proxy statement with the SEC in connection with a program of fraudulent stock acquisitions, and the merger of six recently acquired companies into NSMC. The proxy statement contained no more recent audited financial statements than were certified by Peat Marwick as of August 31, 1958. It did contain unaudited financial statements for the nine-month stub period ended May 31, 1959. The Peat Marwick accountants "associated" themselves with the stub period financial statements appearing in the proxy materials. The accountants also drafted a footnote to go into the proxy statement, which would appear to reconcile NSMC's prior reported sales with restated amounts resulting from the pooled companies that NSMC had just acquired.

The footnote was the auditors' last clear chance to permit the reader of the proxy statement to see what NSMC's separate performance truly had been in fiscal 1968, as adjusted for the $1.7 million write-off. Because such separate performance was abysmal, it was a matter of importance for NSMC to conceal the true effect of the write-off, and the auditors readily obliged. They deducted the write-off from the earnings of the pooled companies. There was no disclosure in the footnote, however, that $1.7 million of previously reported NSMC sales had been written off. Pertinent was Judge Friendly's statement in *Simon*: "The jury could reasonably have wondered how accountants who were really seeking to tell the truth could have constructed a footnote so well designed to conceal the shocking facts."[11]

Peter Fleming told me once that *Simon* was the case of a "shitty footnote" that the auditors blessed. *Natelli* was of a piece.

While the auditor has no responsibility for unaudited statements, the accounting profession would admit that he has a duty to correct any false statements of his client with which he associates himself when he knows, or willfully closes his eyes to the fact, of their falsity. The jury convicted both defendants. Judge Tyler sentenced Natelli to 60 days in jail and a $10,000 fine; Scansaroli to 10 days in jail and a $2500 fine. The lenient sentences aside, the principle of holding accountants criminally responsible for slipshod and willfully myopic audits was alive and well in the Mother Court.

As for the relevance of generally accepted accounting principles, Judge Gurfein, in affirming the convictions of Natelli and Scansaroli, had this to say:

> We expound no rule, to be sure, that an accountant in reviewing an unaudited company statement is bound, without more, to seek verification and to apply auditing procedures. We lay no extra burden on the normal activities of accountants, nor do we assume the role of an Accounting Principles Board. *We deal only with such deviations as fairly come within the common understanding of dishonest conduct which*

---

11. United States v. Simon, 425 F.2d 796, 807 (2d Cir. 1969).

*jurors bring into the box as applied to the particular conduct prohibited by the particular statute.* It was not for Judge Tyler in his instructions to deal with the abstract question of an accountant's responsibility for unaudited statements, for that was not the issue.[12]

Judges are in the business of drawing lines; and, in this instance, the line was once again drawn against the accountants.

What I learned about accountants' professional responsibilities served me well long after I left the U.S. Attorney's Office, when I represented accountants charged with fraud for their conduct of an audit. I knew that I must establish their honesty and good faith, and not their blind reliance on professional standards.

Years later, I represented Haskins & Sells in the *Equity Funding* cases. A number of the cases were brought in the Southern District but were then transferred to the Central District of California where they were consolidated with other *Equity Funding* cases for purposes of pretrial proceedings. Equity Funding was a diversified corporation primarily engaged in selling life insurance and mutual funds. Haskins & Sells had been the auditors of Equity Funding's life insurance subsidiary. The company had put bogus life insurance policies on its roster of insurance in force, and then reinsured or co-insured the bogus policies with others for a fee. The life insurance subsidiary's financial statements were then consolidated with those of the parent, which reported on a generally accepted accounting principles basis. Generally accepted accounting principles permitted the company to accelerate recognition of the co-insurance consideration, and amortize it and the related reserve over the life of the policy.[13] This permitted the parent to overstate its earnings based

---

12. United States v. Natelli, 527 F2d 311 at 324.

13. The related reserves for death benefits to be paid to policyholders under the bogus policies were of no moment as the "risk" was transferred to the reinsurers. Under the Equity Funding setup, no fictitious policyholder ever died.

on bogus policies. There were criminal proceedings in California against the parent company's auditor, who was on the take, and civil class actions against the parent's auditing firm, Seidman & Seidman, and my client, Haskins & Sells.

Marshall Grossman, an aggressive and colorful Los Angeles plaintiff's lawyer, led the plaintiffs' class action committee. Marshall had a sense of humor that was sometimes over the top. When the New York cases got transferred to Los Angeles, Marshall thought he had won a great victory. The case would be tried in his own backyard. At the initial hearing, Marshall reached into his briefcase and presented fiery New York defense lawyer Sam Gates, who had opposed the transfer, with a "California apple" to mark the occasion. Everyone in the courtroom, including federal Judge Malcolm Lucas, was flabbergasted.[14]

I remember when William Seidman testified on deposition. Seidman was an economic adviser to President Ford, and he repeatedly asked for recesses so he could take calls from the White House. Finally, in exasperation, Grossman said, "Mr. Seidman, unless it's a call from the Speaker of the House, no more recesses."

Marshall was always good for a laugh.

I defended another accounting firm in a major securities fraud case in the Southern District. This one was the only accounting case I played a role in where there was a serious question of compromise in the auditor's independence. It seemed that the married engagement partner on the account was entertaining his girlfriend in the client's apartment, located in the heart of the Southern District of New York, and there was some suggestion that there might be tapes and films of the couple in flagrante delicto. When I interviewed the girlfriend, she said that the accountant at moments of pillow talk

---

14. Lucas later became chief justice of the California Supreme Court.

expressed concerns that their relationship might be compromising his independence. When I asked her how she knew about independence, she looked at me flirtatiously and said, "How does your wife know what a tort is?" Luckily, the tapes and films never materialized.

The accounting firm retained the legendary criminal lawyer Edward Bennett Williams to advise on possible criminal issues in the case. For anyone who could afford his hefty up-front retainer, Ed was the "man to see" if you got into trouble with the law.

When a grand jury indicted millionaire Boston textile manufacturer Bernard Goldfine, a close associate of President Eisenhower's chief of staff, Sherman Adams,[15] for failing to file tax returns for four years, and defrauding the public of some $800,000, it was natural for Goldfine's personal attorney, Ralph Slobodkin, to call in Williams. Slobodkin was a Goldfine functionary who collected unpaid bills, procured girls, and fetched cigarettes for the nabob. Ed studied the tax case carefully and sorrowfully advised Goldfine that he had no defense.

Goldfine was a Russian immigrant with a thick accent who minced no words in English or in Yiddish. When Williams went to the men's room, Goldfine turned to another of his lawyers and said, "Who does that *momzer* [bastard] from Washington think he is, telling me I have no defense? Defense? If I had a defense, I'd still have Slobodkin." Goldfine went to jail, and Ed loved to tell the story.

When Ed died, relates his biographer, Evan Thomas, the obsequies were at Holy Trinity, a neo-Georgian church in the heart of Georgetown. Senators and Supreme Court justices, felons and

---

15. Adams received lavish gifts from Goldfine, including a vicuña overcoat and an oriental rug, at a time when Goldfine was doing business with the government. Goldfine was also the target of investigations started by various federal agencies. The scandal led to Adams' dismissal from the White House.

bookmakers, waiters and doormen, billionaires, professional ball players, and Georgetown society jammed under the domed ceiling to sit before the plain mahogany casket.

I never met a man with a more mischievous twinkle in his eyes than Ed Williams until the evening I shook hands with Sir Laurence Olivier. Like Olivier, when Ed spoke, it was like magic; both had eyes that literally danced. Ed immediately put me at ease. "I hear great things about you," he said. "Not to worry. This is about a guy who got too close to his client. We'll find a way to figure it out."

I mentioned Duke Zeibert's, a landmark restaurant in Washington that Ed used to frequent with Art Buchwald, the writer and humorist, who was one of Ed's clients. I had met Buchwald in Paris in 1960 when we both worked for the Paris *Herald Tribune* on the Rue de Berri near the Etoile. He was utterly hilarious. Also in Ed's luncheon group was Joe Califano, Ed's partner, who later became my close friend. Joe was the author of the Medicare bill and had served as domestic adviser to Lyndon Johnson and in the Carter cabinet. Ed Williams would say anything for a laugh, and he could never resist a little hyperbole. "I have had enough heartburn from Duke Zeibert for a lifetime," Ed chuckled. "He has killed more Jews with his pickles than died in the Holocaust." Unfortunately, Ed made the same crack in the presence of Duke Zeibert. I am reliably told that Duke didn't speak to Ed for a long time afterward.

I represented Arthur Andersen in the *Fund of Funds* litigation. Andersen were auditors to Fund of Funds (FOF), then controlled by Bernard Cornfeld, and also to King Resources, which sold FOF interests in natural resource assets. John King, the guiding spirit of King Resources, was also an investment adviser to FOF. The situation was riddled with actual and potential conflict of interest. King sold natural resource assets to the fund at what were later characterized as "unreasonably high mark-ups." King then valued the same assets at cost on the books of FOF, since he occupied the dual position of both seller of the assets and investment adviser to FOF. Also involved in the lawsuit was the great Arctic revaluation, where an investment of FOF in the Canadian Arctic was revalued upward based on sham sales with secret buy-back agreements. The claim was that the auditors should have detected and exposed King's machinations.

I remember attending the deposition of FDR's son, James Roosevelt, who had been a director of FOF. My adversary repeatedly asked whether the unreasonably high mark-ups were something Roosevelt, as a director, would like to have known or would like the auditors to have told him about. I objected on the ground that the witness's father would have called that "an awfully iffy question."

In the DeLorean motor car case, in which I represented Arthur Andersen, John DeLorean used a conduit called GPD to siphon off hundreds of millions of dollars that he then used to buy a ski-grooming equipment company in Logan, Utah. The principal source of finance for DeLorean was the British government, which wanted DeLorean to build a plant in Dunmurrie, Northern Ireland, so as to put people to work. They got their plant, less what DeLorean skimmed off, but the automobile project failed.

In the course of the DeLorean litigation, I had the privilege of deposing Margaret Thatcher, who was the prime minister charged with monitoring the British government's investment in the DeLorean motor car project. Asked why the project failed, the "Iron Lady" gave a great answer for the auditors: "Because nobody bought the car."

But as to how and why the GPD money had "gone walkabout," Thatcher's answer was a little less helpful: "That, Mr. Zirin, is why we employ auditors."

I felt that to have gone *mano a mano* with Margaret Thatcher and come up with a draw was a singular accomplishment.

All these cases involved in some degree the defense of generally accepted accounting principles and auditing standards. Would compliance with those standards protect the auditor from criminal prosecution and civil liability even where the auditor had reason to believe that the affairs of the client were not being conducted honestly? We would think not.

Since *Simon* and *Natelli*, auditors have tightened up. But problems still persist. The Public Accounting Oversight Board is charged with reviewing annually the quality of public company audits. In 2009, the first year for which figures are available, the board found something defective in nearly one in every six audits conducted by the Big Four accounting firms. The next year, the proportion doubled to one in three.[16]

Of one thing we can be virtually certain. The Mother Court has not heard the end of criminal prosecutions involving the accounting profession.

---

16. Floyd Norris, *Bad Grades Are Rising for Auditors*, N.Y. TIMES, Aug. 24, 2012, at B1.

# 11

# OF THE LIBEL CASES

*Good name in man and woman is the immediate jewel of their souls.*
*Who steals my purse steals trash, 'tis something, nothing;*
*'Twas mine, 'tis his, and has been slave to thousands;*
*But he that filches from me my good name*
*Robs me of that which not enriches him,*
*And makes me poor indeed.*
—*Othello*, act III, scene 3

Libel is about the power of words to destroy reputation. The law of libel always fascinated me because I am intrigued with the power of words, and honor is necessarily at stake on both sides. Suing for libel, however, can get you in trouble, because truth is a complete defense.

In his book *A Fool for a Client*, Roy Cohn, someone in a position to know, encapsulated the pros and cons of suing for libel:[1]

---

1. COHN, A FOOL FOR A CLIENT 152 (1971).

Among the considerations in favor of suing are: (1) If you don't, some people regard the failure to do so as an admission of the truth of the published statements. (2) When one is libeled, particularly for commercial purposes, why let the people responsible get away with it? (3) Why not get back some of the money their libelous statements have cost you in loss of business, reputation and so on?

Among the factors against suing are: (1) There is a legal difficulty particularly for a public figure, in view of Supreme Court decisions giving great leeway to statements about people in public life under the umbrella of freedom of the press and fair comment. (2) The expense of obtaining counsel, stenographic transcripts, research, investigation, etc. can be substantial. (3) Since a libel suit is predicated on your good reputation, the publication you sue can go into your activities in some depth in an effort to show that you did not have a sufficiently good reputation that could be libeled.

Oscar Wilde, the Irish playwright, was the great case in point. Wilde, who was possessed of an extraordinary wit, was a notorious homosexual. He had sued the Marquess of Queensberry, whose son he had seduced, for writing on a card, "Oscar Wilde, posing [as a] sodomite." Wilde launched a "private prosecution" against Queensberry for criminal libel, confident that he was agile enough to withstand any cross-examination. Edward Carson, one of the great barristers of his day, completely unmasked Wilde in one of the most memorable cross-examinations ever:

Q: Do you know Walter Grainger?
A: Yes.
Q: How old is he?
A: He was about 16 when I knew him. He was a servant at a certain house in High Street, Oxford, where Lord Alfred Douglas had

rooms. I have stayed there several times. Grainger waited at table. I never dined with him. If it is one's duty to serve, it is one's duty to serve; and if it is one's pleasure to dine, it is one's pleasure to dine.

**Q:** Did you ever kiss him?

**A:** Oh, dear no. He was a peculiarly plain boy. He was, unfortunately, extremely ugly.[2] I pitied him for it.

**Q:** Was that the reason why you did not kiss him?

**A:** Oh, Mr. Carson, you are pertinently insolent.

**Q:** Did you say that in support of your statement that you never kissed him?

**A:** No. It is a childish question.

**Q:** Did you ever put that forward as a reason why you never kissed the boy?

**A:** Not at all.

**Q:** Why, sir, did you mention that this boy was extremely ugly?

**A:** For this reason. If I were asked why I did not kiss a doormat, I should say because I do not like to kiss doormats. I do not know why I mentioned that he was ugly, except that I was stung by the insolent question you put to me and the way you have insulted me throughout this hearing. Am I to be cross-examined because I do not like it?

**Q:** Why did you mention his ugliness?

**A:** It is ridiculous to imagine that any such thing could have occurred under any circumstances.

**Q:** Then why did you mention his ugliness, I ask you?

**A:** Perhaps you insulted me by an insulting question.

---

2. Once a witness has committed himself to a position, it does no harm to ask a "why" question because the witness is caught in a trap from which he cannot conceivably extricate himself, whichever way he goes.

Q: Was that a reason why you should say the boy was ugly? [The witness began several answers almost inarticulately, and none of them he finished. Carson's repeated sharply: "Why? Why? Why did you add that?" At last the witness answered]:

A: You sting me and insult me and try to unnerve me; and at times one says things flippantly when one ought to speak more seriously. I admit it.

Q: Then you said it flippantly?

A: Oh, yes, it was a flippant answer.

Wilde dropped the case, and the court acquitted Queensberry of criminal libel. Wilde was bankrupted by court costs under England's "loser pays" rule. Later, he was prosecuted for homosexuality and "gross indecency." After serving two years in Reading Gaol, he died in Paris after three years in exile, a broken man.

And all because he had brought a libel case.

## PEGLER V. REYNOLDS

Not all libel cases have ended badly for the plaintiff. Quentin Reynolds was a celebrated World War II correspondent. He had won a national and international reputation as a journalist, author, and lecturer. His writings appeared regularly over a period of 17 years in a leading national magazine. He was a fixture on radio and television programs under the sponsorship of well-known national concerns, and his books enjoyed a wide distribution. Reynolds' reputation for personal integrity and general standing was indisputable. In 1954, Reynolds, represented by noted lawyer and writer Louis Nizer, won a jury verdict in the Southern District before Judge Weinfeld against right-wing Hearst columnist Westbrook Pegler and two Hearst Corporation defendants, which had "with reckless indifference" published Pegler's 26-paragraph column defaming Reynolds. The verdict was for $1 in compensatory damages, and $100,000 in punitive damages against Pegler; $50,000 in punitive damages against Hearst Corporation; and $25,000 in punitive damages against Hearst Consolidated Publications. At the time it was the largest libel judgment ever. Weinfeld found that each of the 26 paragraphs contained "defamatory strictures upon the plaintiff." Describing the column, Weinfeld wrote,

> A sampling of but a few of the maledictions cast upon the plaintiff conveys some idea of the general vituperative nature of the article. The article said of plaintiff that he was ". . . largely an absentee war correspondent"; that ". . . the fact was not to be established until we got the war which he had been howling for, that his protuberant belly was filled with something else than guts"; that, although an "'interventionist'" and loathing "'isolationists'" and ". . . though he was a giant and a bachelor, he let several million kids about 18 years old do the fighting"; that ". . . by forceful, opportune promotion, [he] became one of the great individual profiteers of the war"; that one whom he had opposed for public office had ". . . peeled him of his mangy hide and nailed it to the barn door with the yellow streak glaring for the world to see"; that he ". . . and his girl friend of the moment were nuding along the public road."[3]

The court of appeals upheld the award of punitive damages. Reynolds' attorney Louis Nizer devoted to the case an entire chapter to his book, *My Life in Court.*

---

3. Reynolds v. Pegler, 123 F. Supp. 36, 40 (S.D.N.Y. 1954), *aff'd*, 223 F.2d 429 (2d Cir. 1955)

## GOLDWATER V. GINZBURG

Public figures bringing libel actions have encountered significant obstacles. Ever since the Supreme Court decision in *New York Times v. Sullivan*,[4] decided a decade after the Reynolds case, a public figure had the almost insuperable burden of establishing by "clear and convincing evidence" not only that the defamatory statement was false, but also that it was uttered with knowledge of the falsity or "reckless disregard for the truth." Lawyers call this final element "constitutional malice." I watched three Southern District libel cases, brought by important public figures, where the plaintiff obtained various degrees of satisfaction.

Senator Barry Goldwater ran as the Republican presidential candidate in 1964 against Lyndon Johnson. In its September–October 1964 issue, *Fact* magazine published a cover story titled "The Unconscious of a Conservative: A Special Issue on the Mind of Barry Goldwater."[5] Goldwater responded with a libel action against *Fact*, managing editor Warren Boroson, and publisher Ralph Ginzburg.

Goldwater alleged in his complaint that *Fact*'s statements about him were "false, scandalous and defamatory," and published with "actual malice, or with reckless disregard for whether such statements were false or not."

The evidence was that Ginzburg and Boroson had together watched the July 1964 Republican convention, and were displeased by Goldwater's views. Political liberals, how they must have shuddered at the famous line in Goldwater's acceptance speech: "Extremism in the defense of liberty is no vice! And let me remind you also that moderation in the pursuit of justice is no virtue!"

The two decided to publish a "Goldwater issue" of *Fact*, a psychobiography of Goldwater.

---

4. 376 U.S. 254, 279–80 (1964).
5. This was of course a play on Goldwater's book title, *Conscience of a Conservative*.

Before any research or polling began, Boroson wrote a letter to Walter Reuther, head of the United Autoworkers Union, who was politically opposed to Goldwater. The letter stated in part,

I'm writing an article for *Fact* about an old enemy of yours—Barry Goldwater. It's going to be a psychological profile, and will say, basically, that Goldwater is so belligerent, suspicious, hot-tempered and rigid because he has deep-seated doubts about his masculinity. . . .

Boroson then began his research, in which he selectively culled material appearing in newspaper stories, magazines, and books about Goldwater, and concluded in a "research draft" submitted to Ginzburg that Goldwater was an "authoritarian personality." Ginzburg ignored the "research draft," and reached his own conclusion that Goldwater suffered from paranoia, and was mentally ill.

At about the same time, *Fact* sent a questionnaire to a list of 12,356 psychiatrists asking the question, "Do you believe Barry Goldwater is psychologically fit to serve as President of the United States?" The recipients of the questionnaire were deliberately skewed. According to a survey conducted by *Medical Tribune*, "two-thirds of the psychiatrists favor[ed] a Democratic candidate." Only 2,147 of the alienists responded to the questionnaire, and *Fact* published a "sampling of their comments."

Comments in the article, such as that Goldwater had a "nervous breakdown," "unmistakable symptoms of paranoia," "delusions of persecution," and the "death-fantasy of another paranoiac woven in Berchtesgaden and realized in a Berlin bunker," proved to be baseless, made up, or insufficiently sourced.

The Southern District trial was before the staunchly Republican Judge Harold Tyler. The jury trial consumed 15 days, and the spectators' seats were jammed.

The dramatic highlight of course was the testimony of Senator Goldwater, whose charm and diffident manner made him highly sympathetic on the witness stand. Harris Steinberg and Stanley Arkin, both superb trial lawyers, represented Ginzburg. Goldwater turned over his medical records to the defense, and Judge Tyler, as was appropriate, gave Steinberg great latitude in cross-examination as he probed Goldwater's medical and psychiatric history. The cross went something like this:

> Q: And then you saw the doctor and got an injection of 200 milligrams of testosterone.
>
> A: If that's what it says.
>
> Q: What is testosterone, Senator?
>
> A: Mr. Steinberg, I don't rightly know.
>
> Q: Would it surprise you, Senator, if I told you that you were injected with a male sex hormone that came from the testicles of a bull?
>
> A: If that's what it says.
>
> Q: And the next week you went back to the same doctor and got an injection of 400 milligrams of testosterone.
>
> A: Guess that's right.
>
> Q: Both tanks that time, right Senator?

Steinberg's cross-examination notwithstanding, Goldwater won the case, and the jury brought in a verdict of $1 in compensatory damages against each defendant, $25,000 in punitive damages against Ginzburg, and $50,000 against *Fact* magazine.[6]

---

6. The Second Circuit affirmed Judge Tyler's judgment, and the Supreme Court denied review with Justice Black and Douglas dissenting. The dissenters thought that all statements of and concerning public officials are constitutionally protected. As Justice Black put it:

> This case perhaps more than any I have seen in this area convinces me that the *New York Times* constitutional rule is wholly inadequate to assure the "uninhibited, [396 U.S. 1049, 1051] robust, and wide-open" public debate which the majority in that case thought it was guaranteeing. See *New York Times Co. v. Sullivan*, 376 U.S. 254, 270 (1964). . . . This case illustrates I think what a short and inadequate step this Court took in the *New York Times*

In 1984, I watched with great interest two separate libel cases, conducted almost simultaneously. [7] Both actions, commenced in the Southern District, *Sharon v. Time, Inc.* and *Westmoreland v. CBS*, were tried to a jury and brought by distinguished army generals against large media organizations. The issue in both cases was a balancing of First Amendment free press values against the media's duty to publish only the truth. Both cases demonstrated that in public figure libel cases, courts such as the Mother Court may (or may not) return verdicts, but the verdict of history will necessarily be found elsewhere.

## SHARON V. TIME, INC.

My good friend from U.S. Attorney's Office days, Judge Abraham Sofaer, presided over the *Sharon* trial. Sofaer had a brilliant and thoughtful legal mind. Born in Bombay, India, he and his family were Baghdadis. Baghdadis were Jews of Iraqi origin whose ancestors had moved to South and Southeast Asia in the 19th century to avoid religious persecution. Many Baghdadi Jews, such as the Sassoons of Bombay, achieved wealth, power, and influence in India. Sofaer donated his parents' Iraqi wedding contract to the Jewish Museum in New York City. Long a friend of Israel, he also donated his world-class collection of coins of the Holy Land to the Israel Museum in Jerusalem.

The plaintiff Ariel Sharon had been a commander of the Israeli army since its beginnings as the Haganah in 1948. He was a key military figure in the War of Independence, the 1956 Suez War, the 1967 Six-Day War, the 1973 Yom Kippur War, and as Minister

---

case to guard free press and free speech against the grave dangers to the press and the public created by libel actions.

7. Trial commenced in the *Sharon* action November 13, 1984, and concluded January 13, 1985; the *Westmoreland* trial began October 9, 1984, and concluded February 18, 1985.

of Defense in the 1982 Lebanon War, described as "Israel's Vietnam." In Israel he was deemed to be the greatest field commander in Israeli history, greater than even the legendary war hero, Moshe Dayan. Wherever he went in Israel crowds would chant *Arik Melech Yisroel* ("Ariel, King of Israel").

A chilling incident in the Lebanon War captured the attention of the international media. The Israelis were allied in war with the government of the charismatic Lebanese Christian leader, Bashir Gemayel, against Lebanese elements of the Palestine Liberation Organization and radical Muslims from Syria, who had been attacking Israelis from safe bases in Lebanon.

Palestinian terrorists assassinated Gemayel. In revenge, Christian Phalangists, or militiamen, loyal to Gemayel, invaded the Palestinian refugee camps of Sabra and Shatilla near Beirut and slaughtered some 460 Palestinians. Although Sharon met with Gemayel's family after the assassination and before the attack, there was no evidence that Sharon encouraged the attack or even knew of it before it occurred. Even Israeli intelligence, said to be the best in the world, did not know in advance that the attack was imminent.

Nevertheless, an Israeli commission, headed by Yitzhak Kahan, chief justice of the Israeli Supreme Court, concluded, after a four-month investigation, that Sharon was "indirectly responsible" because he should have foreseen the tragedy. The Kahan Commission found:

> The decision on the entry of the Phalangists into the refugee camps was taken without consideration of the danger—which the makers and executors of the decision were obligated to foresee as probable— the Phalangists would commit massacres and pogroms against the inhabitants of the camps, and without an examination of the means for preventing this danger.
>
> Similarly, it is clear from the course of events that when the reports began to arrive about the actions of the Phalangists in the camps, no

proper heed was taken of these reports, the correct conclusions were not drawn from them, and no energetic and immediate action was taken to restrain the Phalangists and put a stop to their actions.

Kahan concluded that Sharon had personal responsibility "for ignoring the danger of bloodshed and revenge," and for "not taking appropriate measures to prevent bloodshed." According to Kahan, Sharon's negligence in protecting the civilian population of Beirut, which had come under Israeli control, amounted to a nonfulfillment of a duty with which Sharon was charged, and it was recommended that Sharon be dismissed as defense minister.

A *Time* magazine article titled "The Verdict Is Guilty" took Sharon's indirect culpability to the next level. It charged that he had *directly* encouraged the attacks. *Time* falsely reported in February 1983 that Sharon had urged the need for revenge upon the Gemayel family. The public portions of the Kahan Report could not conceivably support this statement. *Time* claimed, however, that a secret addendum to the report, known as Appendix B, gave credence to the tale.

Sharon targeted as libelous one paragraph in *Time*'s story:

One section of the report, known as Appendix B, was not published at all, mainly for security reasons. . . . *TIME* has learned that it . . . contains further details about Sharon's visit to the Gemayel family on the day after Bashir Gemayel's assassination. Sharon reportedly told the Gemayels that the Israeli army would be moving into West Beirut and that he *expected* the Christian forces to go into the Palestinian refugee camps. Sharon also reportedly discussed with the Gemayels the *need* for the Phalangists to *take revenge for the assassination of Bashir*, but the details of the conversation are not known.[8]

---

8. Italics mine. One of Sharon's subordinates, Uri Dan, writes that he sat "slightly to the right and behind Sharon [listening] intently" at the very meeting in 1982 with the Gemayels at which *Time* reported General Sharon had given the green light to Phalangists in Lebanon to massacre Palestinian refugees. *Time*, he writes, "reported something that had never happened."

Sharon's point was that a fair reading of the *Time* story, which interpretation the magazine disputed,[9] was that Sharon instigated the massacre by telling the Gemayels that he "expected" their forces to enter the camps, and that they had a "need" to take "revenge for the assassination of Bashir," and that Appendix B was the basis for the allegation.

The razor-sharp meaning of the words "expected" and "need" could not be clearer. *Time* was charging Sharon with instigating the massacre by directly giving the green light to the Gemayels.

Sharon called *Time*'s article a "blood libel," a reference to the medieval anti-Semitic falsehood that Jews, as part of the Passover ritual, murder Christian children and drink their blood. He felt he had no choice but to sue *Time* to vindicate his reputation. Sharon had no money, as he had been a military man or a farmer all his professional life. But he was determined to retrieve his honor in a libel suit. He sold his house to pay litigation costs, and sued for $50 million.

To prevail in the suit, Sharon faced the same almost insuperable *Sullivan* obstacle to making out his case that had confronted Barry Goldwater, namely that he had to show constitutional malice, namely, actual knowledge of the falsity or reckless disregard for the truth. Or as Judge Sofaer put it, that *Time*'s statements were false, that they defamed Sharon, and that they published with "serious doubts as to the truth."

Milton Gould, a great trial lawyer, represented Sharon; Tom Barr of Cravath, Swaine & Moore, who had represented IBM in its antitrust cases, represented *Time*.

---

9. *Time* claimed that the passage does not accuse Sharon of instigating the slaughter—an interpretation refuted by any fair reading of the paragraph. The article's thrust and substance that Sharon was directly responsible is inescapable.

Milton was sui generis. A born raconteur, he was at home in the courtroom like no one I have ever seen. He was also the author of books and articles about the law and lawyers.[10] Though his baggy pants and crumpled suits belied effable flamboyance, his courtroom manner was impeccable, and he knew all the tricks and played all the angles.

Cross-examiners are supposed to ask questions of witnesses, not argue with them or make statements. Gould, however, was a master at bending the rules. Once I saw him cross-examine a government witness, more or less, as follows:

**Q:** You have pleaded guilty to securities fraud and conspiracy?

**A:** Yes sir.

**Q:** And you are awaiting sentencing?

**A:** Yes sir.

**Q:** And you have been promised leniency in return for your testimony if it convicts my client?

**A:** No sir.

**Q:** It is your hope, is it not, that you will receive leniency on sentencing?

**A:** Yes sir.

**Q:** You don't want to go to jail?

**A:** No sir.

**Q:** And you made the decision to cooperate with the government when you knew they had you and you might go to jail for a long time? That's the way you decided to go?

**A:** Yes sir.

---

10. *E.g., The Witness Who Spoke with God and Other Tales from the Courthouse.* Another Milton book, *A Cast of Hawks*, is about the Nagle case, in which the Supreme Court sided with a federal marshal who, in protecting U.S. Supreme Court Justice Stephen J. Field, killed Field's sworn enemy, former California Justice David S. Terry, after Terry accosted and threatened Justice Field. It was the Wild West in those days.

Q: And the government told you they would make your cooperation known to the sentencing judge and ask for leniency?

A: Yes sir, but that the sentence would be up to the court.

MR. GOULD: *You bet!* Sorry, your Honor, that was spontaneous, I couldn't contain myself, and I apologize to the court.

Nobody ever did it better. In the *Sharon* case, when Judge Sofaer told him in his cross-examination of a witness, "You are getting argumentative," Gould sighed, "Yes I suppose so, your Honor." Milton was so much fun to watch.

"This man Sharon," Gould told the jury in summation, "is a minister, a general, a soldier, a farmer and a hero in his own country." If what *Time* said was true, he said, it would amount to an accusation that a national hero was guilty of mass murder.

"That was a lie," Gould told the jury. There was a "terrible crime" committed against the Palestinians, but the Phalangists committed the crime, not Sharon. "It falls to you, six Americans,"[11] he said to the jury, "to do your duty and eradicate this infamy."

Barr's theory in *Time*'s defense was that Sharon was the subject of "tough press" for some time preceding the article, and that this would rebut malice. Barr contended that what was at stake was the ability of the press to seek and print the truth. "This involves a news story of how a horrible, brutal, insensible massacre of women and children took place," he said. "That is what the press's job is: to dig at things like this, to pick at things that may not be pleasant or comfortable for the people involved, to try to get as much of the story as possible into the hands of the public so that the public can make decisions about how we want to run our lives."

To defend a libel case on the ground of truth and fair comment, it is basic that the truth must be as broad as the alleged libel. The

---

11. In the Southern District, a criminal jury consists of 12 people; a civil jury is six.

riddle of the case came down to whether Sharon had *instigated* the massacre, or at least whether this was the conclusion of the Kahan Commission as reflected in Appendix B, on which *Time* claimed to have relied. Barr intimated to the jury that Appendix B would prove that Sharon had suggested revenge to Gemayel's family and the Phalangists, but that the Israelis had thwarted *Time*'s efforts to see what was there.

David Halevy, *Time*'s veteran Jerusalem correspondent and author of the memorandum that was the purported basis for the story, conceded under questioning by Judge Sofaer that he had no source for his information that Appendix B indeed contained the incriminating evidence. He testified, however, that he had heard from four other sources that at Sharon's meeting with the Gemayels, the participants had discussed revenge. He said he had "deduced" the information in the Appendix "based on [his] 43 years of living in Israel." Pretty thin! *Time* conceded that it had no basis for its story that the secret Appendix B had concluded Sharon told the Gemayels he expected the Phalangist forces to go into the camps, and that he discussed with them the need to take revenge. *Time* claimed, however, that four sources, independent of what was in the Appendix, informed its reporter that Sharon had discussed revenge. Of course, that was not what *Time* said in the article. *Time*'s case was a moving target.

Gould sharply questioned *Time*'s William E. Smith, who had written the story in New York, as to why he had changed the wording of Halevy's memorandum from the statement that Sharon had given the Phalangists the "feeling" that "he understood their need to take revenge," to what appeared in the article: namely that "Sharon also reportedly discussed with the Gemayels the need for the Phalangists to take revenge for the assassination of Bashir."

To this Smith lamely sputtered, "I read that to mean words, words. . . . To my mind . . . there [was] a discussion going on."

Judge Sofaer conducted lengthy negotiations with the Israeli government to gain access to the secret Appendix. His approach was to have Israeli lawyers for both sides meet with Kahan, and to have him answer on a confidential basis an interrogatory propounded by Sofaer as to whether the Appendix "contain[ed] any evidence or suggestion" that Sharon discussed revenge with the Phalangists, or "knew in advance that the Phalangists would massacre civilians." Kahan certified his answer in the negative. After eight weeks of trial and 14 witnesses, the case went to the jury.

Judge Sofaer's invaluable contribution to this and future libel cases involving public figures was his jury charge. Instead of asking for the usual general verdict, either for General Sharon or for *Time*, the judge instructed the jury to come back to the courtroom as soon as it had an answer to each of these crucial and separate questions:

Was *Time*'s story defamatory?

Was it false?

Was it written with constitutional malice?

This three-part special verdict made it possible for each side to claim vindication in the verdict: General Sharon, when the jury found *Time*'s story false and defamatory, and *Time* when the jury found it not guilty of constitutional malice and, therefore, innocent of libel.

The result: case dismissed with both sides claiming victory in the court of public opinion.

As the trial drew to a close in late 1984, I met Ariel Sharon at a dinner sponsored by a Jewish organization at the Pierre. Guard dogs were in the dining room sniffing for bombs. Also present was Benjamin Netanyahu, who was then Israel's U.N. ambassador. Shimon Peres, who did not attend the dinner, was prime minister. I attended at the invitation of Milton Gould. I liked Sharon's face and admired his fighting spirit. He projected the bravery and heroism of a great warrior. As a result of the Kahan Report, he had been relieved of his portfolio as defense minister and served his government as minister of industry, trade, and labor. Sharon made some brief remarks about the trial and advised his audience to "come to Israel."

## WESTMORELAND V. CBS

The *Westmoreland* case also left both sides claiming victory in the court of public opinion, although Westmoreland's victory was less arguable.

William Westmoreland commanded U.S. military operations in Vietnam from 1964 to 1968, at the height of the conflict. He was a distinguished general, decorated many times for valor, who also saw combat in World War II and the Korean War. When given the Vietnam post, Westmoreland had already held at least six commands and had been superintendent of the U.S. Military Academy at West Point.

On January 23, 1982, CBS aired a Mike Wallace documentary, "The Uncounted Enemy: A Vietnam Deception," alleging that Westmoreland engaged in a "conspiracy at the highest level" to suppress and alter assessments of enemy troop strength; that Westmoreland did so for political reasons so as to prolong the conflict; and that Westmoreland's assessments were lower than what would have been had he included Communist civilian organizations in the mix. The broadcast was by any standard biased and unfair—in short, a hatchet job.[12]

The program was hardly a success, finishing last in the ratings for the week it ran (reason enough not to sue for libel). The documentary spun its conspiracy theory, carefully crafted by a paid CBS consultant, former CIA analyst Sam Adams, that in order to delude the Pentagon and the country into thinking the war was winnable,

---

12. Among the many examples of unfairness was the interview conducted by Wallace with Westmoreland himself, during which the camera panned on Wallace, showing him tanned and relaxed, but zoomed in on Westmoreland's jowly face, making him appear shifty, unattractive, and unbelievable.

Westmoreland deliberately understated enemy troop strengths in a key military document known as the Order of Battle.[13]

The documentary in thrust and substance accused Westmoreland of juggling enemy troop figures to produce an artificially low count and please President Johnson.

Westmoreland heatedly denied the charges in the documentary, claiming he had been "rattlesnaked." Westie sued Wallace, CBS, Adams, and producer George Crile for libel in the Southern District, stating that his honor was at stake, and claiming $120 million in damages.

The issue was not whether the CBS report was fair and unbiased. Unfairness does not a libel make. The First Amendment protects journalists and others from libel actions based on biased and unfair interpretations of public figures. Since the segment involved a public figure, the issue was whether the publication was false, and whether it was published with either knowledge of the falsity or reckless disregard for the truth; in short, the same legal issues involved in the *Sharon* case.

*Westmoreland* was a case for the ages. Not only were First Amendment values at stake, but the case also put both the honor of a distinguished general and the conduct of the Vietnam War on trial. All this drama was to unfold before Judge Pierre Leval in a Southern District courtroom.

Pierre Leval began his career as a law clerk to Judge Henry Friendly, a harsh taskmaster. Leval is fond of illustrating Friendly's critical approach with a note Friendly made in the margin of some unfortunate law clerk's memorandum to the judge. "What is new here is not good," Friendly wrote. "And what is good is not new." Friendly, himself a law clerk to Mr. Justice Brandeis, had a number of outstanding clerks, including now Chief Justice John Roberts.

13. The theory is counterintuitive. One might suppose a field commander would want to overstate enemy strength in order to justify additional personnel and materiel. Actually, by understating enemy troop strengths, the commander can argue that there is "light at the end of the tunnel," and that if the nation patiently "stays the course," the army can emerge victorious.

President Clinton elevated Leval to the Second Circuit in 1993, where he continued to enjoy an outstanding judicial career.

Leval is a great judge. He has perhaps the finest legal mind I have encountered in my professional experience. Urbane and sophisticated, he appreciates fine arts, music, and literature. Most of all, he is intrigued by and interested in people and ideas. Some might say he is in the idea business. He is a prolific and gifted writer. As a judge, he particularly valued international human rights and the protection of artistic expression in the copyright laws. Off the bench, he wrote and lectured extensively about both subjects. A libel case, involving a public figure, was just up his alley.

A litigation is not unlike a bullfight, with its phases divided into three parts: discovery, motions, and trial. In the bullring, the stages in the battle are called *tercios*. The bullfight proceeds to the *faena*, the last part, where the matador makes a series of passes with the cape before attempting to kill the bull.

In the discovery phase of a trial, the parties take depositions and review relevant documents in the possession of the other side either to be used as impeachment or as affirmative evidence. Then there is the motion phase, where someone might seek summary judgment because there is no "genuine issue of fact" to be tried.

It was inevitable that CBS would make a summary judgment motion, and it was almost inevitable that the motion be denied. The Second Circuit described summary judgment as follows:

> [U]nder the Federal Rules, "a law suit is a search for the truth and the tools are provided for finding out the facts before the curtain goes up on trial...." The summary judgment procedure ... is just such a "tool" because it enables the court to determine if the "curtain" should be raised at all.[14]

---

14. Fitzgerald v. Westland Marine Corp., 369 F.2d 499 (2d Cir. 1966).

The case bristled with triable issues. Leval narrowed the issues for trial to four significant instances where Westmoreland alleged, and CBS denied, there was knowingly (or recklessly) misstated evidence in the broadcast:

a. *Col. Hawkins' characterization of figures:* Colonel Gains Hawkins was a member of the MACV [Military Assistance Command Vietnam] intelligence team who in 1967 was sent as part of a delegation to represent MACV at a conference of the National Intelligence Estimate [NIE] Board. The conference was held to try to resolve differences of opinion among various agencies on the enemy strength. When CBS interviewed him in preparation of the broadcast, Hawkins had said:

> *Now prior to this when we had the old figures that we inherited from the South Vietnamese forces,* there was never any reluctance on my part to tell Sam [Adams of the CIA] or anybody else who had a need to know, that these figures were crap. They were history. They weren't worth anything.

In editing this statement for the broadcast, CBS excised the italicized portion and presented the balance in a context suggesting that Hawkins was applying the labels of "crap," "history," and "worthless" to the figures that he and the MACV delegation were sponsoring at the NIE conference. Hawkins' derogatory remarks in fact referred to a different set of figures—older figures that had earlier been provided to MACV by the South Vietnamese forces. The earlier figures had nothing to do with Westmoreland.

Westmoreland claimed that by so editing and distorting Hawkins' statement, the broadcast gave it a different meaning and made it seem as if an important member of General Westmoreland's intelligence staff was making an accusation he had in fact not made. He argued this was a deliberate distortion, a knowing falsification of evidence and, therefore, an instance of [constitutional malice].

b. *Misdescription of Col. Hamscher's Statement and Status.* The broadcast contained the following passage involving Colonel George Hamscher:

> Wallace: CBS REPORTS has learned that Colonel Hawkins was in fact carrying out orders that originated from General Westmoreland. Westmoreland says he doesn't recall these orders. But the head of MACV's delegation told us that General Westmoreland had, in fact, personally instructed him not to allow the total [estimate of enemy strength] to go over 300,000....

Westmoreland claimed that this passage would be understood by the viewer as asserting that Hamscher had been the "head of [Westmoreland's MACV] delegation" and told CBS "that General Westmoreland had, in fact, personally instructed him not to allow the total [estimate] to go over 300,000."

In fact, Hamscher was not the head of the MACV delegation, nor even a member of it, nor even under General Westmoreland's command. He was an intelligence officer assigned to Admiral Sharp, the Commander-in-Chief, Pacific (CINCPAC), who participated as a representative of the Defense Intelligence Agency (DIA) in multi-agency meetings with MACV intended to arrive at a consensus on enemy strength. Moreover, Hamscher did not state that he had received such orders from General Westmoreland.

c. *The McChristian hypothetical.* Another instance of claimed falsity in the documentary involved the interview of General Joseph McChristian, who had been General Westmoreland's Chief of Intelligence until June 1967, when he was given the command of an armored division. McChristian had found and had reported a constantly increasing enemy strength during his tenure in Saigon. There was speculation in the press at the time that his transfer was occasioned by Pentagon displeasure over his continually increasing estimates. McChristian believed Westmoreland was disturbed by the large increase in the intelligence figures and concerned that the release of those figures "would create a political bombshell." McChristian, however, never stated that General Westmoreland had given orders to hold down the estimate. To the contrary, he flatly denied that any such thing had happened. In the CBS interview, Crile asked McChristian a hypothetical question as to how he would characterize an order to place an arbitrary ceiling on the estimate of enemy strength. He answered that such an order would constitute "falsification of the facts." On TV, the hypothetical became a reality when this segment of his interview was shown on the program (shortly following the passage quoted above that seemed to attribute to Hamscher the assertion that he had received such an order from General Westmoreland); it was preceded by an introduction by Wallace, saying,

WALLACE: Colonel Hawkins assumes full responsibility for his actions. But we went to General McChristian, his [Westmoreland's] old intelligence chief, to ask what we should think of *General Westmoreland's instructions.*[15]

CRILE: To put a ceiling on enemy strength estimates, to tell an intelligence operation that it is not permitted to report enemy strength estimates over a certain number—

GENERAL MCCHRISTIAN: Uh-hmm.

CRILE:—what does that constitute, sir?

GENERAL MCCHRISTIAN: From my point of view, that is falsification of the facts. . . .

---

15. Italics mine.

Because of Wallace's reference to "General Westmoreland's instructions," the audience surely would have understood this passage as McChristian's acknowledgement that Westmoreland had given such an order. It was undisputed that General McChristian said no such thing.

d. *Misattribution of a cable.* In a segment that became part of the broadcast, the following questioning occurred:

**WALLACE:** Isn't it a possibility that the real reason for suddenly deciding in the summer of 1967 to remove an entire category of the enemy from the Order of Battle, a category that had been in that Order of Battle since 1961, was based on political considerations?

**GENERAL WESTMORELAND:** No, decidedly not. That—that—

**WALLACE:** Didn't you make this clear in your August 20th cable?

**GENERAL WESTMORELAND:** No, no. Yeah. No.

**WALLACE:** I have a copy of your August 20th cable—

**GENERAL WESTMORELAND:** Well, sure. Okay, okay. All right, all right.

**WALLACE:** —spelling out the command position on the self-defense controversy.

**GENERAL WESTMORELAND:** Yeah.

**WALLACE:** As you put it in the cable, you say the principal reason why the self-defense militia must go, quote, was "press reaction." That cable, dated August 20th, 1967, spelled out General Westmoreland's predicament: "We have been projecting an image of success over the recent months. The self-defense militia must be removed," the cable explained, "or the newsmen will immediately seize on the point that the enemy force has increased." The cable went on to say that "No explanation could then prevent the press from drawing an erroneous and gloomy conclusion. . . ."

General Westmoreland, in point of fact, was not the author of the cable to which Wallace referred. General Creighton Abrams, the deputy commander of MACV, sent the cable from Saigon while Westmoreland was away, a fact concededly known to CBS.

The triable issue here was whether the inaccurate attribution of the cable to General Westmoreland was a knowing falsification of evidence designed to strengthen CBS's case against him.

Judge Leval denied CBS's summary judgment motion and ordered the case to proceed.[16]

The case went to trial October 9, 1984, and consumed 18 weeks of testimony. Anticipating a long and complicated trial (it would last 62 days), Pierre Leval, always a master of trial innovation, crafted an imaginative and unprecedented approach to help the jury understand the proof—the interim or "mini-summation."

The court allowed each side up to 120 minutes between opening and closing argument in which the lawyers might have a chance to address the jury directly with their interpretations of the evidence, as the case unfolded.

Under Leval's procedure, the lawyers could use their mini-summation time whenever and however they saw fit (in blocks of time or as short or long as necessary) to explain the point they were attempting to make.[17] This was the first time the technique had ever been used, and it serves as a model for efficient trial management of complex litigation to this day. It worked, and it worked well.

The issue came down to whether the allegations against Westmoreland were true, and whether CBS was entitled to rely on the statements of high-ranking military officers who stuck to their stories when they testified at trial under oath.

---

16. Westmoreland v. CBS, 596 F. Supp 1170 (SDNY 1984).

17. The only restriction on an overly clever lawyer was that he was not permitted to pepper his adversary's presentation with mini-summations or interfere with the court's schedule.

General McChristian, assistant chief of staff for Intelligence under Westmoreland, testified that when he had presented new increased enemy troop strength assessments, Westmoreland said that sending these figures to Washington would "create a political bombshell" and would embarrass the president. McChristian testified that in being loyal to the president—his commander in chief—and in withholding the figures, Westmoreland was "disloyal to the country."

Another military intelligence officer, Colonel Gains Hawkins, followed McChristian on the stand. Hawkins basically reaffirmed what he had said on the CBS program.

Courtroom observers said that David Dorsen, who assisted chief plaintiff's counsel Dan and at the trial, scored some major points against both McChristian and Hawkins on cross-examination.[18] The two officers, who were the chief military witnesses for CBS and whose testimony was so potentially damaging to General Westmoreland, did not in fact acquit themselves well on cross-examination, providing little or no direct evidence of any cover-up or intelligence manipulation.

Once Dorsen completed his cross of Hawkins there would be summations, and the court's charge.[19] Then, the jury's deliberations would begin. Leval said that he would propound special verdicts to the jury as Sofaer had done in the *Sharon* case.[20] The last phase

---

18. This is the same David Dorsen who wrote the biography of Judge Friendly referred to earlier.

19. At the close of the evidence and following summations, the judge instructs the jury as to the law governing the case. Lawyers call this "the charge." In the federal court, the judge may summarize the evidence. Some lawyers believe this to be the most important part of the trial.

20. A general verdict would have been: Do you find for the plaintiff or for the defendant? Under this scenario, if Westmoreland lost the case, he could argue to the world that the jury found the program to be false but that he had failed to establish constitutional malice. A special verdict would be to have the jury answer the specific questions: (1) Was the program false in any material respect? (2) Was it defamatory of General Westmoreland? (3) Did CBS know it was false or did they publish the broadcast with reckless disregard for the truth?

of the trial, the *faena*, was at hand, and the parties awaited the "moment of truth."

But the "moment of truth" was not to be. Cross-examination was to continue on February 18, 1985, when Dan Burt entered the courtroom and announced that Westmoreland had settled with CBS. The announcement stunned both Dorsen and George Leisure, Westmoreland's local counsel, who had not been previously informed. The settlement left Westmoreland with no money from CBS and no apology. Both sides released public statements about the case. Far short of an apology, CBS said that it never intended to say "General Westmoreland was unpatriotic or disloyal in performing his duties *as he saw them*."[21] Westmoreland said he respected "the long and distinguished journalistic tradition of CBS and the rights of journalists to examine the complex issues of Vietnam and to present perspectives contrary to his own."

The settlement was astounding and still remains unexplained. Some speculated that Westmoreland ran out of money, and that his contributions from conservative think tanks dried up. Others said that Westmoreland's trial watcher had told him he was going to lose.

On February 26, 1985, the week after they announced the settlement, I wrote a piece for the *New York Law Journal* titled "Westmoreland's Capitulation: A Trial Lawyer's Perspective," arguing that Westmoreland was wrong to quit at the finish line. I wrote that the sharply contested issues involved in his case, instinct with public interest, should have been tried out before a judge and a jury, not to a court of public opinion. Ex parte statements espousing partisan positions may influence a court of public opinion. The public may not have heard all the evidence. What it has heard may be biased,

---

21. (Emphasis mine). I suspect that the "as he saw them" language was the handiwork of CBS's lawyer, David Boies.

particularly in a case of this kind where the movers and shapers of public opinion, the media themselves, are interested parties.

Some would prefer the court of public opinion for cases such as this, arguing that libel actions, even if groundless, impose a chilling effect on a free press. True, it costs a publication an enormous sum in legal fees merely to go to trial, and the Supreme Court of the United States has indicated that since public officials' libel actions turn on questions of state of mind, they must normally go to trial, rather than be decided on a motion for summary judgment. The argument comes with lesser force, however, when one knows that these costs are defrayed by insurance, which publications normally have in coverage sufficient to deal with such contingencies.

The court system, however imperfect, is peculiarly well-equipped to accommodate competing considerations of the duty of a free press to be accountable within the narrow corridor permitted by the First Amendment for malicious falsity in its statements about public officials, and the correlative right of the press to be unfettered in its expression of ideas by the chilling apprehension of large libel judgments. And courts can give a final answer in the particular case and put the issue to rest. The verdict of history, however, may be capricious or mercurial.

It is, therefore, too bad that General Westmoreland capitulated just as his last campaign was about to be decided. Had the jury verdict gone against him, the general could have publicly rejected the decision or ascribed his defeat to the betrayal of subordinates. He might even have blamed the nearly insuperable obstacle of the First Amendment, which Ariel Sharon could not surmount, in his case against *Time* magazine. And, as many believe, he might have won a total or, like Sharon, a partial victory.

Now these opportunities are lost, and in hindsight one may say that Westmoreland would have been better served not to sue in the first place. His reputation as a warrior was in worse shape than it was before he filed suit. The lawsuit resurrected the charges against him, long since forgotten or dismissed, with a born-again vitality that sully the record of a career committed to duty, honor, and country.

And CBS could claim a victory, not based on success in a court of law or the vindication of its broadcast practices, but on Westmoreland's irresolution and mistrust of the decency of an American jury, which would have rendered no harsher verdict than that which he self-inflicted in the court of public opinion.

CBS was terribly unfair to a man who had dedicated his life to public service. One need only read Judge Leval's opinion denying summary judgment to see that a jury could readily conclude that the thrust and substance of the program was both false and defamatory.

Judge Leval said, following announcement of the settlement, "Judgments of history are too subtle and too complex to be satisfied with a verdict. It may be for the best that the verdict will be left to history." As the judge said, the verdict would be "left to history."

# U.S. V. ROY M. COHN

*When I went to the Bar as a very young man (said I to myself, said I)*
*I'll work on a new and original plan (said I to myself, said I)*
*I'll never throw dust in a juryman's eyes (said I to myself, said I)*
*Or hoodwink a judge who is not over-wise (said I to myself, said I).*
—W.S. Gilbert, *Iolanthe*

*[L]egal principles are . . .an argumentative technique—in other*
*words, . . .an arsenal of offensive and defensive weapons to be used*
*in litigation. Inventiveness and ingenuity. . .are actually far more*
*important in legal battles than scholarly learning.*
—Thurman Arnold

Not all the trials I knew of in the Mother Court resulted in convictions. Here are some acquittals I know about, all involving the same defendant, Roy Marcus Cohn.

If John Gotti was the "Teflon Don," Roy Cohn was the "Teflon Rogue." For some, he was a picaresque hero, for others, the very personification of evil. In the 1960s, Bob Morgenthau as U.S. Attorney for the Southern District indicted Cohn three times in six years on charges ranging from extortion and blackmail to bribery, conspiracy, securities fraud, and obstruction of justice. None of the charges stuck.

Cohn was the strangest looking man I ever met. He would have been neatly typecast as Richard III, or maybe even Caliban. His body seemed to be perpetually atilt, and his diminutive zigzag frame presented the overwhelming impression that he wasn't quite straight. Roy's characteristic pose was whispering conspiratorially to someone with his hand over his mouth, lest he be overheard plotting some piece of skullduggery. His face was contorted in a perpetual ugly sneer that seemed to project an air of unbridled malevolence.

Cohn was a child prodigy. He graduated from law school at age 20, and had to wait until his 21st birthday to be admitted to the bar. At 24, he prosecuted the Rosenbergs, and helped send them to the electric chair. At 25, on the recommendation of J. Edgar Hoover, he became chief counsel to Senator McCarthy's Senate Permanent Subcommittee on Investigations. Judge Murphy used to refer to him derisively as "the young lawyer."

Despite his chilling affect, Roy had his fans. Although those on the political Left thought of him as an unscrupulous opportunist, a Communist witch hunter, a headline-seeker, a fraudster, and a menace, those on the Right saw him as a great American, a vigorous advocate against global Communism, and an engaging rogue who became a lightning rod for political persecution. Some even called him "Jesus Christ." His anti–New Left politics were the bane of the liberal establishment.

Roy befriended the most ardent apostles of anti-Communism, some of them quite powerful politically. Atop a spiral staircase in his law office, located in an Upper East Side Manhattan townhouse where he also lived, was a wall festooned with autographed photographs of Cardinals Spellman and Cooke, J. Edgar Hoover, and even Richard Nixon. Cohn was particularly proud of a plaque sent him by Rumson, New Jersey, High School:

To Roy M. Cohn, outstanding patriotic American, brilliant young attorney, fearless crusader and defender of the faith against Godless Communism.

When Cohn was acquitted of obstruction of justice charges in 1964, Cardinal Spellman sent him a message of congratulations.

Cohn readily cast himself as the victim of three unjust indictments, resulting in four trials and three acquittals.[1] The political Right, rallying to Cohn's defense, readily bought into Cohn's accusation of a political vendetta. William F. Buckley, brandishing his characteristically acerbic wit, wrote in the *National Review*:

The zeal with which the U.S. Attorney in New York has gone after Roy Cohn over a period of years suggests either that Mr. Cohn is soon to be revealed as head of SMERSH or that the U.S. Attorney is suffering from a devil fixation.[2]

A master of the vicious public counterattack, Cohn's defense indulged the time-honored tactic of vilifying his accusers. He contended that Kennedy and Morgenthau were "out to get him," and claimed they were responsible for prejudicial articles about him appearing in *Life* magazine—a "smear job" he said that was intended to prejudice the jury. Cohn claimed this vendetta started with Bobby Kennedy when the two were rivals for the job Cohn eventually won

---

1. As will be seen, the first trial resulted in a mistrial when a juror's father died during deliberations. On the retrial, Cohn was acquitted.

2. SMERSH is a Soviet counterintelligence agency featured in Ian Fleming's early James Bond novels as Agent 007's nemesis. Ironically, when Cohn was disbarred in 1986, just a month before his death, Buckley's *National Review* referred to him as "an ice-cold sleaze."

with McCarthy. Cohn and Kennedy never liked each other. During the Army-McCarthy hearings in 1954, their mutual animosity boiled over to the point that they almost came to blows.

Cohn assailed Morgenthau for "generational pay-back." According to Cohn, as counsel to a subcommittee chaired by Senator Karl Mundt of South Dakota, he had investigated Morgenthau's father, Treasury Secretary Henry Morgenthau Jr. After World War II, the Soviets had attempted to get U.S. occupation-currency printing plates. Cohn alleged that Henry Morgenthau overruled objections of Budget Director Daniel Bell, and turned over the plates to the Russians. He claimed that Treasury economist Harry Dexter White, later exposed as a Soviet spy, manipulated Morgenthau into passing the plates to the Soviets, who then printed currency with abandon. Treasury officials gave the plausible explanation that restricting Soviet use of the plates in the Russian sector would needlessly endanger postwar cooperation. While this episode was catnip for those on the far Right, economic histories of the period suggest that there was little evidence of Soviet abuse. The investigation went nowhere.

Nevertheless, Cohn claimed that Kennedy and Morgenthau harbored some sort of political grudge against him, and wanted to settle old scores. Morgenthau responded by saying that "a man is not immune from prosecution merely because a U.S. Attorney happens not to like him." This did not seem to silence Cohn's supporters. All this made for good media copy, but had no bearing on the fortunes of the three prosecutions, which inevitably turned on the evidence and the credibility of the witnesses.

In his 1964 trial for perjury and obstruction of justice relating to an underlying stock swindle, including an allegation that Cohn had conspired to bribe a U.S. Attorney, Cohn twice cheated the hangman. The first trial, before Judge Archie Dawson, ended with

,

the jurors leaning toward conviction on three out of seven counts, when during deliberations a juror's father suddenly died. With no knowledge of how the jury stood, Judge Dawson asked the parties to consent to a verdict from a jury of 11. The government said they would agree, but Cohn's premier lawyer, Frank Raichle, would not agree, and so there was a mistrial.[3]

The government proceeded to try Cohn again. A retrial usually favors the defendant, because he has already had both a preview of the government's case and a go-round with the government witnesses, which can be used for impeachment. On the retrial, interestingly enough, Raichle asked to be relieved of the case because of the illness of his 90-year-old mother. Cohn volunteered to continue in his own defense, heedless of the old truism that "every man who is his own lawyer has a fool for a client." The judge forced Raichle to continue, and Cohn was acquitted the second time around.

In his 1969 trial, prosecutors charged Cohn with bribing a New York City appraiser with $25,000 to obtain secret appraisal data coming from the city files, which would have been of enormous assistance to Cohn and his associates in the condemnation proceeding the group brought when the city seized Fifth Avenue Coach Lines.[4] Allegedly, Cohn paid the bribe money to an intermediary named Bernard Patrusky on June 16, 1964, outside Courtroom 110 of the Foley Square Courthouse, where Cohn was standing trial on the first indictment. The indictment also charged that Cohn

---

3. Hundreds of people reportedly gathered outside the courthouse to congratulate Cohn on the mistrial. At the edge of the crowd, according to the *New York Times*, was Helen Sobell, wife of Morton Sobell, who was tried with the Rosenbergs and was then in jail serving out his sentence. Mrs. Sobell said that she had followed the case with interest and thought Cohn should have agreed to a verdict by an 11-person jury.

4. The Fifth Amendment to the Constitution provides that private property may not be "taken for public use, without just compensation." When it is, a party may test the adequacy of the compensation award in what is known as a condemnation proceeding. New York's highest court, the Court of Appeals, awarded Fifth Avenue Coach $55 million for the assets the city had seized.

extorted stock for himself from his "friend," Lawrence I. Weisman, president of Fifth Avenue Coach, by threatening Weisman that he would expose his role in the bribery scheme.

The judge in the case was Inzer B. Wyatt. Like Judge Woolsey, who wrote the landmark decision in the *Ulysses* case, Wyatt hailed from the South. A bon vivant, he had been a partner in Wall Street behemoth Sullivan & Cromwell and owned a house and a restaurant in the south of France. A resident of New York for at least 45 years, he often spoke with a mellifluous Southern twang, which he could readily turn on and off.[5]

The proof against Cohn came from government witnesses, who had by then admitted their own complicity in the alleged crimes. Cohn did not take the stand in the two-month trial. The proceeding took an amazing turn. At the conclusion of the evidence, Cohn's seasoned criminal trial lawyer, Joseph Brill, who resembled a whirling dervish replete with bald head, handlebar mustache, and goatee, suddenly collapsed in the courtroom—the apparent victim of a heart attack. EMT workers rushed Brill to the hospital.[6] Just before collapsing, Brill had completed the cross of the government's last witness.

Cohn immediately suggested to Wyatt the same gambit he had considered in his prior trial when Frank Raichle asked to be relieved. Cohn described what happened next:

I had decided to take the stand. We had spent many hours preparing an outline of my testimony. Cross-examination did not worry me,

5. When Wyatt died in 1990, his passing was noted on the obituary page of the *New York Times*. The headline read, "Federal Judge Inzer B. Wyatt, 82; Presided at Acquittal of Roy Cohn."

6. The hospital released Brill shortly after the trial concluded. There was the lurking suspicion that Cohn had somehow staged the whole thing, as the government never asked for a court-appointed doctor to examine Brill to determine when he might be fit to resume the defense of the case. Wyatt never seemed to consider the possibility of delaying the trial for a week or ten days, so that Cohn would have an opportunity to engage new counsel. Brill died of cancer some six years later.

since I would be telling the truth and had sufficient background not to be trapped. But Mr. Brill's heart attack changed our strategy. We had two voids to fill: presentation of our witnesses on our direct case and the summation to the jury. Tom [Bolan, Cohn's partner] agreed that if I testified, I should not sum up, and that if I summed up, I should not testify.[7]

Cohn made the right decision. He asked to sum up in his own behalf, and it was a masterstroke. Cohn hadn't taken the stand where he might have been cross-examined on his murky financial dealings, and the true nature of his business relationships.

The courthouse was abuzz with the news of Brill's purported heart attack. I wondered whether there might be a mistrial. I ran into Al Gaynor in the hallway. Al had unsuccessfully prosecuted Cohn's partner, Daniel Driscoll, for failure to file three years of tax returns. I asked Al who Cohn might get to take over the case on such short notice to sum up for the defense. Tom Bolan, his law partner, who sat beside him at the trial? A new lawyer? "I think the new lawyer will be Roy Marcus Cohn," Al said. I thought to myself, "Boy, I had better see this one." and entered the courtroom just in time to hear Tom Bolan announce, "Mr. Cohn is now ready to sum up in his own behalf."

The jury hadn't heard a word from Cohn during the two-month trial, nor did they have his take on the events that formed the basis for the indictment. If convicted on all five counts in the indictment, he might have been sentenced to a maximum of 45 years in jail. Facing the jury, he spoke without notes for about five hours. This was his shot, and it was a tour de force:

---

7. Cohn, A Fool for a Client 90 (1971).

This is the first time in my life that I ever addressed a jury in behalf of a defendant in a criminal case. When I went to law school, little did I dream that my first time in this role would be in my own behalf . . . The only thing we have before us are the issues in this indictment. If I have done anything good in my life, I expect no credit for it in this case. Nor do I expect to be blamed here for any position I've taken with which you might not agree.

Addressing the credibility of the government witnesses, he refrained from railing against them in rancor:

The prosecutor will follow me in summation. I was once a prosecutor, and if I may say so a pretty good one. Frequently, prosecutors say of the government witnesses, "You heard the defense attack them as thieves and liars and crooks, but they weren't my friends, they were [his] the defendant's." In fact, most of these witnesses were never my friends, all except Larry Weisman. He was my friend, and he betrayed my friendship. I can't understand why he would say the things he said which are so untruthful. Maybe it's so he wouldn't go to jail. I guess that's how the system works. That's life. Larry said that I extorted stock from him to gain control of the company. But after the alleged extortion he wrote me a letter, which is in evidence. "Roy," he wrote, "I'll always be able to count on you as one of my friends." Of course, this is just the sort of letter you write to your friendly blackmailer. After the alleged extortion, I was invited to Weisman's wedding, attended a cocktail party in his home—all the things you do for a friendly blackmailer.

Then came the crusher.

After the alleged extortion, Weisman gave me this silver pitcher.

Cohn brandished the one-foot-high silver pitcher to the jury.

It contains this engraved inscription, which I'll read you. "To the Second Best lawyer in the United States. With Regard and Affection of L.I.W.-No. 1."

Cohn then came to the knockout punch of his summation, expressing his faith in the U.S. jury system:

There is one final thought I wish to share with you.... The indictment does read, "The United States of America against Roy Cohn"....

I do not believe for one second that the United States is against me.... The mere concept bothers me as much as anything in the world.

As I was thinking of that concept and looking over the record preparing to address you, I came across a quote which Judge Wyatt gave to the jury....It was a quote from Ecclesiastes ... "It is better the ending of a thing than the beginning thereof."

I tried to apply that to this case, and the beginning was the testimony of Lawrence Weisman. He was the first witness.... Lawrence Weisman lied to the grand jury.... That was the beginning.

Then I thought of the end. I remember when one of the members of the prosecution staff [Assistant U.S. Attorney John Allee, who in fact was the lead prosecutor in the case] stood up and said "The United States of America rests," and just before that statement was made, a witness had walked off the stand, the ending witness, and that man was Bernard Patrusky.... who admitted lying to two grand juries, who did lie to a third one, and who did lie to you in here in this courtroom....

So that was the ending. Well, I thought back on the quotation from Ecclesiastes, and ... it was difficult for me to see how the ending with Patrusky was very much better than the beginning with Weisman. But then I realized two things. I realized that Weisman and Patrusky are not the United States of America: In this case, as the sole judges of the facts, as the only people in the world representing our system of law and justice, who pass on the facts and the truth under a system of law the finest known to mankind, devised in a country a lot of people like to knock, but I know which you all believe is the greatest country in the world, under that system you are the sole representatives of the United States of America in passing upon the facts and truth in this case.

And then I realized the second thing: I realized that the end had not come when Bernard Patrusky walked off that witness stand. I realized that the end can come only when you have spoken and rendered your verdict, and I hope and know, if you will, I pray that when that end does come it will indeed be better and brighter than was the beginning.

The emotion was so thick in the courtroom, you could have cut it with a knife. Everyone was blown away. One female juror wept.

In his charge, Judge Wyatt told the jurors, "It seems clear that your verdict depends on the determination of the credibility of the witnesses." The jury took less than four hours to reach a verdict of acquittal. The jury foreman, who throughout the trial had worn an American flag in his lapel, announced the verdict. When asked later about the basis of their verdict, one of the jurors said, "We didn't believe the witnesses—not one." As Judge Weinfeld commiserated later with one of the disappointed prosecutors, "You can't do the testifying for your witnesses."

The third case was a cakewalk for Cohn. Morgenthau charged he had lied in the proxy materials submitted to the stockholders of Fifth Avenue Coach by concealing a $350,000 advance he received from the company. At the start of the trial, the government dropped six

of the ten charges against him. Cohn's defense was that the money
was a legal fee that did not have to be reported. In cross-examining
one of the government witnesses, Cohn's lawyer and partner, Tom
Bolan, somehow got before the jury the fact of the prior acquittal in
the Fifth Avenue Coach case. The Southern District judge, Charles
H. Tenney, denied the government's motion for a mistrial.[8] Cohn
did not take the stand in his defense. Judge Tenney dismissed the
conspiracy count at the close of the evidence, leaving three counts
of false statements to go to the jury. The jury did not spend much
time on this one, only one hour of deliberation. It was "been there,
done that" for Cohn, and he walked out of the courthouse to freedom, never having uttered an audible word in the course of the
proceeding.

Roy could get away with anything—at least for a while, until
things caught up with him. His glibness was amazing.

I once saw him argue an appeal in a New York appellate court.
The presiding justice opened the proceeding in a way that seemed
quite ominous for Cohn. "Mr. Cohn, in your brief at page 31, you
cite the case of *Jones v. Smith*. My law clerks and I have searched the
authorities for *Jones v. Smith*, and we can find no report of the case
where you cite it—indeed no report of it anywhere. Are you sure
that this case exists?"

Without blinking an eye, Cohn responded, "I'll have a letter on
your Honor's desk at 10 tomorrow morning."

Although Roy cheated the hangman three times in the Mother
Court, eventually life caught up with him. The IRS audited his tax

---

8. Even if the motion had been granted and the government then contended that Bolan had
provoked the mistrial with his improper statement, government motions for a mistrial after the
jury is impaneled are virtually unknown since the double jeopardy clause of the Constitution
(Amendment V: "[N]or shall any person be subject for the same offense to be twice put in
jeopardy of life or limb. . . .") may bar a second bite of the apple once a jury has been impaneled.
Case closed.

returns 20 years in a row. His assets were concealed in a maze of corporations. His misconduct seemed to go from bad to outrageous. He advised witnesses before the grand jury, "It is no crime not to remember." He even approached witnesses about to appear before the grand jury and gestured with his open hand, as though to show moral support. Prosecutors I knew believed that this "high five" gesture was a "bench signal" to take the Fifth. Amendment. He entered the hospital bedroom of his comatose dying client, Lewis Rosenstiel, and induced him to scribble an illegible signature on a codicil making Cohn one of his beneficiaries. You can't make this up.

In 1973, a mysterious fire broke out aboard Cohn's 95-foot yacht, the *Defiance*, once owned by Malcolm Forbes, aboard which Cohn customarily entertained politicians, prelates, and other notables.[9] The ship sank. The captain and two crewmembers survived, but another crewmember, Charles Martenson, lost his life. Martenson's father charged that Cohn ordered the *Defiance* scuttled to collect on a $200,000 insurance policy, and was hence responsible for his son's death. Cohn used the insurance money to pay off the mortgage on the yacht and cover some of his personal expenses.

In a weird development in 1974, Cohn entered the primary race for New York County District Attorney, taking on Richard Kuh and his old nemesis, Robert Morgenthau. In the campaign debates, Cohn, the former McCarthy counsel, argued that Morgenthau was a "pseudoliberal" who had conducted a personal vendetta against him, using unauthorized wiretaps, mail watches, and other unconstitutional techniques. Cohn's claims fell on deaf ears with the electorate. Morgenthau won handily, and served with great distinction as District Attorney for 34 years.

---

9. Cohn used to invite Carmine DeSapio and other Tammany Hall leaders out for cruises to talk over the perennial topics—"who was in, who was out, and who wanted what from whom."

Roy Cohn's father, Albert Cohn, was a highly respected justice of the New York State Supreme Court's Appellate Division. In June 1986 the court his father had served disbarred Cohn for dishonesty, fraud, and deceit in cases dating back as far as 20 years. The court cited the Rosenstiel matter and the insurance proceeds of the *Defiance* fire as but two of the multiple instances of Cohn's misconduct. The appellate division ruled that following the yacht's sinking, "the events which ensued cast serious doubts upon" Cohn's "professional conduct and integrity, both as an attorney and as an escrow agent."

Roy Cohn died of complications from AIDS a month after his disbarment, lying to the end about the nature of his ailment and the high-risk behavior that had brought it about.[10]

---

10. Cohn's ambivalence and hypocrisy about his deeply closeted homosexuality is treated in Tony Kushner's 1993 Pulitzer Prize–winning play *Angels in America: A Gay Fantasia on National Themes.*

I

# 13

# U.S. V. THEM

*These memories, which are my life—for we possess nothing certainly
except the past—were always with me. Like the pigeons of St.
Mark's, they were everywhere under my feet, singly, in pairs, in little
honey-voiced congregations, nodding, strutting, winking, rolling the
tender feathers of their necks, perching sometimes, if I stood still, on
my shoulder or pecking a broken biscuit from between my lips; until,
suddenly, the noon gun boomed and in a moment with a flutter and
sweep of wings, the pavement was bare and the whole sky above dark
with a tumult of fowl.*

—Evelyn Waugh, ***Brideshead Revisited***

"We have some planes," radioed Mohamed Atta from the
flight deck of American Airlines Flight 11, minutes
before he flew the Boeing 767 into the north side of the north
tower of the World Trade Center complex known as One World
Trade Center. My large corner office on 9/11 happened to be on
the 54th floor of One World Trade Center. When I joined my firm
in 1993, I knew that the building had been the target of a terrorist
attack earlier that year, and that the jihadists had vowed to do it

again. I never really thought about it as each day I swiped my key card on the concourse turnstile that admitted me to the building.

The Mother Court was no stranger to terrorist trials prior to 9/11. As early as 1965, Steve Kaufman and Pierre Leval prosecuted three terrorists for plotting to dynamite the Statue of Liberty in New York Harbor, the Liberty Bell in Philadelphia, and the Washington Monument. All three were tried, convicted, and sentenced to jail.[1]

In the spring of 2001, Mary Jo White, the first female U.S. Attorney for the Southern District, reported four successful prosecutions of terrorists plotting death and destruction in New York City:[2]

- The 1994 trial of four defendants for the World Trade Center bombing;
- The 1995 trial of 12 defendants for the Day of Terror plot, a diabolical scheme of mass destruction simultaneously to blow up the Holland and Lincoln Tunnels, and the FBI's New York office across the street from the Foley Square courthouse;
- The 1996 trial of three defendants for the Manila Air attack, a horrific plot hatched in the Philippines by Ramzi Yousef, one of the masterminds of the WTC bombing and a fugitive from American justice. His goal was, in a single 48-hour period, to blow up a dozen U.S. jumbo jets bound for U.S. destinations; and
- The 1997 trial of Ramzi Yousef, who had been arrested in Pakistan together with the driver of the Ryder van used in the World Trade Center bombing who in turn had been arrested in Jordan and brought to the Southern District for trial.

Terrorist indictments in civilian courts work. In 1998, the United States indicted 21 defendants, including Osama bin Laden, for

---

1. United States v. Bowe, 360 F.2d 1 (2d Cir. 1966).
2. Mary Jo is now chair of the Securities and Exchange Commission.

complicity in the bombings of two of its embassies, one in Nairobi, Kenya, and the other in Dar es Salaam, Tanzania. Twenty-four died in the attacks, including 12 Americans. The indictment was filed in the Mother Court. The results were excellent. Of the 21, three remain fugitives; non-U.S. forces killed two; U.S. forces killed six; and one died of natural causes while in custody. Of the remaining nine, six are serving life sentences, and three are awaiting trial. As we have seen, one of these involved the 1993 bombing of the World Trade Center that left six people dead, over 1,000 injured, and the entire New York City population permanently scarred.

It is eminently manageable to try and convict terrorists in civilian courts, with a speedy public trial and elaborate protection of their constitutional rights. Some have argued that a defendant's rights in a civilian trial to see relevant evidence in the government files may conflict with national security interests, and thereby make such cases untriable. But judges are very good at winnowing out what is relevant to a case from what may be too sensitive for disclosure; names of informants, sources, and methods of intelligence, and antiterrorist strategies would never be exposed to the prying eyes of terrorists and their lawyers.

Few of us can forget where we were on September 11, 2001. It was one of the transforming events of a lifetime, comparable to the Kennedy and King assassinations, or to the day Neil Armstrong walked on the moon. As it had when Armstrong took his "one small step for a man," the whole world stopped that day, and we knew it would never be the same.

It was a particularly clear day that autumn morning. I jogged around the Central Park Reservoir, as was my routine, and prepared for a busy day at the office. Some time before nine o'clock my wife, Marlene, and I were waiting for the elevator in our apartment building on our way to work. Marlene worked at JP Morgan Chase as head of Global Philanthropic Services. Her office was in midtown. The phone rang.

It was my Princeton classmate, Tom Pulling, a prominent New York investment banker with offices at Seven World Trade Center who had lost some of the hearing in one ear as a result of the 1993 bombing. Tom happened to be in midtown on 9/11. An ex-Marine, he was invariably early at his post. His midtown appointment may have saved his life.

"A plane has crashed into the high floors of One World Trade Center," he said. "You have to be joking," was my response. He said, "I would never joke about such a thing. Turn on the television." It was on all day. Fortunately for us, Marlene and I had been leaving for work together, and she knew I was not going to my office, so she didn't have to worry. She left for work, and Pulling soon joined me at home, where we stayed glued to the television. There was no phone service for several hours.

When Pulling reported the first strike all I could think of was an incident I remembered from childhood, when a small plane had accidentally crashed into the Empire State Building. It made the front page of the *Daily News*. The childhood memory nurtured my denial of what had surely occurred. But, accident this was not. When I turned on the television, a far darker picture emerged. Before my eyes on the screen, a second plane crashed into the 80th floor of Two World Trade Center, the south building of the twin towers. I wanted to believe it was just a videotaped rerun of the first crash, and then I realized it wasn't. This was terrorism on a cataclysmic scale.

Pulling and I broke for lunch at Swifty's, a small but popular restaurant on Lexington Avenue between 72nd and 73rd Streets. There, we encountered the columnist Liz Smith, having lunch with a friend, and talked about how we all are so vulnerable to history. We toasted life and expressed the hope we would meet there at the same time the next year. We did. When we left the restaurant, I glanced south on Lexington Avenue. There was a sickening plume of black smoke that clouded the sky. I felt myself recoil in horror.

Back home, phone service eventually resumed. The first call was from Pierre Leval. "Boy, am I glad to hear your voice!" he said. If for nothing else, I shall always love him for that one.

My law firm occupied floors 54–59 at One World Trade Center, the north tower. The strike hit some 30 floors above us at 8:46 a.m., in the vicinity of floor 98. Fortunately, in human terms, our firm was not so hard hit as most. We had roughly 125 people on site that morning. In another hour we would have had 300. Almost all escaped the building by descending over 50 flights of stairs to the street. The exception was our switchboard operator, Rosemary Smith, who sat on the steps to rest. She went down when the building collapsed at 10:28 a.m., roughly 70 minutes after the strike.

One of our heroes that day was our office manager, John Connelly, who, like the captain of a sinking ship, made sure every office was evacuated and every computer was turned off before he went down the stairs. He escaped the building with only minutes to spare, retrieving the priceless gift of life. He was the last of us to leave the doomed building. Our office was totally destroyed.

No loss that occurred that day was more tragic than the senseless and horrific loss of innocent human life, next to which the loss of my office and its contents is surely trivial. The dead were robbed of their future; I was merely robbed of the papers that reflected my past.

New Yorkers waited on line at the hospitals to give blood for the injured, though the number of injured was few. Those trapped in the building had embraced oblivion.

As I sorrowfully went to bed that night, thinking about the horrific events of the day, I could not help but have a feeling of immense pride in our country. Americans are an extraordinary people. Blessed with a rugged individualism, they have at the same time a remarkable ability to pull together in crisis, and unite to defend shared values and common purposes. As expressed in the magnificent preamble to our Constitution: it is "We, the people ... [who] establish justice, insure domestic tranquility, provide for the common defense, promote the general welfare, and secure the blessings of liberty to ourselves and our posterity." The preamble expresses more than the "power of words." It embodies our strength, our common values, and it is why we are the greatest nation on the planet. Whatever our differences, we all pulled together that day.

My partner and friend, Roger Hawke, another graduate of the Morgenthau U.S. Attorney's Office, was one of those who made it to safety. Two weeks after 9/11, Roger and I attended the annual meeting of the American College of Trial Lawyers in New Orleans, where he was to be inducted as a Fellow. I had proposed him for membership. As might be expected, there was almost no one on our Continental Airlines plane, which departed Newark Airport where United Airlines Flight 93 had taken off only a fortnight earlier with four terrorists aboard. The terrorists headed that plane for the U.S. Capitol building or the White House. But for a passenger revolt, they would have succeeded. The plane crashed in a field near Shanksville, Pennsylvania, about 20 minutes by air from Washington, D.C.

The president of the American College of Trial Lawyers, former Watergate prosecutor Earl Silbert, called Roger to the podium to receive his certificate in the presence of about 800 members and guests from all parts of the country and Canada. Also present was Justice Scalia, who was about to address the group. Roger is a brilliant advocate, a "just the facts, ma'am," low-key kind of guy. He told the sobering tale of his near-death experience for being early at his post—a shaking building, a "place where no one would want to be," air redolent of foul-smelling black particulate, and groups of fearful, traumatized people filing down the stairs in orderly fashion, and then running for their lives when they reached the street. He told of his searing recurring nightmare of the earnest faces of young firemen in full battle dress running up the stairs as he descended. The shoes he wore that day, later photographed and framed for the wall of his office, were covered with a powdery filth and grime.

In introducing Roger, Silbert invited him to tell how terrorism might have changed his life. Roger said, "Will terrorism change my life? I am proud to be a trial lawyer. I was preparing for trial when it happened. It's what I have done all my life. No terrorist will ever change that." There was a standing ovation that must have lasted five minutes. Men and women had tears in their eyes.

There were almost 3,000 victims of the 9/11 attacks, excluding the 19 suicide hijackers. Of these, 2,606 were at the World Trade Center.[3] The random loss of human life that day still shocks the civilized conscience.

I lost the mementos of my career. On the wall of my office at Ground Zero was my certificate of appointment as an Assistant U.S. Attorney, signed by Attorney General Ramsey Clark in May 1997 and countersigned by the then Solicitor General Thurgood Marshall.[4]

There was a photograph of my swearing in by Bob Morgenthau in a conference room of the Foley Square Courthouse. I was unable to replace it.

There was a signed photograph of J. Edgar Hoover inscribed "For James D. Zirin With best wishes," and the date. He had sent it to me after I had successfully prosecuted a multimillion-dollar bank fraud case.

---

3. Reporters of the event tend to gloss over those who died at the Pentagon and the innocent passengers aboard the four planes. One of the murdered passengers was my client, the marvelous photographer Berry Berenson. Not one of whom is ever to be forgotten.

4. I was able to get a duplicate original of the certificate from the U.S. Department of Justice, and I persuaded former Attorney General Ramsey Clark to re-sign it for me.

There was also a photograph of lawyers on the steps of the Foley Square Courthouse taken in 1947 by the great French photographer, Henri Cartier-Bresson, as part of his New York series. The photograph is on the cover of this book.

Also on the wall was a treasured photograph of Margaret Thatcher and me in evening clothes. After I took the deposition of the "Iron Lady" in the *DeLorean* litigation in the Southern District, we had remained in touch, and when she came to New York to make a speech, she called and asked if I would meet her for a photograph that we both might like to have. She had an unbelievable vocabulary and spoke in a distinctive cadence that gave her words a magical elegance. She also had a remarkable memory for people and events. She started her professional life as a lawyer.[5]

There was also a piece of notepaper torn from a pad with a line of poetry signed by Robert Frost, whom I met in Princeton in 1957. After the iconic poet spoke to a group of undergraduates, I asked for his autograph. He said that if I would write out one of his verses, he would sign it. I wrote on a piece of undergraduate notepaper, "'Good fences make good neighbors.'" He inserted the single quotation marks as they appeared in the poem and signed his name. I have thought of this line many times since 9/11, as we see the delicate fault lines in the Middle East setting off tremors that intermittently unleash metastatic attacks on Western civilization, such as the one in Benghazi on September 11, 2012, or the one in Boston on Patriots Day 2013.

I went to funerals of people I knew who had perished in the tragedy. I also went to funerals of children of people I knew until I

---

5. Five months after 9/11 I met with her in London, and we took another photograph that hangs in my office today. After the photo op, the "Iron Lady" and I sat down to tea for several hours and did a *tour d'horizon* of the international situation from Islamic terrorism to George W. Bush's "axis of evil." It was an honor to be with her.

couldn't take it any more. I went to the Council on Foreign Relations to hear retired generals and national security experts talk of the military options, and what was to be made of the fact that of the 19 hijackers, 15 were Saudis.

The 9/11 Commission offered an explanation of the horrific events that only unsettled us further:

> We learned about an enemy who is sophisticated, patient, disciplined, and lethal. The enemy rallies broad support in the Arab and Muslim world by demanding redress of political grievances, but its hostility toward our values and us is limitless. Its purpose is to rid the world of religious and political pluralism, the plebiscite and equal rights for women.

Life goes on. The pain eased, but I don't think it will ever disappear. We wondered how such a tragedy could possibly have occurred on American soil. The government to which we had entrusted our safety had failed us. As the 9/11 Commission explained it,

> We learned that the institutions charged with protecting our borders, civil aviation, and national security did not understand how grave this threat could be, and did not adjust their policies, plans and practices to deter or defeat it. We learned of fault lines within our government—between foreign and domestic intelligence and between and within agencies. We learned of the pervasive problems of managing and sharing information across a large and unwieldy government that had been built in a different era to confront different dangers.

The 9/11 Commission proposed reforms that they said would make us safer. More agencies, fewer silos, more initials, more acronyms. We emerged safer and stronger as a people.

This was a crime of horrific proportions. Some spoke of it as a criminal act or an act of war, but I believe it to have been a crime against humanity, and a crime against the United States. Churchill said, "[T]he mood and temper of the public with regard to the treatment of crime and criminals is one of the most 'unfailing' tests of the civilization of any country." We are about to face that unfailing test with regard to the prosecution of the 9/11 defendants in Guantanamo.

The attacks on September 11 were vicious, cowardly senseless criminal acts. Being, as the reader may gather, a card-carrying "Mother Court-ist," I believe that the case should have been prosecuted in the Southern District of New York, since New York is the "State where the . . . Crimes . . . [were] committed."[6] Instead, the 9/11 defendants are moving for discovery and making pretrial motions before a military commission in Guantanamo that will eventually try them for their crimes some years down the road. Had the case been promptly brought in the federal court, it would have long since been concluded.

The major players in the plot should have been prosecuted in the Southern District, less than a quarter mile from Ground Zero. Probably, some would have pleaded guilty as so many terrorists have, and their allocutions in which they admitted their guilt would be taken before a judge in open court. It is interesting that al Qaeda operative Anas al Libi, wanted in connection with the 1998 U.S. embassy twin bombings in Kenya and Tanzania, will await trial in the Mother Court. U.S. Special Ops forces seized al Libi in Tripoli, Libya on October 5, 2013. Federal authorities then transported him to a place of detention in Manhattan.

---

6. U.S. CONST. art. III, § 2.

If there were a trial in the 9/11 case, I would not worry about impaneling a fair and impartial jury in the Southern District. 9/11 was a New York–centric crime, but after so many years it would be possible to find jurors from such a large jury pool who would be fair and unbiased. Of course, they would have to be questioned closely for bias by the trial judge.

After the late Osama bin Laden and his successor, Dr. Ayman Mohammed Rabie al-Zawahiri, the most culpable in the attack was one of bin Laden's principal lieutenants, Khalid Sheikh Mohammed (KSM), whom the 9/11 Commission, headed by the excellent former New Jersey Governor Thomas W. Kean, found to be the "principal architect of the 9/11 attacks."

Prior to 9/11 KSM primarily operated as a freelance terrorist. He was the uncle of Ramzi Yousef, lead bomber in the 1993 bombing of the World Trade Center, and played a cameo role in that attack. Our intelligence community just dropped the ball. No one had linked KSM with bin Laden or al Qaeda. A CIA report dated June 12, 2001, said that KSM was actively recruiting people to travel outside nests in Afghanistan to carry out terrorist activities for Osama bin Laden in various places, including the United States. Officials were alerted throughout the world. CIA Director George Tenet said that "the system was blinking red" in the summer of 2001. Yet no one connected the macro threat, known to the CIA, to the presence of known terrorists in the United States, which had been reported on by the FBI. The two silos just weren't talking to each other.

KSM was largely educated in the United States. Following his graduation from secondary school, he left Kuwait to enroll at Chowan College, a Baptist school in North Carolina. Subsequently, he transferred to North Carolina Agricultural and Technical State University in Greensboro, where he earned a degree in mechanical engineering in 1986.

KSM's animus against the United States came not from his experiences in North Carolina, but from his virulent disagreement with U.S. foreign policy in the Middle East. His plot was as clever as it was diabolical. For two years he was a fugitive from justice. The CIA seized KSM in Pakistan in 2003. Waterboarded, he gave his confession. The CIA removed him to Guantanamo, where he has been ever since. Following his arrest, during hearings at Guantanamo, he again confessed his responsibility for the attacks, stating he "was responsible for the 9/11 operation, from A to Z." KSM was a particularly brutal and vicious killer. No waterboarding that time.

KSM confessed to a multitude of terrorist plots and attacks over the past 20 years, including a cameo role in the World Trade Center 1993 bombings, the Operation Bojinka plot, an aborted 2002 attack on the U.S. Bank Tower in Los Angeles, the Bali nightclub bombings, the failed Richard Reid shoe bombing of American Airlines Flight 63, the Millennium Plot, and the decapitation of *Wall Street Journal* reporter Daniel Pearl. He confessed to cutting off Pearl's head personally. He is a monster. His was a trial made for the Mother Court.

Human rights organizations and a number of retired generals urged President Obama to order a trial for KSM and the other terrorists in the Southern District rather than before a military commission with newly minted rules and fewer procedural guarantees. They pointed out that 195 international terrorists have been convicted in federal courts since 2001. Obama appeared to agree, and then changed his mind.

There are great advantages to a civilian trial from the perspective of our institutions. Article III judges are independent of the executive branch of government. They are there for life. Military judges are not immune from command influence, as they report ultimately to the president. There will be the inevitable perception (if not the reality) that they will be answerable to their commands if something goes wrong with the trial, the jury fails to convict, or the sentence is deemed too lenient. In the Southern District, the trial would be public for the entire world to see; the defendants' rights would be elaborately protected; the procedures would be stern and familiar, burnished by over two centuries of jurisprudence; and justice would be done.

George W. Bush described the Military Commissions Act as "one of the most important pieces of legislation in the war on terror."[7] "Important" as it may be, military commissions just don't provide the procedural safeguards afforded to criminal defendants in civilian courts. It is hard to see with all its cost what trial by a military commission accomplishes—except a host of delightful legal questions about the tribunal's constitutionality, which are likely to linger for generations.

Is the cost of the commission really worth it? Are there any benefits at all in a military trial that would not be offered by trial in a civilian court? I can't think of any. We have spent millions paying military lawyers to warm over the rules of the military tribunal, sprinkling into the mix a right here and a right there—familiar rights available for centuries in the civilian courts. Our purpose is to make the trial "fair," but have we succeeded?[8]

Trial by military tribunal will be inevitably suspect in the eyes of the world, because the defendants' procedural rights are not the same. Unlike a trial in a federal court, hearsay evidence before a military tribunal is admissible. This vitiates the constitutional right of an accused to be confronted with the witnesses against him.[9] In a military tribunal, coerced statements of witnesses (but not defendants or suspects) are admissible. When coupled with the open floodgates of hearsay, the military trial smacks of the Kafka-esque, as a coerced "battlefield statement" could be legally read to the jury

---

7. Remarks on Signing the Military Commissions Act of 2006, 42 Wkly. Compo Pres. Doc. 1831 (Oct. 23, 2006).

8. Most notably, this would include the right to a public trial. The commission proceeding has achieved greater transparency by commendably allowing the public access to a televised proceeding piped to an army base at Fort Meade, Maryland.

9. The Sixth Amendment provides that "in all criminal prosecutions, the accused shall enjoy the right . . . to be confronted with the witnesses against him."

without the appearance of the witness for cross-examination.[10] The Guantanamo trial will be to a jury of 12 military officers, none of whom are lawyers,[11] so where is the cross-section of the community that is at the heart of our jury system?

Throughout the Muslim world, and perhaps elsewhere, the commission proceeding will be called a sham because the outcome is "heads I win, tails you lose." If a defendant were acquitted, he would not be set free, as is usually the case in an Article III court. Instead, he would be subject to further indefinite detention as an "enemy combatant." For the government to conduct a fair trial, it must be prepared to free defendants who are acquitted. Otherwise, we have a travesty. That has always been our justice system.

President Obama, himself a trained lawyer, reversed himself on a civilian trial for KSM and his cohorts for reasons that are largely unclear. Some suggested the presidential decision involved local security issues, or else politics. Mayor Michael Bloomberg, however, was willing to have the trial in New York City, though he initially did express concerns about the economic impact on the city, which he later agreed could be obviated. Police Commissioner Ray Kelly was confident that the NYPD could provide the necessary security in Foley Square. Moving the trial venue to secure locations in the Southern District such as Governor's Island or Stewart Air National Guard base in Newburgh, New York, was another alternative. So, why not a trial before a civilian court?

As Jane Mayer posted for the *New Yorker*, "A guilty verdict arrived at in front of the world, in a public trial, with ordinary citizens

---

10. A coerced "battlefield statement" might be where a jihadist, after being waterboarded, told the CIA that "Mohamad Jones" was a member of the conspiracy. That statement would be admissible against Mohamad Jones. It is unclear that the jury would hear such a statement to the effect that Mohamad was *innocent* of any involvement. The prosecutor would surely object to it as hearsay. Both declarations would be inadmissible in a federal court as unreliable hearsay.

11. Under the commission rules, military lawyers are excluded from jury service.

sitting in judgment of KSM, would be internationally accepted as legitimate, in a way that no military tribunal ever will be."

Americans have always believed that a "delicate balance" must be struck between order and liberty. As Justice Jackson put it,

> The choice is not between order and liberty. It is between liberty with order and anarchy without either. There is danger that, if the court does not temper its doctrinaire logic with a little practical wisdom, it will convert the constitutional Bill of Rights into a suicide pact.[12]

But does "practical wisdom" prevent a fair trial in the best civilian trial court in the world? Unless we are prepared to abandon our fundamental values altogether, the rule of law must retain its vitality in war and in peace, even when terrorists topple our buildings into rubble and senselessly murder our citizens in the American homeland.

Terrorism comes in waves, and it is no comfort that since 9/11, Islamic terrorists have killed a handful of Americans on our soil, almost all of them members of the military.[13] This may be, as General Wesley Clark has said, because the "A-Team" went down with the planes they had commandeered on 9/11. Other members of the "A-Team" may have died in drone attacks. But whether it is Benghazi, where al Qaeda murdered our Ambassador Chris Allen and three others, or the Boston Marathon, with three dead and

---

12. Terminiello v. Chicago, 337 U.S. 1 (1949) (Jackson, J., dissenting). The case involved the prosecution of an anti-Semitic priest for inciting to riot under the Illinois breach of the peace statute.

13. A terrorist imam, Anwar al-Awlaki, radicalized a military doctor, Nidal Malik Hasan, at Fort Hood, Texas. In November 2009, the doctor went on a shooting spree at the base before he was himself shot in the chest. At his court-martial in August 2013, Hasan admitted to and was convicted of 13 counts of premeditated murder and 32 counts of attempted murder. He is currently incarcerated at Fort Leavenworth, Kansas, awaiting execution. Al-Awlaki died in a drone attack in Yemen in 2011.

hundreds more brutally maimed or injured, the lesson is that we must never let down our guard.

The dead on 9/11 will find a measure of justice only with the conviction of KSM and his cohorts after a fair trial, and that conviction must stick. Sadly, this will not occur in the Mother Court for the entire world to see. This is where the atrocity occurred. This is where the wrong to the American people should be vindicated.

# 14

# SOME OF MY FAVORITE JUDGES

*Enter the Lord Chancellor followed by his trainbearer.*
*Lord Chancellor:*
*"The Law is the true embodiment*
*Of everything that's excellent.*
*It has no kind of fault or flaw.*
*And I, my lords, embody the Law."*
**—W.S. Gilbert,** *Iolanthe*

Judges "are the keepers of our sacred right to justice," declared Judge Walter Mansfield. Judges are the most important figures in the dramatis personae of the trial—even a trial by jury. They have been called the 13th juror, and the jury's "alter ego." This is particularly true in the federal court, where the trial judge may comment on the evidence. The judge stands between an innocent defendant and an unjust conviction, or between a wronged society and an unjust acquittal.

It is important to give life and personality to judges. Judges, for whom everyone rises when they enter and leave the courtroom, appear to assume a superhuman quality, sitting on an elevated bench, garbed in judicial robes, making rulings here and decrees there, and exercising all the whims and caprices of an enlightened despot. The reality is that judges are people like everyone else, and their character may be inferred from what they say and do—just like everyone else.

The Southern District judges I regularly appeared before were of diversified backgrounds and varying ethnicities. Some of them I greatly admired; others not so much. Here are those I appeared before who are particularly outstanding in my memory.

## SOME OF THE BEST

The great Southern District judges I knew in the 1960s were, in my perspective, iconic figures, who projected the very spirit of justice. There were "giants on the earth" in those days. You may not have known them, but I want you to.

### EDWARD WEINFELD[1]

I was lucky indeed to have my first trial, and many trials after that, before Edward Weinfeld. Judge Weinfeld had a slight figure, penetrating eyes, and a national reputation for rigorous fairness. His gaunt, Lincolnesque face of ascetic expression was mounted above the signature bow tie on his neck. At times I thought his penetrating gaze peered into the souls of all he encountered—even into the beyond. He was every inch a judge.

---

1. Judge Weinfeld served on the Mother Court from 1950 until his death in 1988.

Weinfeld was known as the "Dean of American Trial Judges." Justice William Brennan of the Supreme Court found a fitting tribute hard to compose. "It would be easier to salute him," Justice Brennan said, "if he'd been more noisy, if he had laid claim to some innovative legal philosophy or sought attention through 'great' opinions or a monopoly of 'important' cases." Instead, Judge Weinfeld's career was distinguished by "the purity of its devotion and its quiet dedication to the business of judging." No one would challenge Justice Brennan's conclusion "that there is no better judge on any court."

He was an unusual man, much like the unusual men who founded our country and made it great. He was someone of extraordinary quality, and it showed in everything he did. Men are often bounded by their ambition. It was not enough for Weinfeld to be a good judge or even an excellent judge. He wanted to be a great judge, and his ambition was not for recognition, but in the professional satisfaction that comes only with true accomplishment.

He hated it when administrators began amassing statistics of cases disposed of as a measure of more efficient management. He rejected the notion that it is better to dispose of the case than to dispose of it correctly. "Litigants," Weinfeld often said, "are not ciphers—they are people."

He was at his desk every morning at 6 o'clock, at times even earlier. He would walk to the courthouse from his home on the Lower East Side of Manhattan and often awaken the sleeping security guard to admit him. Once, according to a *New York Times* report, a deranged porter from a neighboring Lower East Side building attacked him. His face and eyes bruised, he went on to the office anyway. The crazed assailant later cut his own throat while in custody. Weinfeld went to court to testify against him.

Weinfeld had a tremendous capacity for work. Normally, he worked a 12-hour day. Priest-like in his devotion to duty, he worked six days a week, sometimes seven, and most holidays. Freud said, "Love and work are the cornerstones of our humanness." Weinfeld either got only the memo about the work part or found the two to be synonymous. He inscribed a photograph of himself, which he gave to one of his law clerks, "To Frank, who shared with me the joy of work."

He was rarely, if ever, reversed on appeal when he sat nonjury. This was because he made meticulously well-grounded findings of fact on which the disposition turned. As every trial lawyer knows, an appellate court must accept the fact-findings of the trial judge when he sits nonjury unless they are "clearly erroneous." His scholarly opinions were superbly crafted and always quite substantive. He said once that he wrote his opinions with his "life's blood." Most of them are good law today.

Among Weinfeld's law clerks were some extraordinarily successful lawyers: Marty Lipton, who founded the Wachtell Lipton Firm; Barry Garfinkel, one of the first partners at Skadden Arps; Frank Tuerkheimer, an accomplished lawyer and law professor; and John Koetl, who himself became a distinguished judge of the Mother Court.

For exercise, Weinfeld would walk daily across the Brooklyn Bridge, sometimes alone, or with other judges, or with his clerks. He also played handball at a nearby indoor court, often with defense attorneys who, like himself, had come up the hard way from the Lower East Side.

He was a New Yorker of the old school. Before ascending the bench, he served for four years as New York's first state commissioner of housing under Governor Herbert Lehman. The salary was $12,000 a year. There, he administered a pioneering program under which $300 million in loans and $5 million annually were distributed to communities throughout the state so as to make housing available to low-income families.

Lehman as Senator, whom Weinfeld eulogized as a "man of matchless courage and rare integrity," recommended him to President Truman for appointment to the bench of the Mother Court. The *New York Times* applauded the appointment, describing Weinfeld as "a man of fairness and high personal integrity . . . [who] will, we are confident, be a respected judge." In his almost 40 years on the bench, Weinfeld did not disappoint.

He demanded that the lawyers who came before him be thoroughly prepared. Almost always, they were. There was the story told in the U.S. Attorney's Office of the defense lawyer who beseeched Weinfeld for leniency toward his client on sentencing. He grounded his plea on the fact that the defendant was an orphan.

Deadpan, Weinfeld observed, "Yes, I see from the presentencing report that he murdered both of his parents."

When on trial, Weinfeld stretched court hours, taking the bench at 9:30 in the morning instead of the customary 10 o'clock, much to the irritation of court personnel and U.S. marshals. Woe betide the lawyer or the juror who was even a minute late. Weinfeld never waited in the robing room until all were present, as many judges do. He took the bench stony faced and reviewed his trial notes. When the tardy miscreant burst into the courtroom breathless, Weinfeld would say sharply, "Court begins at 9:30. Let's proceed."

Weinfeld believed that decorum in the courtroom was important—as well it should be. During the administration of the oath, everyone at the counsel table was expected to remain seated and pay close attention. No one was allowed so much as to lift a pencil, let alone talk. If I called a witness, I learned to wait until Weinfeld had written something in his trial notebook, and I caught his eye before I proceeded. He would nod to me, feigning impatience, but always appreciative that I recognized that he was the master of the courtroom.

I tried my first criminal case in the courthouse before Weinfeld and a jury, and it was a baptism in fire. The case was against a small-time fraudster named Abie Sutton, who falsified his application for an FHA loan. The false statement was the omission to disclose a prior FHA loan, which was information requested on the form. The evidence was that when the FBI asked Abie why he had done this, he said that he knew "if you had one FHA loan you couldn't get another." He was right.

I called to the stand the FBI agent who had interviewed Sutton, and he testified that he had shown Sutton the FHA application, and that Sutton had admitted he signed it. I thought that it was enough with the admission to establish a prima facie case, so I rested. I hadn't learned yet that the law is rigorously agnostic when it comes to proving a prima facie case.

"No, you will not rest," said Weinfeld outside the presence of the jury. "You have not proved that he signed the loan application. I will throw this thing out."

"But your Honor," I argued, "the FBI agent said he showed the defendant the application, and he admitted it was his." "No," said Weinfeld, "he didn't say he showed him the *original* application. This case requires a handwriting expert. Is this your first trial?"

I was soaking wet with perspiration. "Yes, your Honor."

Said Weinfeld, "In the exercise of discretion, I will allow the government to reopen its case. And [turning to defense counsel] you will not tell me I am unfairly siding with the government. The government lost $15,000 in this case. Court is adjourned until tomorrow morning at 9:30."

I called handwriting expert Luciano Caputo, whom we had hastily recruited from the Bureau of Alcohol, Tobacco, and Firearms. After carefully studying the matter overnight, Caputo testified that the signature on the original application matched the signature on the fingerprint card that Sutton signed when he was arrested. Fortunately, there was no cross-examination as to how much time the witness had spent studying the matter. The issue disappeared when Sutton took the stand in his own defense and admitted that he had signed the application. The jury did not believe Sutton that it was all a big mistake, and I had won my first case before Judge Weinfeld.

When Sutton announced he would appeal his conviction, I opposed bail on the ground that the appeal was frivolous.

Weinfeld said, "The Court admires the sincerity with which you speak, Mr. Zirin. You want to see the judgment of the court vindicated."

Before I could say, "Yes, your Honor," Weinfeld had admitted Sutton to bail pending appeal. He didn't go to jail until several months later, when the conviction was affirmed on appeal.

Weinfeld had a reverence for the trial process. Speaking at Fordham Law School in 1984, he expounded the philosophy of the trial judge:

> The trial judge sees the actual litigants and their witnesses and decides the facts. In jury cases, he shares responsibility with citizens who are called upon to play a role in the administration of justice. Important and unimportant cases do not exist; each case is important, and each is demanding. Indeed, this is the first lesson that I learned in practice, and it is the first lesson that I impart to my law clerks: each case is important, whether or not it will make new law, because the outcome can bring either triumph or disaster to the litigants and their families.

The trial judge knows that his final judgment may have a profound impact on individuals who have appeared before him. It will affect their well being for better or for worse, their property, their reputation and, at times, their very liberty. Indeed, the daily grist of cases runs the gamut of every conceivable problem of law and society.

Then there is the final analysis, sometimes of agonizing concern, particularly where liberty or life is at stake. The judge confidently hopes that he has reached the right, fair and just result within the law. That final and ultimate ruling is his alone. It is not a shared effort with a peer. The trial judge treads a lonely path; ofttimes it is a soul-searching vigil. Thus, service at the trial level is markedly different from that performed by the appellate judge. It is challenging and demanding, yet it is also a rewarding and fulfilling experience. I truly believe that there is no more satisfying service in the entire judicial system than that experienced by the trial judge.

Weinfeld's signal cases included the *Keogh* obstruction of justice trial discussed earlier; the ruling that Senator McCarthy's subcommittee lacked the authority to investigate socialist author Corliss Lamont; the proposed horizontal merger between Bethlehem Steel and Youngstown Sheet & Tube, which he blocked; and the Quentin Reynolds-Westbrook Pegler defamation trial, in which he wrote the seminal opinion on punitive damages in a libel case.

Writing of his service, Weinfeld said, "When, at a fairly early hour in the morning, I put the key into the door of my darkened chambers and walk across the room to start the day's activities, I do so with the same enthusiasm that was mine the very first day of my judicial career. What one enjoys is not work. It is joy."

Many lawyers wanted to see Weinfeld on the U.S. Supreme Court. His judicial home, however, was meant to be the Mother Court, which he called "the greatest court in the country, bar none."

But for all his gravitas, Weinfeld never forgot his humble beginnings on the Lower East Side of Manhattan. He always kept up with old cronies from his early days, joining them for a game of handball or a casual "schmooze."

One of the old cronies was a criminal defense lawyer called Moses Kove. He was named for the guy the princess found floating in the bulrushes. Mo was a bantamweight, about five foot four, who dressed the part to the nines. He wore a cat's eye ring on his pinky finger, pinstriped suits, a boutonniere in his wide lapel, elevated patent leather loafers, and a pencil-thin mustache that made him look like a floorwalker at Macy's. He reminded me of the character "Nicely Nicely" Johnson in *Guys and Dolls*.

While many defense lawyers treated the prosecutors at arm's length, Mo was their friend. He cozied up to the Assistants and had morning coffee with them in the courthouse cafeteria. It was impossible to dislike Mo Kove, particularly since all he wanted was an adjournment so he could collect his fee. Undoubtedly, he also bragged to his clients about his relationship with the U.S. Attorney's Office that won him no favors but gave him an undeserved reputation in the underworld that he could perhaps fix a case. That reputation helped keep him in patent leathers.

Mo was always good for a laugh over coffee. When we indicted New York City Water Commissioner James Marcus for bribery, the trial was before Weinfeld. Though he was not serving as counsel in the case, Mo went to the courtroom as a spectator, keenly observing when Herbert Itkin, the government's informant and star witness, took the stand. Itkin testified he received hundreds of thousands of dollars in unaccounted-for fresh cash (he called it "green") to bribe public officials, and then turned the wrappers over to the FBI to be used as evidence. Mo told how Weinfeld had called him up to the bench in a recess to ask why he was there. As Mo told it, he said to the judge, "I just wanted to be sure I never met the son of a bitch." He reported that Weinfeld roared with laughter. Mo and Weinfeld went back a long way.

Weinfeld, like Judge Learned Hand, was the paragon of judges. Weinfeld, like Hand, left a profound impression on all who appeared before him. As one seasoned trial lawyer put it, "When you're in his court, you know you're before the bar of justice."

## THOMAS MURPHY[2]

Thomas Murphy was a giant of a man, with a deep booming voice. He always had a special way about him. In winter, he wore a black bowler hat that reminded of a Magritte painting; in summer, a turn of the last century style straw boater identified with barbershop quartets. Standing well over six foot five, he had a formidable walrus mustache and mountainous shoulders bulging from the black pup tent that was his judicial robe. The shoulders must have been a family trait; his brother, Johnny "Fireman" Murphy, was a right-handed relief pitcher who had 93 wins in his 12 years on the New York Yankees. When Judge Murphy learned that I had studied French literature in college, he told me that he had a fondness for the French novel, and had read all seven volumes of Proust's *Remembrance of Things Past* in the original French.

No one on the federal bench had a sharper or quicker wit than Judge Murphy. He had a droll, sardonic sense of humor in and out of the courtroom. One of a judge's many duties is to expedite the proceeding. When counsel dragged his feet on putting a question to a witness, most judges would say icily, "Proceed, Mr. So-and-so!" Murphy peppered his judicial obligations with characteristically laconic humor that always put him a step ahead of the brightest lawyer. He took no prisoners. If a lawyer hesitated over his notes,

---

2. Judge Murphy served on the Mother Court from 1951 until his death in 1995.

there was no "proceed, counsel." Instead, Murphy would deliver the crusher, "Can we pick up the anchor . . . and go?"

Having been a star prosecutor in his day, Murphy had a decidedly progovernment bent in criminal cases, although he was the fairest of judges. He had a quick and sharp wit. Often, he was hilarious. Among his gems:

He arraigned a Black Muslim defendant on a narcotics charge, and the colloquy was as follows:

**MURPHY:** Do you have a lawyer?

**THE DEFENDANT:** Your Honor, Allah is my counsel.

**MURPHY:** Who represents you locally?

At a conspiracy trial I conducted where the witness for the prosecution was a colorful hijacker named Jo-Jo Betancourt, and the defendants were the fences:

**BY MR. ZIRIN:** Did there come a time when you saw a man named Irving Adler (an unindicted co-conspirator)?

**A:** That I did, sir.[3]

**Q:** Did you have a conversation with him?

**A:** That I did, sir.

**Q:** What did you say to him and what did he say to you?

**DEFENSE COUNSEL:** Objection, your Honor.

**MURPHY:** On the ground that?

**DEFENSE COUNSEL** (turning to the jury in feigned triumph): Upon information and belief, Mr. Adler is dead.

**MURPHY** (addressing the witness): Was he alive when you talked to him?

**A:** That, he was, sir.

**MURPHY:** I'll allow it.

---

3. Betancourt's style was not to answer questions yes or no.

Murphy hated sidebar conferences where, with the jury in the box, the lawyers crowd around just below the bench and whisper to the judge about housekeeping or evidentiary matters. He required counsel to state their objections and arguments in open court. When a lawyer asked for a sidebar because what he had to say in front of the jury might be prejudicial, Murphy replied, "Then you say it at your peril."

When a lawyer requested such a commonplace conference, the colloquy before Murphy would often go something like this:

DEFENSE COUNSEL: May I approach the bench, your Honor?

MURPHY: No.

COUNSEL: I need to discuss an important matter with your Honor outside the presence of the jury.

MURPHY: I am the boss here. Say it in open court.

COUNSEL: I have talked with all of my colleagues at the defense bar, and we all agree that the matter we propose to discuss must not be within the hearing of the jury.

MURPHY (sighing): I guess that makes it Holy Writ. I'll permit it.

At a high-profile mail fraud case I prosecuted where the defendant was a relative of the Queens Borough president, a tenacious defense lawyer named Maurice Edelbaum pounced on a government witness called Crake. Crake admitted that he had recorded certain telephone conversations that were not part of the case, and that he had turned the tapes over to the government.

MR. EDELBAUM: Your Honor, I demand the production of the Crake tapes.

MURPHY: On the ground that?

MR. EDELBAUM: Under the rule of *Brady v. Maryland* [a landmark case in the Supreme Court (which Murphy knew well) where the prosecutor suppressed the fact that someone other than the defendant had confessed to the crime].

MURPHY (sarcastically): What is the rule of *Brady v. Maryland*? [Of course, he knew.]

MR. EDELBAUM (turning dramatically to the jury): It stands for the proposition, your Honor, that the government must turn over anything that is exculpatory to the defense.

MURPHY (addressing the prosecutor): Is it exculpatory?

THE PROSECUTOR: No, your Honor.

MURPHY: Denied.

MR. EDELBAUM: I demand the production of the Crake tapes under Rule 16 of the Federal Rules of Criminal Procedure.

MURPHY: Which says what? [Murphy knew goddamn well what it said.]

MR. EDELBAUM: It says that the court must turn over documents to the defense.

MURPHY: It says the court *may*. Denied.

MR. EDELBAUM: I have one further reason why your Honor should order the production of the Crake tapes.

MURPHY: I hope you saved the best for last.

MR. EDELBAUM (again turning dramatically to the jury affecting an attitude of helplessness): I implore your Honor to direct the prosecutor to turn over the Crake tapes in the interests of justice.

MURPHY: And suppose I order him to turn over the tapes in the interests of justice, and he tells me to go to hell. What do I do then?

MR. EDELBAUM (looking at the jury in pain as though stung by a hornet): Thank you, your Honor.

MURPHY: Don't thank me. I get paid at the end of the month.

When a lawyer applied for a "brief" adjournment to study a bundle of documents just produced to him by the government, Murphy's response was as terse as it was vintage Murphy: "Application granted—adjournment over."

Murphy was a tough sentencer. In the days before the federal sentencing guidelines and mandatory minimum sentences in most cases, the court had broad discretion to fashion an appropriate punishment. He might sentence the defendant to a term of years, impose probation, or suspend sentence altogether. At each sentencing, the defendant had the right to address the court directly and ask for leniency. This was called the allocution. Murphy disliked allocutions, but he was required by law to entertain them. One sentencing before Murphy I recall involved a white-collar criminal defendant who, like his wife, was a cultural anthropologist. In his allocution he told Murphy that he and his wife had discussed the matter and that both agreed there was no useful purpose to be served by a term of imprisonment. So the following colloquy occurred:

> THE DEFENDANT: Is there anything I can do to avoid your Honor's sentencing me to jail?
> MURPHY: RUN!

In a March 1961 trial before Murphy, a Southern District jury convicted troubadour Pete Seeger of contempt of Congress for refusing to answer questions put to him by the House Un-American Activities Committee.[4] On the sentencing, Judge Murphy inquired of Seeger whether he wanted to say anything. Seeger, who had brought his guitar to the courtroom, concluded his allocution as follows:

> THE DEFENDANT: The House committee wished to pillory me because it didn't like some few of the many thousands of places I have sung for. Now it so happens that the specific song whose title was mentioned in this trial "Wasn't That a Time" is one

---

4. The Second Circuit later reversed Seeger's conviction on technical grounds.

of my favorites. The song is apropos to this case. I wonder if I might have your permission to sing it here before I close?

MURPHY: You may not. One year.

THE DEFENDANT: Well, perhaps you will hear it some other time. A good song can only do good, and I am proud of the songs I have sung. I hope to be able to continue singing these songs for all who want to listen, Republicans, Democrats, and independents. Do I have the right to sing these songs? Do I have the right to sing them anywhere?

Without answering, Murphy strode off the bench.

Murphy was someone with a steel-trap mind who understood that the truth, particularly in a criminal case, is "attended by a bodyguard of lies."[5] In this regard, he took no prisoners. First-rate lawyer Dan Murdock told me about the interstate transportation of stolen property case involving three valuable paintings, one of which was a Degas. The defense was that the defendant lived with the victim in a deteriorating homosexual relationship, so he took the paintings off the wall of their shared apartment and shipped them down to his uncle's farm in Texas in the hopes of attracting the victim's attention and winning him back. When the defendant made the dubious pitch that his were the irrational acts of a scorned lover, Murphy muttered sotto voce to his bailiff, an ex-NYPD detective, "He's a fucking liar."

Steve Kaufman, who was the chief of the Criminal Division when I served in the office, told me another Murphy story about a criminal antitrust trial where former Mother Court Judge Simon Rifkind represented the defendant. Murphy and Rifkind never got along. Rifkind was fond of the old trial lawyer's trick in cross-examining

---

5. Paraphrasing Churchill: "In wartime, truth is so precious that she should always be attended by a bodyguard of lies."

a witness, of cupping his ear, pretending not to hear a favorable answer, and then asking the witness to repeat himself. The witness would then have to say it again, and the repetition, Rifkind hoped, would make a lasting impression on the jury. After this happened a few times, the witness became exasperated at having to repeat himself. So the next time Rifkind professed not to have heard the answer, the witness asked Judge Murphy, "Do I really have to say it again?" Murphy replied in his characteristically booming voice, "You don't have to repeat yourself. *Mr. Rifkind can hear the grass grow.*"

Murphy projected the persona of a strong judge. Appearing before him, I was often reminded of Ethel Barrymore's retort when someone asked what she would do in the theater if someone coughed during one of her great soliloquies. She said, "I never let them cough. They wouldn't dare!"

Never was Murphy's ability to keep order more tested than on a hot day in August 1967, when he presided in Courtroom 318 over the arraignment and bail hearing of the black activist H. Rap Brown. I was there.

Brown had been in the 1960s the chairman of the Student Non-violent Coordinating Committee and had served as "Minister of Justice" during SNCC's brief alliance with the Black Panther Party. He was notorious for his observation, apt to this very day of assault weapons and high-capacity magazines, "I say violence is as American as cherry pie." He also had made the incendiary statement, "If America don't come around, we're going to burn it down." I guess we came around.

In July 1967, a local civil rights group invited Brown to address a rally in Cambridge, Maryland, where he urged the crowd of about 400 to fight fire with fire. About four hours later, the Pine Street Elementary School in Cambridge burned to the ground. It had been torched twice before and was a shell at the time. Brown fled the state. He was charged in Maryland with inciting to arson and riot, and landed on the FBI's most wanted list.

On August 14, a federal grand jury in New Orleans indicted Rap Brown on a charge of carrying a .30 caliber rifle across state lines while under state court indictment. The grand jury charged that Brown fled New Orleans with the weapon and returned to New York with the weapon two days later, where he was arrested. The New Orleans federal court set bail at $25,000, and Brown sought a reduction.

Murphy was sitting in Courtroom 318 on August 22 when Brown's bail application came on to be heard. He frequently sat in August while other judges were on vacation, and ran a "summer calendar" in which he called old cases for trial back-to-back. Unruly Brown supporters filled the large courtroom. The situation was all the more terrifying because in those days there were no metal detectors at the entrance, and no one inspected anyone's ID.

Underscoring the importance of the case, both Bob Morgenthau and Steve Kaufman appeared for the government. Steve was as elegant and eloquent a lawyer as we had in the office.

Kaufman had a worthy adversary in radical lawyer Bill Kunstler, who represented Brown. After Brown entered the courtroom surrounded by a squadron of U.S. marshals, Kunstler's argument had little to do with the question of bail: "Your Honor, the black man in this country has had it up to here."

Almost immediately, there was an outburst from the audience, which began to chant, "Black power! Power to the people!" Murphy rose and walked off the bench. The message was clear: a federal judge presides over a court of justice, not an unruly mob.

When Murphy returned, the bail hearing continued. Kaufman quoted from one of Brown's speeches, which he contended showed Brown had no respect for the laws of the United States: "But black people fall for that same argument, and they go around talking about law breakers. We did not make the laws in this country. We are neither morally nor legally confined to those laws. Those laws that keep them up keep us down."

Immediately, there was another outburst of "Black power, power to the people."

Murphy addressed the crowd. He said, "Ladies and gentlemen, I can adjourn this, and the defendant will remain in prison until we reconvene."

Order restored, Kunstler's argument became more focused. He pointed out that lower bail had been set that day for defendants who had more substantial criminal records than Brown. Murphy took the matter under advisement, and remanded Brown to the Federal House of Detention. The hearing had consumed one hour. Brown was not in the courtroom when Murphy announced his decision to reduce bail by $10,000.[6] If ever there was a prouder day for the Mother Court, it was that August morning in 1967, when the rule of law triumphed over the passions of the mob.

Tom Murphy was a giant of a judge as he was a giant of a man. I loved him.

## WALTER MANSFIELD[7]

Walter Mansfield was a great judge to appear before. He had a keen legal mind, a gentle demeanor, a military bearing, and a cobra-like smile. He spoke in a low voice, reminding me of the Psalmist's: "His words were softer than oil, yet they were drawn swords."[8]

---

6. Brown was more dangerous than a mere rabble-rouser. He is currently serving a life sentence following the 2000 shooting of two Fulton County, Georgia, sheriff's deputies, both African American. One of the deputies died of his wounds.

7. Judge Mansfield served on the Mother Court from 1966 until 1971, when he was elevated to the Second Circuit. He thereafter served on the appellate court until his death in 1987.

8. Psalm 55:21.

Mansfield had a fascinating background. Son of the former Mayor of Boston, he was a war hero who served under the legendary OSS chief "Wild Bill" Donovan.[9] During World War II, Mansfield was secretly parachuted into Yugoslavia to assist the partisans fighting with Mihailovich against the Nazis. At a Federal Bar Council convention in Mazatlan, Mexico, in 1981, when he was 70, I saw him parasail wearing that signature smile pasted across his face, his arms expertly cradling the cords that attached him to his parachute.

In 1953, then Captain Mansfield recalled his wartime experiences:

> There is no nation which would, more than you Serbs, appreciate human freedoms and rights. Not only appreciate, but give everything for them. It happened on Kosovo, the Salonika Front and Ravna Gora. The first thing that I learned from your brothers in your mountains was "Freedom or Death." The great law and ideal for great men and times.
>
> . . . I have not many opportunities to meet many great men. One of them is my good and never forgotten Chicha [General Mihailovich]. He will live in my heart as long as I last. I observed him in all conditions, mostly difficult ones. Then one can see better. It made no difference whether the gunpowder was burning the eyes, or death was waiting, or injustice was hurting. He was always great and sincere in victory as well as in defeat. He loved his country, his people and the cause of freedom, sacrificing himself for the glory of living . . .
>
> Calm, courageous, and resourceful, during all operations from Ivanjica, Drina, Zlatibor, Valjevo and Sabac, he remained always legendary. I remember one night near Rudo, when a battle lasted three hours and the Germans were firing on us from all sides and from the air, Chicha went from one to another, from one part of the battlefield to another,

---

9. Mansfield joined Bill Donovan at the Donovan Leisure firm, where he became a litigation partner.

bringing fate and force into our weakened bodies. To him we have to be grateful for breaking out of the encirclement. Yes, I might add, and for our lives. If there was no General I would not be alive today . . .

During the very difficult winter of 1943, together, we were pushing to break out of the Valley of Death. Already the perspective was changing. . . . The naïve Allies, to accommodate Stalin, nurtured a snake in their bosoms.

On his account fables were converted into history. Other people's successes into his red feather. We were in Rogatica after Ostojic's troops won the victory at Visegrad. That same night the BBC gave our victory to Tito and announced that he was victorious. Partisans had entered Rogatica. We, the Yugoslav Army of the Homeland, were in Rogatica. At that time, around the town there was not a single German or a Tito Commie.

When we parted after a brotherly hug, Chicha was smiling but his eyes were sad. We knew what kind of days were to follow.

Few on or off the bench could tell of having such a ringside seat at the defeat of fascism and the advent of Soviet Communism. I met with Walter Mansfield shortly before I left the Office in 1970. He had some good things to say about a summation I had given in a case before him, and we reminisced for a while about some of the matters we had together. He told me that I didn't know it then, but I had learned valuable lessons that would stand me in good stead my entire professional life. He was spot-on about the lessons part.

I think he liked me. I certainly liked and respected him. We corresponded after I left the Office and exchanged some happy letters, which are lost somewhere with the contents of my office in the rubble of One World Trade Center.

Mansfield died of a stroke at age 75 in Christchurch, New Zealand, where he had been vacationing. The *New York Times* remembered him for participating in the selection of special counsel to investigate the Iran-Contra scandal, and for upholding the $1 billion bond required of Texaco to secure the $13 billion judgment against it obtained by Pennzoil.

There was so much more to him than that. He will be remembered as a true patriot and a loyal servant of justice.

### HAROLD R. TYLER, JR.[10]

It is hard to conceive of a more engaging man than Harold Tyler. At first blush, he appeared to be smiling, benign—almost oblivious. His smile had a characteristic benignity, projecting the indelible impression that he was especially pleased with himself. His mind was sharp as a tack.

Tyler hailed from upstate New York—Utica, to be precise. A commanding presence with a bald head atop his towering height of six feet four inches, he had a certain folksy, almost cornball, way about him. He had played basketball at Exeter, where he earned the nickname "Ace." The nickname followed him to Princeton and then to Columbia Law School.

Ace Tyler liked lawyers. He believed in a fraternity of lawyers. When I entered his courtroom he would say, "Ah, Mr. James David Zirin, welcome." No one ever had called me "Mr. James David Zirin." I confess to having been more than a little flattered, particularly since he greeted my mentor, the amazing trial lawyer Peter Fleming, as "Mr. Peter Emmet Fleming."

If a lawyer made some frivolous argument, Tyler would never become upset. He would say something like, "Don't hand me that

---

10. Judge Tyler served on the Mother Court from 1962 until he resigned in 1975 to become Deputy Attorney General of the United States.

malarkey." If someone asked for an adjournment, he would sigh, "Oh these boring adjournments. I am ready to rule."

When he sentenced Democratic kingpin and Tammany Hall boss Carmine DeSapio to two years' imprisonment on conspiracy and bribery charges, he said, "Mr. Carmine Gerard DeSapio, there is nothing personal about this. I know that if I met you under other circumstances, I would like you very much—even invite you to my home." I never heard anything quite like that before from a sentencing judge.

I hope he was not taking a leaf from Irving Kaufman's book in imposing sentence on a drug dealer I prosecuted. "Mr. Nelson Crespo, I went to church last night and got on my knees and asked my maker about you." There is no indication that his maker fashioned the sentence.

He loved the phrase "as follows." It permitted him to crystallize his thinking. "The judgment of the court is as follows" or "My ruling is as follows." I always waited with bated breath to see what came next.

Tyler loved the give and take of the trial court. He turned down a seat on the Second Circuit because that was not where the action was. President Kennedy appointed Ace Tyler to the bench of the Mother Court. A middle-of-the-road Republican, Tyler served as the head of Justice's Civil Rights Division in the Eisenhower administration. He resigned from the bench to become Deputy Attorney General under President Gerald Ford.

Tyler was a man of principle. In 1982, he resigned his membership in New York's exclusive University Club to protest the Club's decision not to admit women. When the Club reversed its stance in 1987, he refused to rejoin.

Tyler was chairman of the ABA judicial qualifications committee, which, in a split decision, gave its highest rating to Robert Bork, nominated by President Reagan for a Supreme Court seat in 1987. You will remember Bork as the federal judge who terrified women with a ruling that the American Cyanamid Company did not violate federal law when it required women to undergo sterilization in order to continue working in jobs that exposed them to chemicals likely to harm a developing fetus. Bork did not appear to understand that there are moral boundaries imposed on judges, even when they are thinking they follow the law. As Brandeis put it, "[L]aw is not a system of artificial reason, but a logical system of ethical ideals—with freedom at its core." Bork's view of the world seemed off the spectrum.

There were four dissenting votes on the 15-person ABA panel, which recommended confirmation. Tyler was one of them. The unusual split vote was seen as giving ammunition to Bork's detractors. Though he defended the committee's findings as unbiased and nonpartisan, Tyler wrote a letter to Senator Howard Metzenbaum, a Democratic member of the Senate Judiciary Committee, who was a point man for the anti-Bork faction in the Senate, stating that a favorable rating of any nominee should not be seen as a recommendation that the Senate should vote for confirmation, "since the committee expressly disclaims any opinion upon issues which we assume that the Senate can and does consider." Tyler also released a statement to the Senate Judiciary Committee explaining the dissenters' position as skepticism about Bork's compassion, open-mindedness, and sensitivity to the rights of women and minorities. In an official written statement, Tyler told the committee at Bork's confirmation hearing that the four dissenters also expressed concerns about Bork's "comparatively extreme views" on applying the constitutional guarantee of equal protection of the laws. Bork failed Senate confirmation, and many conservatives blamed the divided ABA report as a decisive factor.

After he left the government, Tyler threw himself into the private practice of law. He was always eager, however, to accept some quasi-governmental assignment. Thus, he authored a report commissioned by the State Department on the 1980 killings of four American churchwomen in El Salvador, which put an end to criticism that the Reagan administration had been lax in not pressing harder for swift prosecution of the killers. In behalf of Major League Baseball, he investigated Yankee owner George Steinbrenner for paying a gambler named Howie Spira $40,000 to dig up "dirt" on star right fielder Dave Winfield. The investigation led to Steinbrenner being banned from day-to-day-management of the team. He also authored a report on the "Bess Mess," involving lurid allegations leading to the resignation of former Miss America Bess Myerson as New York City cultural affairs commissioner.

Ace loved to teach young lawyers by syllabus and by example. He was the quintessential mentor. He taught as an adjunct professor at New York University Law School from 1965 to 1974. I participated with him in many continuing education panels on advocacy. He loved teaching how to do it, and his comments and criticisms were delivered in a cheerful and generous manner reflective of the grand gent that he was.

Ace Tyler was an independent man with a strong libertarian streak, who never shrank from speaking his mind or his conscience. He personified the excellence and the fairness of a Southern District judge.

## EDMUND PALMIERI[11]

An Eisenhower appointee, Ed Palmieri was a former federal prosecutor. When he spoke, he always seemed to have an agonized

---

11. Judge Palmieri served on the Mother Court from 1954 until his death in 1989.

expression on his face, as though someone had just extracted a molar. An urbane man, he was fluent in Italian and French, and loved grand opera. My pal Jim Tripp tried a criminal case before Palmieri in which Tripp prosecuted Renata Tebaldi's Bayonne, New Jersey, tax adviser for preparing false tax returns for the diva.[12] Tebaldi, who critics said had the "voice of an angel," was the star witness for the prosecution. Still going strong at La Scala and the Met, she came to Foley Square in a black dress, which revealed her pronounced embonpoint. On her tax return was an item of deduction for "claque," money spent by many opera performers to plant stooges in the audience to start the applause or shout for an encore. Tebaldi testified indignantly that she never used claque. The defense lawyer was Louis Bender. Lou Bender was a tall, lanky, hatchet-faced man with a soft voice. His manner projected total sincerity. Lou had been an All-American basketball player at Columbia, and looked the part. When Lou rose to cross-examine, Palmieri called him to the sidebar.

"Please go easy on this woman, Mr. Bender," the judge said with a wry grimace. "I love her."

Of course! Tebaldi was the most beloved lyric soprano of all time. No cross-examination would have changed the facts. The judge believed her story that her applause was earned, not bought, and so did the jury, which returned a guilty verdict.

Palmieri usually found a way to rule for the government, so, as a prosecutor, I was always very happy with him.[13] Judge Palmieri's progovernment predilections appeared in a case involving the *Miranda* shibboleths, which required the government to advise a defendant in custody of his right to remain silent and his right to

---

12. Jim went on to a satisfying career as counsel to the Environmental Defense Fund.
13. Supreme Court Justice Ruth Bader Ginsburg served as a law clerk to Judge Palmieri. Not much is known of her one-year stint with the judge, but she referred to him with affection many times in 1960 when addressing groups of lawyers in New York.

counsel before interrogation could begin. My colleague Andrew Maloney, an able and zealous prosecutor with marvelous trial instincts, once advised a defendant of his Miranda rights during a prearraignment interview. When the defendant said he wanted a lawyer, Maloney was dismissive of the request, telling him, "You don't want to take a risk like that."[14] The defendant thereupon incriminated himself, but later wanted to suppress his statements. Judge Palmieri denied the motion, holding that the warnings were sufficient, and the defendant was "doubly warned": first, that he was entitled to a lawyer; and second, that things might go worse for him if he did not cooperate.

Palmieri presided over a number of high-profile cases. Two separate cases involved the prosecution of Florida millionaire Louis Wolfson. Wolfson first achieved prominence both as a corporate raider and as owner and breeder of the 1978 Triple Crown winner Affirmed. The first case was an indictment for selling unregistered stock of a company called Continental Enterprises; the second involved an investigation into Wolfson's shipbuilding company, Merritt-Chapman & Scott, where Wolfson was found guilty of perjury and obstruction of justice. Southern District juries convicted in both cases. Wolfson appealed, and also sought a presidential pardon. A *Life* magazine investigation into Wolfson's activities uncovered that Supreme Court Justice Abe Fortas, a close friend of Lyndon Johnson, was on the payroll of Wolfson's family foundation to the tune of $20,000 a year for life. So was Fortas' wife. This arose at a time when Fortas knew that Wolfson was under criminal investigation by the SEC and, in all likelihood, would have business before the Court. The government's witness, a close business associate

---

14. The "risk" was not so far-fetched. Lawyers frequently give bad advice to their clients. No wonder Carl Sandburg's verse resonates so strongly: "Why is there always a secret singing / When a lawyer cashes in? / Why does a hearse horse snicker / Hauling a lawyer away?"

of Wolfson, Alexander Ritmaster, reported that Fortas, while a Supreme Court justice, had flown to Wolfson's horse farm in Ocala, Florida, to advise Wolfson on strategy in his pending appeals.

The episode led to Fortas's withdrawing his nomination as chief justice of the United States. Subsequently, he resigned from the Supreme Court.

Defense lawyers loved to accuse the government's witnesses of lying, and the witness Ritmaster was no exception. Since the law is supposed to be a learned profession, such accusations sometimes bristled with literary or Biblical allusion. Frank Raichle, Wolfson's lawyer, who spoke in a tremulous voice, referred to Ritmaster in open court as "that perfidious Ritmaster, this latter day Ananias." Lawyers are our wordsmiths. Who was Ananias? This was well before Google, and Raichle sent me scurrying to the dictionary.[15]

A case I successfully prosecuted in the Southern District before Judge Palmieri was *United States v. Friedland*. My adversary was a hotheaded defense attorney of Sicilian extraction. Eloquence is never misplaced in a courtroom, but excessive anger on the part of counsel can be a problem. The defense lawyer had a bad habit of blasting off at me, at the witnesses, and even at the judge. At times he almost lost it, and eventually Palmieri became annoyed.

"You know," he said to the defense lawyer almost in a whisper, "you and I have a Mediterranean temperament."

"Of which I assume we both are proud," the lawyer almost shouted.

"Of course we are," said Palmieri in a sibilant whisper. "We have to learn in court to keep our emotions in check."

"I'll try, your Honor."

---

15. Ananias was a New Testament character struck dead for habitual lying. Another time, much later on, another lawyer had me running to the dictionary when he referred to me in a brief as "struthious." It means like an ostrich. He thought I had my head in the sand—or perhaps somewhere else.

"Try harder more quietly," said Palmieri.

The defendant in the case, Leon Friedland, was also known by the alias of "Lee Armand." Friedland was a corrupt accountant who helped a conniving businesswoman named Edith Kendall prepare fraudulent financial statements, covered by fake accountants' certificates, which she gave to banks in support of loan applications. Kendall's uxorious husband, Lawrence Banks, was another member of the conspiracy. The financial statements were so convincing that the conspirators mulcted millions of dollars from the banks, which they divided in varying proportions.

Kendall was quite charming. She spoke with a European accent that projected glamour and urbanity. She also had a generously endowed bosom, which she displayed *en décolletage* with great effect on the gullible bankers who relied on her business plan. Armand's day job was as an SEC accountant. He had met Kendall when, in the course of his official duties, he investigated her company for securities fraud. There was an instant chemistry between them. Soon, Armand would spend evenings on the premises of her offices creating the bogus statements. Armand's defense was that Kendall "seduced" him, and that he had spent time in her office in pursuit of a meretricious relationship. Armand's wife came to court every day. Before Judge Palmieri, I cross-examined Friedland on the defense of seduction:

Q: Mr. Friedland, you are a married man?
A: Yes.
Q: When you married your wife, you promised to be true to her?
A: Yes.
Q: That was a lie, wasn't it?
A: Yes.
Q: And before you met Mrs. Kendall, you knew how to make love to a woman?

**A:** Yes.

**Q:** You knew how to hold her hand?

**A:** Yes.

**Q:** You knew how to tell her you loved her?

**A:** Yes.

**Q:** Knew to put your arm around her?

**A:** Yes.

**Q:** Knew how to tell her sweet things?

**A:** What sweet things?

**Q:** That she was beautiful, and you liked her hair or her clothes?

**A:** Yes.

**Q:** Now, when Mrs. Kendall "seduced" you, you held her hand, did you not?

**DEFENSE COUNSEL:** Objection, your Honor, I don't know where he is going.

**THE COURT:** I think I know where he is going. He is testing the defense of seduction. Overruled.

**Q:** Did you hold her hand?

**A:** Yes.

**Q:** Did you tell her that you loved her?

**A:** Yes.

**Q:** Did you put your arm around her?

**A:** I don't remember.

**Q:** Could one forget?

**DEFENSE COUNSEL:** Objection, your Honor. I move for the withdrawal of a juror and the declaration of a mistrial.[16]

**THE COURT:** Denied. Mr. Zirin, I think the proper question should be, "Did you forget?"

---

16. All he had to do was move for a mistrial, although there was no basis for it. Some lawyers used to say, "I move for the withdrawal of a juror." I think this meant that the judge would send one juror home and, there being no jury, declare a mistrial because the case could not proceed any further.

I knew that. I wanted the jury to consider the implications of the bad question.

Q: Did you tell her sweet things?

A: Yes

Q: That you liked her hair?

A: Yes.

Q: Her clothes?

A: Yes.

Q: You lost your head with Mrs. Kendall, didn't you?

A: Yes.

Q: She seduced you?

A: Yes. I succumbed.

Q: Was it mutual?

A: It was mutual.

At this point, Friedland's wife burst into tears and had to be led from the courtroom. The jury didn't believe Friedland. The, defense of seduction failed, and they convicted him on all counts. Palmieri sentenced Friedland to two years in jail.

Palmieri was a fine judge. He had real intellectual stature, and a measured temperament. He demonstrated these qualities in dealing with an obstreperous lawyer named Abe Solomon. Abe was a caricature of himself, a criminal defense lawyer who every once in a while would try a case. A short pepper-pot guy with glasses and a shuffling gait, Abe sounded something like George Burns, but looked like Danny DeVito. When he argued a case, he took George Burns' advice, "Be obscure. Clearly."

Abe liked to try cases his own way, and particularly enjoyed tilting with judges in front of the jury. In a trial before Judge Palmieri, he took umbrage when Palmieri repeatedly overruled his objections. Each time this happened, Abe would turn to the jury and say "exception." Palmieri sharply admonished Solomon that his objection to the ruling was preserved for appeal, and there was no need to say "exception," whereupon Solomon replied, "exception." The judge held Abe Solomon in contempt of court.

Abe bristled. In his closing argument, he said to the jury, "Ladies and gentlemen, sitting here, you may have gotten the idea that I don't like Judge Palmieri. Nothing could be further from the truth. Actually, I think Judge Palmieri is a great judge, one of the greatest judges on the bench 'without exception.'" There was laughter in the courtroom. "Judge Palmieri is Oliver Wendell Holmes, Brandeis, and Cardozo, wrapped into one." Abe's baleful apology would have done proud John Barrymore or even Boris Tomashevsky.

At which point, Palmieri, with his characteristically pained expression reminiscent of John McEnroe, not really enjoying what he was doing even though he was doing it so well, said in a tone so anguished I thought he would burst into tears, "Oh, Mr. Solomon, how can I hold you in contempt when you say something as generous as that? I purge you of contempt." Abe was very grateful. He lost the case with the jury but, duly purged, he slithered out of Foley Square a free man.

## SOME OF THE REST

There were other judges I appeared before who were less iconic. They seemed uncomfortable with the serious business of judging. At times these judges were quite good, and all certainly tried to be fair, but some seemed quite ad hoc in the way they approached their judicial duties. The following judges somehow find a durable place in my recollections of the Mother Court.

## IRVING BEN COOPER[17]

One of the weirdest judges I knew was Irving Ben Cooper. Like the fictional Captain Queeg in Wouk's *The Caine Mutiny*, he was a Freudian delight. Born in London, Cooper was a short man with a pencil-thin Edwardian mustache and a courtly manner that belied his quick tempered and erratic behavior. He called the jurors "ministers of justice" rather than the more traditional formulation, "triers of the fact." He was taken to task for this in the court of appeals. Once, I heard him tell counsel, "Justice doesn't lie with me; it lies with them [the jury]." So what is the judge—a potted palm?

Cooper seemed to be overly sensitive to the possibility that lawyers were baiting him or did not respect him. He often berated and harangued the lawyers, proclaiming proudly in open court that he had been counsel to the fabled Seabury investigation into attorney misconduct, and that he had "thrown many 'shysters' in jail."[18]

Cooper's overblown self-righteous statements were the talk of the courthouse. In taking a guilty plea from some unfortunate felon, he would say, "I see from the alacrity of your responses and your facial expressions that you truly want to plead guilty." Who the hell pleads guilty to a crime with alacrity; and what facial expressions connote voluntariness?

Cooper placed great value on facial expressions, often admonishing young lawyers for "smirking." In one robing room conference I attended during a trial, he whirled on a junior lawyer:

---

17. Judge Cooper served on the Mother Court from 1962 until his death in 1996.

18. In 1930, the New York state legislature appointed Samuel Seabury, a retired judge, as independent counsel to investigate municipal corruption. The inquiry at first focused on crooked lawyers and judges in the magistrate's court and then centered on the "malfeasance, misfeasance and nonfeasance" of Mayor Jimmy Walker. Walker was eventually forced to resign. "This fellow Seabury would convict the Twelve Apostles if he could," Walker wisecracked under questioning by then Governor Franklin Roosevelt.

I've noticed you out there smirking at me. You don't understand. I'm here for life. The trouble with you, Jones,[19] is that you think the judge is a *schmuck*.

Jones didn't answer. Peter Fleming once told me, "The smartest things you learn to say in a courtroom are the things you don't say."

Cooper was fond of expressing the joys of Yiddish on the bench. He proclaimed with seeming pride that he decided with his *kishkes*, rather than his law book. Or he asked a defendant who had decided to plead guilty whether he felt the need to plead guilty in his *kishkes*. For the uninitiated, *kishkes* is a Yiddish expression meaning "guts" that Cooper frequently used in his colloquy with counsel.

A single practitioner from Brooklyn came before Cooper to plead his client guilty. Before entering the plea, he asked the judge what sentence he would impose. "No," said Cooper, "that's the state court practice. Here in the federal court, we don't do that. But, if your client has reservations about pleading guilty and goes to trial, you may be familiar with the expression *och un vey* [Yiddish, "for woe betide"]."

Cooper won the prize for the bloviated judicial utterance. When some criminal miscreant sought to express contrition before Cooper sentenced him to a single count of conspiracy, the defendant addressed the court as follows: "Your Honor, I am sorry. I want to go straight." Cooper replied, "I'm supposed to believe that out of the mouth of slime? The sentence is the maximum penalty of five years. *I wish I had more.*"

One of Cooper's classic jury instructions was a gem:

---

19. I have changed the name to protect the innocent. The incident really happened, not to me, but I was there and bit my tongue hard to keep from laughing.

In the final analysis, then, if you find that the evidence respecting the defendant is as consistent with innocence as with guilt, or that it is more likely that the defendant is innocent than guilty, then you should acquit him. If you find that the law has not been violated you should not hesitate for any reason to return a verdict of not guilty, because that is the law.

While this pious in tone instruction appears to favor the defendant, it is also pernicious in impact, as it actually invites the jury to find guilt "in the final analysis" by a preponderance of the evidence ("more likely that the defendant is guilty than innocent"), rather than beyond a reasonable doubt. The evidence actually may be more consistent with guilt than with innocence but still fall short of guilt beyond a reasonable doubt, the standard universally required in our courts. The court of appeals reversed on this and another issue of plain error in the trial record.[20]

Before his appointment to the federal bench, when he was chief judge of the old gamblers' Court of Special Sessions, Cooper was given to flashes of temper both on and off the bench. For example, he frequently expelled lawyers from his courtroom for being "judge baiters."

Diminutive in stature, he was an unlikely candidate to get physical with a burly bus driver. So it was bizarre indeed when he pedaled his bicycle past a Riverside Drive bus, on two occasions cursed the bus driver who he said crowded him, engaged the driver in a shoving contest on the sidewalk after forcing the bus to the curb, summoned the driver to his chambers, held him in contempt, and ordered him incarcerated. The appellate division was not long in vacating Cooper's "contempt" order.

---

20. United States v. Hughes, 389 F.2d 535 (2d Cir. 1968).

President John F. Kennedy gave Cooper an interim appointment to the Southern District bench in 1961 on the recommendation of Democratic Congressman Emmanuel Celler. The appointment was controversial. Former Attorney General Herbert Brownell spoke out and said, "If there was ever a justice who was not deserving of this appointment, I submit it is Irving Ben Cooper."

When Cooper had his Senate confirmation hearings, a number of people who knew of his erratic behavior testified or submitted affidavits in opposition to confirmation, including the bus driver, who told the story of the bicycle incident on Riverside Drive. Witnesses testified that Cooper was emotionally unstable, abusive, and inclined to exhibitionism.

The venerable and prestigious Association of the Bar of the City of New York, joined by the American Bar Association, filed a brief with the Senate on the subject of Judge Cooper. It concluded:

Call it judicial intemperance, call it emotional instability, call it what you will or what it is, we respectfully submit that the candidate is unsuitable and unfit to serve on the federal bench.

Cooper seemed to suffer from delusions of persecution, which doubtless antedated his confirmation difficulties. He felt, in particular, that White Anglo-Saxon Protestants were out to get him. When my friend Stephen Williams, a talented assistant U.S. Attorney, appeared before him, Cooper was quick to go on the attack. "It was *your kind*, Williams," Cooper began his harangue, "that tried to block my confirmation." Astounded, Williams scarcely had a chance to introduce himself to the court. Steve is now an outstanding federal appellate judge in Washington.

Former Southern District Judge Simon Rifkind, a leader at the Bar, saved the day for Cooper's confirmation by testifying on his behalf before the Senate. So, naturally, after Cooper was confirmed, he and Judge Rifkind enjoyed a special relationship.[21]

Rifkind represented Jacqueline Kennedy Onassis in the 1972 suit she brought to enjoin the "paparazzo extraordinaire"[22] Ron Galella from harassing her and her family.[23] The First Amendment protects journalists and photojournalists from governmental interference with their news-gathering activities. The protection is particularly strong where the targets of the activity are public figures, such as Jackie O and her children, who were legitimate subjects of public interest. First Amendment lawyers call such governmental interference a "prior restraint," an example of which would be the injunction of a publication. First Amendment rights, the Supreme Court has held, are not absolute, and some reasonable restraints are permissible where the activities of the journalist are intrusive, assaultive, frightening, or unlawful. In short, when they come too close for comfort. This was Mrs. Onassis's claim about Galella, who had allegedly made himself an ubiquitous fixture in her daily life.

A prominent trial lawyer, Alfred Julien, represented Galella. Julien told Cooper that he was contemplating an application to disqualify the judge for bias because President Kennedy had appointed Cooper to the bench. Julien never pressed the point. The lawyer probably didn't know it, but Cooper displayed a small bronze bust of JFK on a credenza in his chambers, a reproduction of the famous Robert Berks sculpture. Julien failed to urge the more cogent bias argument, namely that Judge Rifkind had supported Cooper's close confirmation vote.

---

21. Cooper reportedly kept a list in his desk of those lawyers who had testified against him at the Senate hearings. He did not need a list to know that Rifkind was instrumental in putting him in office.

22. The word "paparazzo" originated in the Fellini film *La Dolce Vita*. A character in the film, a satiric look at celebrity culture and the media, is a news photographer named Paparazzo.

23. Mrs. Onassis' suit was brought as a counterclaim. Galella brought the claim in chief against three agents of the Secret Service for obstructing his news gathering. No one took this claim very seriously.

Unsurprisingly, at the nonjury trial, when Julien objected to one of Rifkind's questions, Cooper lamented, "How it pains me, Judge Rifkind, to see you so belittled in my presence!"

Cooper had other bones to pick with the beleaguered Julien. Cooper found, among other things, that Julien made a misrepresentation to the court; that he denounced Cooper for bias, but never formally sought his disqualification; that on one occasion he lost control of himself (the kettle calling the pot black) by forgetting that he had accused Cooper of unprofessional conduct the day before; that on "one occasion he so aroused Judge Rifkind that, it seemed to us, he might have experienced a heart attack while heatedly responding"; that he "roared, mocked and facially expressed his disdain and derision for the other side and spewed his temper. . . . [and w]hen we found ourselves duty-bound to rule against him, his utterances were accompanied by simulated grief"; that he was "obstructive" in rearguing objections following rulings by the court; and that he made "improper extrajudicial statements concerning the case." Bristling with righteous indignation, Cooper said he would refer Julien's conduct to the Bar Association for appropriate disciplinary action.

On the merits, Cooper found, among other things, that Galella's testimony was "so utterly corrupt that its particular value is to demonstrate . . . [his] willingness to lie"; that the "record is studded with instance after instance where plaintiff's testimony was clearly perjurious"; that he "sought to suborn perjury by witnesses who had been subpoenaed"; that Galella's attempts to photograph Jackie were "unnerving and often frightening"; and that Galella "grunts, yells, makes strange sounds, laughs and calls out to Jackie such gems as 'the Marines have landed.'"

While acknowledging that there was great public interest in the activities of Mrs. Onassis and her children, Cooper brushed aside Galella's press freedom arguments and enjoined Galella from coming within 100 yards [a football field away] of Jackie's home,

100 yards of the schools attended by the children, and, at all other places and times, 75 yards from the children and 50 yards from Jackie O, who, of course, won the case.

Troubled by the First Amendment issue, the Second Circuit handed Mrs. Onassis a Pyrrhic victory. The appellate court essentially gutted Cooper's remedy, cutting back the restriction from 100 yards to 25 feet. The appellate court held that the "injunction is broader than is required to protect [Mrs. Onassis]. . . . Relief should not unnecessarily infringe on reasonable efforts to 'cover' her." The court held that "[a]ny further restriction on Galella's taking and selling pictures of defendant for news coverage is, however, improper and unwarranted by the evidence." The evidence was never high on Cooper's list of guiding principles.

As he promised, Cooper referred the conduct of Galella's lawyer, Julien, to the Bar Association for disciplinary action. To my knowledge, the Bar Association never did anything about it, and Julien died 16 years later with an unblemished record.

Another Cooper gem was *United States v. Birnbaum*. In 1966, Cooper sentenced Saul Birnbaum, a wealthy accountant, convicted by a jury of two counts of bribery of an Internal Revenue agent, to a year in jail. On the sentencing, Cooper admitted Birnbaum to bail pending appeal and then made a strange offer. He said that if during the one year that Birnbaum was pursuing his appellate remedies, Birnbaum gave a "hunk of himself" to the community, "I *might*, and I emphasize *might*, entertain a motion to reduce sentence and put you on probation."

Birnbaum, indeed, gave a "hunk of himself." He made large contributions to social welfare programs in Brooklyn's crime-ridden Bedford-Stuyvesant neighborhood, as well as to other charitable organizations. Indeed, the Bed-Stuy community elected Birnbaum its "Man of the Year" for his bounteous benefactions, and cheered as his motorcade paraded through the streets. Birnbaum did pursue his appellate remedies, retaining the very cream of the New York Bar, David Peck, Ben Herzberg, and eventually Arnold Bauman, to attack Cooper's conduct of the trial—precisely the scenario that Cooper hoped to avoid by dangling the carrot of probation in front of Birnbaum's nose. When Birnbaum came again before Cooper on the motion to reduce sentence, Cooper rigidly adhered to the one-year jail sentence, leading Birnbaum to contend that Cooper had reneged on his "promise" to put Birnbaum on probation in exchange for a year of community service.

So Birnbaum brought on a motion to vacate sentence, which came on before another Southern District judge, Inzer B. Wyatt.[24] Bill vanden Heuvel, representing the Bedford-Stuyvesant community, was noted for his grandiloquence. He made an impassioned pitch for Birnbaum. "Who in the United States Attorney's Office," Bill argued with characteristic rhetorical flourish, "has walked the streets of Bed-Stuy, as Birnbaum has?" He continued, "When a court says to a criminal defendant, 'I might,' it is surely saying to him 'I will.'" Judge Wyatt would have nothing of Bill's argument. In his disarming Alabama drawl, Wyatt sounded like an evangelical preacher spouting that old time religion when he said, "I am sorry, Mr. vanden Heuvel, if Birnbaum gave to the community, that was good for his soul—*good for his soul.*"

Birnbaum went to prison, as was richly deserved.

In his motion to vacate Cooper's one-year jail sentence, Birnbaum contended that the bizarre procedure permitted the judge to reward Birnbaum if he pulled his punches in the appellate court, thus chilling vigorous prosecution of his appellate remedy. Judge Wyatt denied the motion, the Second Circuit affirmed his order,

24. I have already mentioned Judge Wyatt in Chapter 12, dealing with Roy Cohn.

and the Supreme Court refused to hear the case. Dissenting from the Supreme Court's denial of review were Chief Justice Warren and Justice Douglas, who wrote a sizzling opinion excoriating Cooper over the impropriety of his bizarre sentencing procedure.[25]

Other proceedings before Judge Cooper were not without their humorous moments. I heard about a Mann Act conspiracy trial he conducted where the unexpected occurred. The Mann Act makes criminal the interstate transportation of women for immoral purposes. It is the statute that the government strangely decided not to invoke against former Governor Eliot Spitzer. In the case before Cooper, the defendants were the pimps, and the witnesses were the hookers. There are always spectators at salacious cases like this one, and, true to form, the spectators' seats were filled to capacity. Witnesses were permitted to sit with the spectators unless the court ordered their exclusion, which usually occurred to prevent the tailoring of any one witness's testimony to that of another.

Once the jury was impaneled, the defense lawyer moved for the exclusion of witnesses, the only defense motion that Cooper granted in the case. There ensued this colloquy with the Court.

THE PROSECUTOR: May I approach the bench, Your Honor.

THE COURT: Certainly, with counsel.

---

25. Birnbaum v. United States, 394 U.S. 922 (1969).

"The impropriety of this sentencing procedure rests not on the fact that the punishment was disproportionate to the offense because it was not. The crime could have supported a punishment greater than that accorded. . . . The impropriety of the sentencing procedure rests instead on the fact that the defendant's meaningful right of appeal was prejudiced, and that he was led to believe that if he contributed to certain charities approved by the judge, he would not be imprisoned, and that after contributing $100,000 and 18 months of personal service to them, he was told unceremoniously that his efforts were of no avail. This was neither in keeping with the statutory procedure nor with the fairness of the judicial process."

A judge should never meet on a case with one side of a controversy outside of the presence of the other side. Lawyers call this an ex parte communication, and it is a no-no. The colloquy continued:

> THE PROSECUTOR: Your Honor ordered the exclusion of witnesses, and there is someone among the spectators who appears to me to be a woman of easy virtue.

The lawyers and the judge glanced back at the spectators' gallery. Seated in the first row was a lanky blonde wearing long earrings, leather pants, a low-cut top revealing her ample cleavage, and a white boa about her voluptuous shoulders. Her mouth was open as she chomped on a piece of chewing gum.

> THE COURT: Gentlemen, what do you know of this?
>
> DEFENSE LAWYER: That's my wife, Judge.

A lawyer must never be too quick to jump to conclusions. There were a million funny stories to come out of Judge Cooper's courtroom. He was sui generis.

## LLOYD MACMAHON[26]

Judge Lloyd MacMahon had the reputation of being the most intemperate judge on the bench. All didn't share this view. Rudy Giuliani, "America's Mayor" and perennial presidential candidate, had clerked for MacMahon and venerated the judge for his toughness in the courtroom and his conduct of trials.[27] MacMahon

---

26. Judge MacMahon served on the Mother Court from 1959 until his death in 1989.

27. Giuliani avoided military service during the Vietnam War. Upon graduation from NYU Law School in 1968, he was classified 1-A, available for military service. He applied for a deferment but was rejected. In 1969, Judge MacMahon wrote a letter to Giuliani's draft board, asking that he

was chief assistant U.S. Attorney under U.S. Attorney J. Edward Lumbard, a pillar of probity, and served briefly as U.S. Attorney when Lumbard went on the Second Circuit bench. As U.S. Attorney, MacMahon held the distinction of having prosecuted Frank Costello for tax evasion.

MacMahon, given to flashes of anger, often snarled at lawyers and never hesitated to hold them in contempt for real or imagined transgressions. The offense of contempt may be regarded with some skepticism these days, as we see the Attorney General of the United States cited for contempt of Congress, but contempt of court is a serious business. Contempt is a particularly dangerous weapon in the hands of an irascible judge with a hair-trigger temper. Once, when a lawyer remonstrated over one of MacMahon's rulings, the judge growled, "Tell that to those idiots upstairs" [meaning the court of appeals]. The lawyer did, and he prevailed.

Another MacMahon gem: "They can take this glorified notary public's job and shove it."

I remember he held in contempt a friend of mine, Jay Gold. Jay was an effective prosecutor with a pleasing demeanor that always made me smile. His manor was not unlike that of the TV detective Columbo, played by Peter Falk. MacMahon was presiding in Courtroom 318, where Gold had consented to a defense request for an adjournment, but MacMahon ordered the case to trial anyway:

MR. GOLD: That's not right, Judge.

THE COURT: What's not right?

MR. GOLD: Your ruling.

THE COURT: What's your name?

MR. GOLD: Jay Gold. J-A-Y G-O-L-D.

THE COURT: You are fresh, F-R-E-S-H. You are in contempt.

---

be reclassified as 2-A, civilian occupation deferment, because Giuliani, who was then a law clerk for MacMahon, was an "essential" employee. The draft board granted the deferment.

Only the intervention of Sil Mollo, who knew MacMahon well from the old Lumbard days, saved Jay from the hoosegow. Jay Gold went on to become a productive state court judge.

MacMahon's paranoia may have stemmed from a mobster drug conspiracy case, *United States v. Bentvena*, which involved 14 defendants and took almost three months to try.[28] As a student, I attended part of the first *Bentvena* trial before the crusty Judge Levet. The trial ended in a hung jury after the foreman on the eve of summations broke his back. The mishap resulted from an unexplained midnight fall down a flight of stairs in an abandoned building. Levet declared the mistrial because no alternate jurors remained.

The prosecutor was William Tendy, born William Tendesco, an iconic figure in the U.S. Attorney's Office. Tendy was the "Iron Man" head of the narcotics unit, which we called the "junk unit." He was a career prosecutor who served three decades as head of the junk unit, as chief assistant U.S. Attorney, and later as deputy assistant U.S. Attorney. A smart, pragmatic, and cagey trial lawyer, with extensive experience in narcotics conspiracy cases, Bill grew up the hard way on the streets of New York. Among his protégés were Charlie Rangel (everyone knows what happened to Charlie), Rudy Giuliani (everyone knows what happened to him too), and Frank Thomas (later to become head of the Ford Foundation). A dynamic leader, Tendy was especially hard on drug peddlers because they corrupted youth. But he never forgot his early experiences and repeatedly reached out to young people who faced overly harsh sentences where they might have been rehabilitated.

---

28. It appeared that some of the defendants attended the infamous meeting in Apalachin, New York, which I describe in Chapter 8.

After the mistrial before Judge Levet, the *Bentvena* retrial fell to Judge MacMahon. While some of the defendants were obstreperous before Judge Levet, they misbehaved outrageously before MacMahon. At the jury selection, one of the defendants, Salvatore Panico, called MacMahon a "bastard" and a "lousy bum." He later climbed into the jury box, walked inside of the rail from one end of the box to the other, pushing jurors in the front row and screaming vilifications at them, the judge, and the other defendants.

And that is not all. Here is how the court of appeals described one of the more startling events at trial:

> On another occasion, while the defendant Mirra was being cross-examined by the Assistant United States Attorney, Mirra picked up the witness chair and hurled it at the Assistant. The chair narrowly missed its target but struck the jury box and shattered. . . . Suffice it to say that more abhorrent conduct in a federal court and before a federal judge would be difficult to conceive.

The chair-throwing incident lives in the annals of the Southern District. MacMahon leaped to his feet white-faced as jurors gasped. Mirra's 13 co-defendants rose from their chairs, shocked at what had happened. The 15-pound chair crashed into the wall ten feet from the witness box. MacMahon had its remnants marked as an exhibit for future contempt proceedings. A phalanx of marshals subdued Mirra and dragged him into a detention pen along with the other defendants. When Mirra returned, his hands and legs were manacled. He chewed gum and smirked at the jury. The prosecutor chose not to continue his cross-examination, and the judge instructed the jury to "put out of your mind" what had happened. As though anyone could. Most witness chairs in the Southern District are bolted to the floor to this very day.

The miscreants, quite appropriately, spent the rest of the two-and-a-half month trial gagged and manacled. Eleven defendants were punished for contempt for their behavior during trial. Thirteen of the 14 were convicted and received heavy sentences.

On appeal, the defendants claimed that they were prejudiced by a "mass conspiracy" trial, with the consequent spillover effect coming from the outbursts and violence in the courtroom. Rejecting these arguments, the court of appeals declared:

> Law enforcement and fair trial for those accused of violations is not to be limited to the pattern chosen by defendants. The administration of criminal justice in the federal courts will not be delivered into the hands of those who could gain only from its subversion. Our decision in *Aviles* is as applicable to a trial of two defendants as it is to a trial of fourteen. *It may take two to conspire but it takes only one to throw a chair at a prosecutor.*[29]

The unnerving chair-throwing incident may have been a factor in MacMahon's irascibility. It is basic in a criminal case that defense lawyers are given broad latitude in cross-examining government witnesses, particularly when they are trying to impeach credibility. The Confrontation Clause of the Constitution guarantees cross-examination.[30] It is only when there has been full cross-examination of witnesses that we have some assurance that the trial has been fair and justice has been done.

---

29. United States v. Aviles, 274 F.2d 179, 193 (2d Cir. 1960). If obstreperous "conduct of a co-defendant at trial were to require a retrial it might never be possible to conclude a trial involving more than one defendant; it would provide an easy device for defendants to provoke mistrials whenever they might choose to do so."

30. The Sixth Amendment to the Constitution provides, among other things, that "In all criminal prosecutions, the accused shall enjoy the right . . . to be confronted with the witnesses against him. . . ."

Defense attorney Lou Bender, whom I have already mentioned, was cross-examining a prosecution witness before MacMahon in an IRS bribery case in which he represented a corrupt accountant, one David Barash.[31] The government witness, one Clyne, was a corrupt IRS agent, who testified that he had never coerced the defendant. Bender proceeded to cross-examine on the basis of tape recordings of a "bull session" made by an undercover agent in which Clyne boasted of his practice of putting pressure on accountants to pay off. Bender intended to use the tapes to contradict the witness and impeach his testimony. MacMahon admonished Bender, "You are needlessly prolonging this cross-examination and going into all this stuff, and you are not using it for purposes of impeachment. Now cut it out."

Judge Friendly in the Second Circuit analyzed the incident as follows:

> If the judge had followed his own bent and prevented any cross-examination as to the tapes, the convictions on the twenty counts relating to Clyne would surely have to be reversed. However, due to the United States Attorney's lack of objection, defense counsel was able to get a large amount of the recordings before the jury—enough to include the point in his summation. Under such circumstances we would normally decline to entertain a claim of erroneous exclusion of evidence in the absence of an offer of proof that would enable us to determine whether the evidence was relevant and more than cumulative [citing cases]. But we are not disposed to be this insistent when an attorney who, while pursuing an appropriate line of

---

31. One of the prosecutors on the case was David Dorsen. I have already related that David, a great mentor of mine in the Office, went on to write a brilliant biography of Judge Friendly.

cross-examination in a criminal trial, has been curtly commanded to "cut it out."[32]

MacMahon was as brilliant as he was nasty. In the administration of justice, however, a short fuse is always undesirable in a judge.

## DAVID EDELSTEIN[33]

There must be a special place reserved in the history of the Mother Court for Judge David Edelstein.

Knowing him, I was always reminded of the marvelous short story by I.L. Peretz called "Bontsha the Silent." Bontsha was a meek, undistinguished man who demanded nothing of life and eventually went to heaven. He said very little, and little of what he said had any substance.

David Edelstein served as chief judge of the Mother Court for nine years, from 1971 to 1980. He was 48 years on the federal bench. Prior to his appointment, he served as a staff attorney in the claims division of the Department of Justice, making slow and steady progress through the mid-level ranks of the bureaucracy. He was President Truman's second choice (the first choice candidate didn't quite pan out) for the Southern District, and achieved Senate confirmation despite American Bar Association objections that he lacked sufficient trial experience.

Edelstein was best known for his long reign over the marathon IBM nonjury antitrust case brought by the government, which went on for decades. The government alleged that IBM sought to monopolize the computer business. The remedy sought was the breakup of IBM into several competing entities. The Department of

---

32. United States v. Barash, 365 F.2d 395 (2d Cir. 1966).
33. Judge Edelstein served on the Mother Court from 1952 until his death in 2000.

Justice brought the case in 1969 at the close of the Johnson administration. The case was out of Dickens; it never wanted to end.

The trial unfolded in a near-empty courtroom. Most judges in
nonjury cases do not allow the endless reading of depositions but
require counsel to hand up the transcripts, together with summa-
ries of the passages of testimony they rely on. Not so in this case
before Edelstein. The trial consisted mostly of paralegals and young
lawyers reading thousands of pages of deposition transcript into the
record. This was done in open court. What is particularly absurd is
that during the virtually endless, monotonous reading Edelstein was
not there. Where he sat was an empty chair.

Edelstein's trial rulings were undeviatingly adverse to IBM.
When he prevented the company from interviewing adverse witnesses, refused to file IBM's papers so IBM could make its record
on appeal, and refused to entertain oral motions in open court,
instead insisting on written submissions, IBM took the unusual step
of bringing on a petition for mandamus in the Second Circuit in
mid-trial. In an unprecedented ruling, the Second Circuit ordered
Edelstein to reverse himself. The situation became so over-the-top
that the appellate court eventually removed him from the case for
bias—an extraordinary rebuke to a district judge.

Chief Judge Jon O. Newman, writing for the Second Circuit,
with unnecessary deference described Judge Edelstein as "one of
the ablest and most experienced judges" in the Southern District
of New York. But, Judge Newman wrote, "[W]e think it manifestly
clear that a reasonable observer would question the judge's impar-
tiality on the pending issue."

Edelstein rarely fared well in the Second Circuit. He presided
over the 1984 trial of New York State Senator Joseph R. Pisani on
charges of tax evasion and embezzling campaign funds. The jury
convicted Pisani on 18 of 39 counts in the indictment and acquitted

him of 11 counts, but was unable to reach a verdict on ten counts that made up a large chunk of the government's case, including allegations that Pisani used $20,000 in state funds to buy a summer house. Pisani's conviction on the 18 counts was reversed on appeal. The trial record was riddled with error.

According to the *New York Times*, he made some bizarre rulings. In 1983, he ordered six wholesale bakers who had been charged with price-fixing in supplying doughnuts and pastries to coffee shops and restaurants to provide the needy with $1,200 worth of free baked goods each week for two years. And in 1987, he allowed the government to seize the property of a defendant in a drug case, with which the defendant proposed to hire a high-priced defense lawyer. Edelstein reasoned:

> In the same manner that a defendant cannot obtain a Rolls-Royce with the fruits of a crime, he cannot be permitted to obtain the services of the Rolls-Royce of attorneys from these same tainted funds.

In the late '60s, I had a nonjury trial before Edelstein, which he said he would conduct in his darkened chambers. It was the first matter I ever had with him, and I did not know what he looked like, as he rarely appeared in open court. When I arrived for a pretrial conference, three tieless men in their shirtsleeves were sitting around a table playing Pinochle. When I inquired after the judge, to my chagrin, one of them answered, "I am the judge." It was David Edelstein.

I attended a dinner tendered to Edelstein by the Federal Bar Council. The roastmaster was Second Circuit Judge William Mulligan, former Dean of Fordham Law School, where Edelstein had received his law degree. Mulligan was merciless, and the roast went something like this.

I wanted to give a learned address on the contributions of David Edelstein to the jurisprudence of the Mother Court [laughter], and I asked two of my most brilliant law clerks to help me with the research. They spent months in the library and eventually came back to me with dismayed expression on their faces, saying, "Judge, we could find absolutely nothing."

Perhaps hyperbole, but it drew a big laugh.

## CONSTANCE BAKER MOTLEY[34]

Constance Baker Motley followed Edelstein as Chief Judge of the Mother Court. She was in a class all by herself. Tall, gracious, stately, extraordinarily sensitive and compassionate, she personified realization of the American dream. Her father had been a chef at Yale for the exclusive secret society Skull and Bones, the members of which had included Tafts, Harrimans, and Bushes. She was a potpourri of firsts:

- First African American woman to be accepted at Columbia Law School.
- First African American woman to become a federal judge.
- First woman to become Manhattan Borough president.
- First African American woman to serve in the New York State Senate.
- First African American woman to argue before the Supreme Court. (She argued ten cases; won nine.)

In the 1950s, Judge Motley was a close associate of Thurgood Marshall, who led the NAACP's Legal Defense and Education Fund. There, she joined Jack Greenberg, future Judge Robert Carter

---

34. Judge Motley served on the Mother Court from 1966 until her death in 2005.

of the Southern District, and a few other lawyers in bringing court case after court case to end the odious practice of segregation. She drafted the complaint and worked on the briefs in *Brown v. Board of Education*.[35] She was instrumental in gaining the admission of James Meredith to "Ole Miss." Her autobiography, *Justice under Law*, tells of her education and adventures fighting for racial justice. Many Assistants were wary of Judge Motley because she was thought to be prodefense or a legal lightweight, and the product of affirmative action. She was quoted as saying that she found law school boring, and knowledge of the law was not her long suit. She was, however, a gracious human being to appear before.

Motley brought a unique personal perspective to her judging, as all good judges do. But she made that perspective her signature. While a legalist such as Henry Friendly might think judging is all about finding the closest precedent to fit the facts, Motley tried to inform her judging with the blood, sweat, and tears of her life's experience.[36]

I remember prosecuting mobster Vincent Alo for obstruction of justice, and the case came before Motley. Alo, a member of the Genovese crime family, gave false and evasive answers before the grand jury, all of which were the same: "My best recollection, I don't remember."

Q: Mr. Alo, where do you live?
A: My best recollection, I don't remember.
Q: What do you do for a living?

---

35. 347 U.S. 483 (1954).
36. Supreme Court Justice Sonia Sotomayor, herself a former judge of the Mother Court, also argues in her marvelous autobiography, *My Beloved World*, that a judge inevitably informs his legal decisions out of his own life's experiences. This may be truer on the Supreme Court than in the trial court where the judge is expected to inform his decisions out of the decisions of the superior federal courts.

**A:** My best recollection, I don't remember.

**Q:** How old are you?

**A:** My best recollection, I don't remember.

And so the litany went on. Repeated disclaimers of recollection in response to questions where the witness obviously knows the answer is an obstruction of justice, for which crime the grand jury proceeded to indict Alo.

The case was styled *United States of America v. Vincent Alo a/k/a "Jimmy Blue Eyes."* Jimmy Blue Eyes was mentioned in the indictment because a number of witnesses knew him only as "Mr. Blue Eyes." He had earned the moniker as a young hoodlum who got into so many fights that his eyes were usually blackened. I shudder to think what the other guys looked like. Before Motley, defense counsel moved to strike the indictment's reference to "Jimmy Blue Eyes" as prejudicial. Motley's response was, "Counsel, I always thought that blue eyes were a mark of beauty in this society." She denied the motion.

Alo was convicted before Motley of obstruction of justice. In announcing the conviction, Bob Morgenthau said, "Alo is one of the most significant organized crime figures in the United States. He is closely associated with Meyer Lansky of Miami, who is at the apex of organized crime."

I had another case before Motley involving a barrel of "Panama Red" marijuana that someone tried to smuggle into the country with an import declaration describing the contents of the barrel as "household goods." Panama Red, renowned for its potency, had a high street value and was popular among cannabis aficionados of the 1960s and 1970s. We kept the barrel of Panama Red with other evidence in an ill-ventilated walk-in vault on the fourth floor of the courthouse. The barrel gave off a pungent aroma, and I often thought that some in the Office spent an inordinate amount of time in the vault pleasurably inhaling the characteristic scent of what was stored there.

I was apprehensive about trying the case before Motley, as I knew of her hostility to drug laws, particularly those involving marijuana and crack cocaine. As it happens, crack cocaine (which is smoked) is the narcotic of choice among blacks, while powdered cocaine (which is usually sniffed) is the drug of choice among affluent whites. Definitive studies have shown there is no justification for treating crack cocaine as more dangerous than powdered cocaine; nevertheless, mandatory sentences for crack were 100 times as harsh. Thus, there was a mandatory five-year sentence for the possession of five grams of crack, as there was for possession of 500 grams of powder. In 2003, when the Federal Sentencing Commission proposed reducing the guideline ratio, the proposal was withdrawn after congressional leaders made clear that it was a nonstarter. Motley regarded this as terribly unfair, which it was.[37]

I decided to go forward with the Panama Red case if only to get the barrel out of the vault. The defendant took the stand to deny that he knew what was in the barrel. He was the addressee of the barrel, which had been shipped to him from Mexico. On cross-examination, I removed the cover from the barrel and asked him to look inside.

**Q:** Look in the barrel, what do you see there?

**A:** I don't want to look in the barrel.

**THE COURT:** Please look in the barrel.

**A** (looking): I don't see anything.

**Q:** You don't?

---

37. In 2010, Congress enacted the Fair Sentencing Act, which reduced the ratio to 18 to one.

**A:** No.

**Q:** Do you see any household goods?

**A:** Maybe.

**Q:** What household goods do you see?

**A:** I don't know.

**Q:** Tell us what you see.

**A:** Looks like grass.

**Q:** Not household goods?

**A:** No.

**Q:** Isn't that grass Panama Red?

**A:** I couldn't tell you.

**THE COURT:** You never heard of Panama Red?

**A:** No.

**Q:** Never heard of it as a kind of high-priced marijuana?

**A** (shaking his head): No sir.

The jury convicted. Motley knew he was lying.

Unlike many judges, she was street smart. Summing up her personal world view, she said once, "Living at the YMCA in Harlem dramatically broadened my view of the world." Do gender and ethnicity play a role in judging? When I read Justice Sotomayor's famous line, "I would hope that a wise Latina woman with the richness of her experiences would more often than not reach a better conclusion than a white male who hasn't lived that life," I thought of Judge Motley.

# THE COURT TODAY

*There are more things in heaven and earth, Horatio, than are dreamt of
in your philosophy.*
—*Hamlet*, I, 5

This book is about the Mother Court, and its unique culture.
But the Mother Court lives today in a digital age. The digital age will inevitably change the character of what goes on in the
courts. With changing times and evolving community standards,
some of the cases I have described (Communist spies, obscenity,
political censorship) may seem largely irrelevant to today's digital
world. Others (mobster trials, white-collar crime, First Amendment press freedoms, terrorism) may present issues that will likely
be with us for some time to come. Technology may make the court
system more efficient; it may also bring about major reforms in how
we dispose of contested issues. Whatever the outcome, the Mother
Court, and whatever the judicial business that goes on there, will
remain embedded in the fabric of American society. This common
thread will certainly continue despite the profound impact of the
Internet and the social media.

## THE LAUNCH OF THE DIGITAL COURTROOM

In case you weren't looking, the world today has gone digital. Just go into a restaurant, and you see patrons manipulating their smartphones as they talk to friends across the table. The Internet has given us an ability to communicate instantly, and to organize. Our children get most of their information from a screen. If we want to read a newspaper or magazine, we go online and get the very latest. There is something of the "retrosexual" in all of us. If we want to look up an old flame, we go to Facebook or Twitter and are connected instantaneously. If we want to mouth off, we don't send our opinions to an editor, who will cut, paste, and rearrange; we post a blog on some platform, and thousands read it within minutes. No gatekeeper and no space limitations. Privacy, decency, brevity, and civility are all abandoned at the laptop keyboard. Texting, sexting, and Instagram photosharing abound. We are all connected, and we all have had to adapt.

So why not the courts? In some respects, the Mother Court has met the challenges of the digital age. Court papers today are filed electronically. Judges write, edit, and save their opinions on the computer. Most use e-mail. Much legal research is digitally conducted. All this saves time and money. But for the Mother Court, the digital age has been a Procrustean bed. Cameras are not yet permitted in the Mother Court. The media feeding frenzy of a televised O.J. Simpson case is anathema to the Southern District judges. In some respects, the judges have seen technology as improving court administration and the efficiency of trials. In others, it is dreaded as a clear and present danger to the integrity of the judicial system.

The modern-day courtroom in the Mother Court is more like Captain Kirk's bridge on the starship Enterprise than the courtrooms I knew and grew up in. Often, I wonder what Judge Weinfeld, who would sit on the bench with his ledger-size trial notebook, would think of the high-tech digital courtroom we see today.

The high-tech courtroom in a case of any complexity has two laptop screens for the judge; one so he can read the exhibits, the other so he can get a transcript of the testimony in real time. In the old days transcripts were only made available that evening at the earliest, and only if someone ordered costly daily copy. Otherwise, the transcripts might not be available until the trial was over.

Now each lawyer also has two screens with the same information as the judge. At the right hand of lead counsel no longer sits an eager associate fresh from a judicial clerkship or a leading law review. Instead, we find a a techie badly in need of a shave ready to translate any instruction into digital display, and a large projection screen worthy of any dreadnought movie house to facilitate the jury and the spectators in viewing whatever evidence is introduced.

As the lawyer presents his case, he may want to offer a document in evidence. If the judge receives the document in evidence, the lawyer barks "publish," his nerdy assistant presses a button, and in a trice the document is projected on the screen for the jury to see. If the document is an e-mail and the lawyer wants to draw everyone's attention only to the third paragraph, he says to the jury, "Ladies and gentlemen, please look at the third paragraph of the e-mail." The techie presses a button and the third paragraph appears framed in black or highlighted in yellow or green or some other sharply contrasting color. If the third sentence of the third paragraph is key, the lawyer reads it to the jury; and, as he reads the words from his position on the podium, an operator, using a touch screen, can highlight the desired language for all to see on the projection monitor.

At a trial in Courtroom 2013 otherwise dull evidence can come alive. Counsel can feature a passage in a document, play a segment of a videotaped deposition, use animation, draw a picture, explain a chart, or otherwise demonstrate that a picture is worth a thousand words. A witness can also use a special pen to underscore a sentence in a document, and the scored excerpt immediately displays on the screen. There is also a "kill" switch next to the judge and counsel, so that the monitors in the courtroom go off and the judge and counsel can review together disputed items of evidence outside the presence of the jury.

In the good old days before the courtroom went high-tech, when I tried a case, I was always worried about organizing the documents and handling the papers. Today, the lawyer worries about how to handle the technology. The judge no longer looks at the witness; he looks at the real-time transcript. If the witness covers his face with his hands, there is no Judge Cooper to say as he often did, "Take your hand away so the jury can see your full face." The judge in Courtroom 2013 misses much of the action and most of the drama. The modern trial has become a digital screening with the techies in the director's chair.

I developed an instinct, perhaps a subtle intuition, when I heard a bad question in a courtroom. In an instant, I would decide whether to object or not. "Objection, your Honor." The judge would instantly make a ruling based on how he had heard and interpreted the question. "I'll allow it," "Rephrase the question," or "Objection sustained." Today, the judge gets the transcript in real time on the screen in front of him. Often, he goes back to the question, studies it, and then makes his ruling. The result is the same, but the intellectual process is very different. So is the drama. I also learned from early days in the U.S. Attorney's Office to keep a trial notebook with loose-leaf pages inside. On each page I would draw a vertical line. On the left of the line were my notes of the important part of the direct examination. On the right of the line were my cryptic notes of how to attack the unfavorable or perhaps burnish the helpful point that had been made on direct. Often, I would use a red pen to highlight what I wanted to do on the cross. Then, I would move in for the kill. There is no single correct way of doing it, but here's how I might use a prior inconsistent statement to contradict the witness:

Q: Did you testify on direct examination that the bills were tens and twenties?

A: Yes sir.

Q: Do you stand by that testimony?

A: Yes sir.

Q: Do you remember that your deposition was taken a year ago under oath in my office?

A: Yes sir.

Q: On your deposition, were you asked these questions, and did you give these answers?

"QUESTION: What denominations were the bills in?

ANSWER: Fifties and hundreds."

DID YOU SO TESTIFY ON DEPOSITION?

A: Yes sir.

Q: Was your memory of the event better then or is it better now?

A: I can't say, sir.

Today, the trial lawyer reads the transcript as the testimony comes in. He has the capability of stopping the screen at the question and answer he wants and marking them for future reference. At the conclusion of the examination, he can go back to the highlighted passages and ask questions about them.

John Sprizzo, a judge of the Southern District of whom I have already spoken, used to say, "Every case is about seven documents. If you rely on more, you have already lost the jury." Forget that in Courtroom 2013. The lawyers in a complex case may wheel into the courtroom what they think are the key documents in a supermarket shopping cart or two. They always did this. But in any kind of case involving electronic documents such as e-mails, attachments to e-mails, charts, PowerPoint presentations, or the like, the lawyer has myriad documents at the ready tagged, indexed, and scanned to an electronic database. There may be literally millions of documents in the computerized files. These are digested, searched, and commented upon in other electronic indices. As soon as a document is offered in evidence the lawyer has it at his fingertips, accompanied by a summary of the document, its significance, and what part of it tends to favor or undercut his case. He also gets links to all related documents. The art form has become an exercise in robotry.

Whatever. Tech is where it's at today. Hillary Clinton said that connectivity is a cornerstone of U.S. foreign policy. The Internet now allows for free expression in most closed societies. It helped bring about the uprising in the Middle East perhaps misnamed the "Arab Spring." It helped the world witness the violence in Syria that has shocked our consciences. It temporarily throttled the Iranian nuclear program, which imperils civilization. It brought us speed, efficiency, reliability, connectivity, and an incredible ability to do serious research. Yet the courts confront technology with great circumspection—like two porcupines mating.

A February 2010 Standing Order, signed by Southern District Chief Judge Loretta Preska, largely forbids anyone from bringing any digital device, including smartphones and iPads, into the courthouse. A lawyer with a special pass may bring one "personal electronic device," which may not be shared. A personal electronic device includes "any cellular telephone, personal digital assistant, Palm Pilot [who uses a Palm Pilot today?], iPhone, BlackBerry, personal digital assistant, and any other comparable device."

There are narrow exceptions. Lawyers, as we have seen, with the permission of the trial judge may bring computer equipment "for use in trials and proceedings in presenting evidence, managing and accessing documents and files, and making use of the Internet access service provided by a private vendor under contract with the Court." Most judges in complex cases will also permit the use of computers to help the jury.

## TWEETING, FRIENDING, AND THE JURY

The use of social media by jurors during trials and deliberations is not a common occurrence. Nevertheless, the interpersonal connectivity and access to information encouraged by social media, and the Internet in general, is alarming to judges of the Mother Court. Stern prohibitions on cell phones and computers in the courthouse make abuses almost impossible. But restrictions against the use of personal electronics end at the courthouse doors. There is no real handle on what may happen outside the courthouse.

Jurors are supposed to get their information in the courtroom, from the witness stand, and from the documents in evidence. How can judges prevent them from Googling or "friending" the witnesses, or the parties?[1] How do courts stop jurors from using GPS satellite photos on Google Earth for a virtual visit to the scene of a crime or accident? If an expert witness testifies, will intelligent jurors want to do their own research, and find other learning in the field to enlarge their understanding?

Twenty years ago, there were more impediments to acting on an impulse to conduct a personal investigation of the case. Inconvenience, expense, embarrassment, and difficulty of such personal inquiry were all inhibiting factors. Now nearly unfettered access to

---

1. One thing that Mark Zuckerberg contributed to our lexicon is the use of the noun "friend" as a verb. So impersonal are our virtual relationships that most Facebook "friends" haven't even met each other.

information is all at our fingertips, and the possible implications to our current jury system are quite troublesome. During the 2001 trial of suspects in the 1998 terrorist bombings of the American embassies in Tanzania and Kenya, a juror researched the concept of "aiding and abetting" on the Internet—a question the jury had asked the court about during deliberations. The court denied a motion for a new trial.

In a suit against Exxon Mobil seeking $104 million for contaminating New York City groundwater, at least five jurors, one of whom was removed before deliberations, did their own independent research online. Southern District Judge Shira Scheindlin, who presided at the trial, sounded the alarm in denying Exxon's motion for a new trial:

> Search engines have indeed created significant new dangers for the judicial system. It is all too easy for a juror to find out more than he or she should by typing a few carefully chosen words into a search engine.[2]

The Mother Court has yet to adopt a hard and fast approach to this problem, which so obviously affects the integrity of jury deliberations. Addressing the issue is left to the discretion of the individual trial judge. The most common strategy is to instruct and remind jurors not to use social media to give or receive communications relating in any way to the case.[3] Of course, this necessitates faith in the fact that such instructions will be followed.

---

2. *In re* Methyl Tertiary Butyl Ether (MTBE) Prods. Liab. Litig., 739 F. Supp. 2d 576, 609–13 (S.D.N.Y. 2010).

3. In January 2010, the Committee on Court Administration and Case Management of the Federal Judicial Center published model jury instructions regarding the use of electronic technologies to research or communicate about a case.

Although most federal judges admonish juries about the use of social media, the Mother Court has yet to catch up with the New York state courts, which have adopted the following model jury instruction for criminal cases:

> You, as jurors, must decide this case based solely on the evidence presented here within the four walls of this courtroom. This means that during the trial you must not conduct any independent research about this case, the matters in this case, and the individuals or corporations involved in the case. In other words, you should not . . . search the Internet, websites, blogs, or use any other electronic tools to obtain information about the case or to help you decide the case. . . .
>
> I know that many of you use cell phones, the Internet and other tools of technology. You also must not . . . use these tools to communicate electronically with anyone about the case. This includes your family and friends. Until I accept your verdict, you may not communicate with anyone about the case on your cell phone or any other device that can access the Internet through email, text messaging, or on Twitter, through any blog or website, through an Internet chat room, or by way of any other social networking websites, such as Facebook, My Space, LinkedIn or YouTube.

Perhaps there is no harm if a juror texts his spouse that he will be home late for dinner. But suppose he tweets or posts about the progress of the case, "We are close to a verdict, but there are two holdouts on the second count. We'll work on them." Will these tweets be used later in a posttrial effort to impeach the jury's verdict?

Of course, when the jury system began in medieval England, the whole idea was that the jurors would know a lot about the facts when they entered the courtroom. This was deemed of invaluable assistance. "Old Giles is accused of horse stealing. He would never do a thing like that." Or, "There goes Giles again; his father was a horse thief, and he is too." Or, "I know what must have happened. It happened to me there too yesterday." But today's juries are not allowed to know things like that. As Mark Twain facetiously said, "We have a criminal jury system which is superior to any in the world; and its efficiency is only marred by the difficulty of finding twelve men every day who don't know anything and can't read." If they know anything, they are dismissed for cause.

Jurors are supposed to adhere to the court's instructions, and we presume they do. If they hear something prejudicial, they are told to disregard it. They are told not to read about the case or discuss the case with anyone or even among themselves until deliberations begin. But will they do it when the information is out there on the Internet and so readily available? Some facts are so egregious that we can't put them out of our minds. How naïve is the law's assumption that the jury will always follow the court's instructions!

## Sentencing by Guidelines

Even federal criminal sentencing has become digitalized in sentencing guidelines.

When I was a federal prosecutor in the 1970s, federal judges had unfettered discretion to fashion appropriate sentences within the statutory maximum prescribed by Congress. And, there was no appeal from the sentence imposed by the lower court. For example, an assault upon a federal officer, whether the defendant knew or did not know of the officer's identity, carries with it a punishment of "not more than" eight years imprisonment.[4] The operative words

---

4. United States v. Lombardozzi, 335 F.2d 414 (2d Cir 1964) (affirming conviction of five gangsters who pistol-whipped an FBI agent in plainclothes who was taking pictures at a mob funeral).

"not more than" gave the judge a broad range of possibilities. He could, with the aid of a presentencing report, take into account the severity of the offense, the criminal history of the defendant, mitigating circumstances, and the like. In short, the judge was free to temper justice with mercy.

Thus, a judge might "throw the book" at the defendant, suspend sentence altogether, or impose a period of supervised or unsupervised probation.

In a revealing article that appearing in the *Atlantic Monthly* of January 1960, Southern District Judge Irving Kaufman, of all people, who as we have seen sentenced the Rosenbergs to death, brooded,

> If the hundreds of American judges who sit on criminal cases were polled as to what was the most trying facet of their jobs, the vast majority would almost certainly answer "Sentencing." In no other judicial function is the judge more alone; no other act of his carries greater potentialities for good or evil than the determination of how society will treat its transgressors.

But the judge in the Mother Court is "alone" no longer when he imposes sentence. At the ready is a raft of guidelines to help him make up his mind.

This is how guideline sentencing got started. In 1973, Southern District Judge Marvin Frankel had an epiphany. A liberal-leaning judge and a man of uncommon intellect, Frankel wrote a book, *Criminal Sentences: Law without Order*, in which he castigated the "gross evils and defaults in what is probably the most critical point in our system of administering criminal justice, the imposition of sentence." The book was intended for "literate citizens—not primarily lawyers and judges but not excluding them," and was an instant success—widely read and tremendously influential. Frankel argued that there was sentence disparity, which was often found in the statutes, but also varied with the predilections of the particular judge in the exercise of discretion. For example, in California the penalty provided by statute for breaking into and stealing something from the glove compartment of a car was up to 15 years, while the maximum penalty was ten years for stealing the car itself. In Colorado the penalty was a ten-year maximum for stealing a dog; a $500 fine for killing a dog.

One defendant might plead guilty to tax evasion before Judge X, some of whose best friends are tax evaders or wish they were, and get a suspended sentence. Another might plead before Judge Y, who thinks tax evasion is a terrible crime, and get five years. The law is supposed to treat people in like circumstances equally. This is the aspiration of equal justice.

As Frankel argued,

> The arbitrary cruelties perpetrated daily under our existing sentencing practices are not easy to reconcile with the cardinal principles of our Constitution. The largely unbridled powers of judges and prison officials stir questions under the clauses promising that life and liberty will not be denied except by "due process of law." The crazy quilt of disparities—the wide differences in treatment of defendants whose situations and crimes look similar and whose divergent sentences are unaccounted for—stirs doubts as to whether the guarantee of the "equal protection of the laws" is being fulfilled.

In a sizzling vote of no confidence on the ability of the federal judiciary to be fair and administer equal justice, Frankel concluded that the "sweeping power of a single judge to determine the sentence as a matter of largely unreviewable 'discretion' is a—perhaps the—central evil in the system." In Falstaff's view, discretion may be the "better part of valor," but its exercise, by judges in the sentencing arena, Frankel argued, led to manifest injustices.[5] Then, he came to his climacteric:

> Beyond codifying the numerous factors affecting the length or sever-ity of sentences, an acceptable code of penal *law* should, in my judg-ment, prescribe *guidelines* for the application and assessment of these factors. While it may seem dry, technical, unromantic and "mechani-cal," *I have in mind the creation eventually of a detailed chart or calculus* to be used (1) by the sentencing judge in weighing the many elements that go into the sentence; (2) by lawyers, probation officers, and others undertaking to persuade or enlighten the judge; and (3) by appellate courts in reviewing what the judge has done. Once more, I mean to paint in broad strokes, leaving the matter for debate and, I would hope, development later on.[6]

However "dry, technical, unromantic and 'mechanical'" guide-line sentencing was just beyond the horizon, Congress did get into the act; there was debate and development. Eve ate the apple, and therein lies the mischief.

Profoundly influenced by Judge Frankel's compelling argument, Congress enacted the Sentencing Reform Act of 1984, creating a U.S. Sentencing Commission, which Judge Frankel's book had also strongly recommended, to publish *mandatory* sentencing guidelines. Because the guidelines were made binding on all federal judges, the Supreme Court had held that they had the force and effect of

---

5. *Henry IV, Part One*, act V, sc. 4.
6. Italics in the original.

law. The primary goal of the guidelines was to avoid "unwarranted sentencing disparities . . . [and] maintain[] sufficient flexibility to permit individualized sentences when warranted."[7] Under the old rule, parole was possible after the defendant had served one-third of his term. Under the guidelines, parole was abolished.

The resulting guidelines were framed in terms of offense levels. The way it worked was that crimes of a given nature are assigned numerical values, which correspond to specific ranges in terms of sentencing. That said, however, no specific sentence was set in stone. The number may be dialed down several levels if the defendant admitted his guilt by pleading guilty, or if he had cooperated with the prosecutors. The number is dialed up several levels if the defendant testified falsely in denying his guilt, a finding suggested by the jury verdict. The result was that the guidelines would point a judge to a narrow range of mandatory sentence for a particular offense. The calculation could be done readily on a computer.

While minor variations can occur, sentencing disparity and judicial discretion came to an end. Gutted, to be true, was the jailhouse perception that street crime carries more severe penalties than white-collar crime: "the more you steal, the less time you get." Nevertheless, money is what it is all about in the sentencing equation. Equal justice is only an aspiration. An entertainment lawyer once crudely said to me, "It's all about money, and what isn't about money, that's about money too." As Anatole France famously said,

> The law, in its majestic equality, forbids the rich as well as the poor to sleep under bridges, to beg in the streets, and to steal bread.

---

7. 28 U.S.C. § 991(b)(1)(B).

The amount stolen, whether obtained by naked theft or artifice, set the base level for calculating the sentence in a fraud or theft case. Aggravating circumstances are all cranked into the formula as though a computer, not a judge, had fashioned the sentence. Departures upward from the guideline range are appropriate for cases that deviate from the garden variety. Upward departures also became the particular cynosure of constitutional controversy, particularly in the area of uncharged crimes that the judge took into account, or where the judge "found," in enhancing the jury finding, that the defendant had more drugs in his possession than the jury had determined in their verdict.

The guidelines give enormous new powers to the prosecutor to coerce guilty pleas, obtain commitments to cooperate, and negotiate the sentence, thereby ousting the court of its authority. Prosecutors and defense counsel began to bargain about what facts will form the basis for the indictment, and therefore the sentencing.

Plea bargains dispose of the overwhelming majority of the criminal cases in federal and state courts. Justice Anthony Kennedy has said that they "have become so central to the administration of the criminal justice system" that plea-bargaining defendants should receive the kind of protections associated with going to trial, a position that Justice Scalia criticizes as elevating the practice "from a necessary evil" to "a whole new boutique of constitutional jurisprudence."

Plea bargains are struck depending on prosecutors' ability to make credible threats of severe posttrial sentences and defense lawyers' ability to resist the pressure of prosecutors. Sentencing guidelines make it easy to issue those threats. The federal guilty plea rate rose from 83 percent in 1983 to 96 percent in 2009, a rise attributed largely to the guidelines. Most importantly, the guidelines newly provide for appellate review of sentencing decisions irrespective of whether the sentence falls outside guidelines ranges.

Frankel, a brilliant intellectual, proved to be too smart by half. The mandatory guidelines he visualized did not work in practice, and raised substantial constitutional questions. There was a "Thermidorian reaction" to the guidelines among lawyers and judges, who argued that the stricture gave too much power to the prosecutor to coerce pleas and straitjacketed the judiciary. Less than a decade later, federal judges began to bridle at the lack of discretion left in the judiciary with regard to criminal sentencing.

Judge Harold Greene, a gifted federal judge in the District Court for the District of Columbia, thought the mandatory guidelines to be as "complicated and detailed as the IRS code."

A good friend of mine, John Martin, was a highly respected judge of the Mother Court, and had served for four years as the U.S. Attorney for the Southern District before President George H.W. Bush appointed him to the bench in 1990. As a judge, Martin was brainy, pragmatic, and sensitive. Thirteen years later, he resigned from the bench to protest the federal sentencing guidelines. He explained his reasons in a letter to the *New York Times* dated June 24, 2003, titled "Let Judges Do Their Jobs." He wrote:

> I have served as a federal judge for 13 years. Having reached retirement age, I now have the option of continuing to be a judge for the rest of my life, with a reduced workload, or returning to private practice. Although I find my work to be interesting and challenging, I have decided to join the growing number of federal judges who retire to join the private sector.
>
> When I became a federal judge, I accepted the fact that I would be paid much less than I could earn in private practice; judges make less than second-year associates at many law firms, and substantially less than a senior Major League umpire. I believed I would be compensated

by the satisfaction of serving the public good—the administration of justice. In recent years, however, this sense has been replaced by the distress I feel at being part of a sentencing system that is unnecessarily cruel and rigid.

For most of our history, our system of justice operated on the premise that justice in sentencing is best achieved by having a sentence imposed by a judge who, fully informed about the offense and the offender, has discretion to impose a sentence within the statutory limits. Although most judges and legal scholars recognize the need for discretion in sentencing, Congress has continually tried to limit it, initially through the adoption of mandatory-minimum sentencing laws.

For example, when an extensive study demonstrated that there was no justification for treating crack cocaine as 100 times more dangerous than powdered cocaine, the ratio adopted by Congress in fixing mandatory minimum sentences, the ... [United States Sentencing Commission] proposed reducing the guideline ratios. However, the proposal was withdrawn when Congressional leaders made it clear that Congress would overrule it. . . .

Congress's most recent assault on judicial independence is found in amendments that were tacked onto the Amber Alert bill, which President Bush signed into law on April 30. These amendments are an effort to intimidate judges to follow sentencing guidelines.

From the outset, the sentencing commission recognized the need to avoid too rigid an application of the guideline system and provided that judges would have the power to adjust sentences when circumstances in an individual case warranted. The recent amendments require the commission to amend the guidelines to reduce such adjustments and require that every one be reported to Congress. . . .

Congress's disdain for the judiciary is further manifested in a provision that changes the requirement that "at least three" of the seven members of the sentencing commission be federal judges to a restriction that "no more than" three judges may serve on it. Apparently

Congress believes America's sentencing system will be jeopardized if more than three members of the commission have actual experience in imposing sentences.

Every sentence imposed affects a human life and, in most cases, the lives of several innocent family members who suffer as a result of a defendant's incarceration. For a judge to be deprived of the ability to consider all of the factors that go into formulating a just sentence are completely at odds with the sentencing philosophy that has been a hallmark of the American system of justice.

When I took my oath of office 13 years ago I never thought that I would leave the federal bench. While I might have stayed on despite the inadequate pay, I no longer want to be part of our unjust criminal justice system.

Heavy stuff! The guidelines, which had appeared to be so promising in the idealistic conception of Judge Frankel, were unworkable in the minds of other more pragmatic judges.

Martin recognized that if there was to be reform, it would not come from Congress in light of its "disdain for the judiciary." He was right. In 2005, less than two years after Martin's resignation, the Supreme Court decided *United States v. Booker*.[8] In *Booker*, the sentencing judge had given the defendant a term of 30 years instead of the 21-year, ten-month term prescribed by the guidelines for the crime reflected in the jury verdict. The jury convicted Booker of possession of at least 50 grams of crack cocaine. The sentencing judge, using a "preponderance of the evidence" standard, found that Booker possessed an additional 566 grams of crack. This, the judge thought, authorized the upward departure.

The Supreme Court disagreed and found the guidelines incompatible with the defendant's right to trial by jury. Accordingly, the

---

8. 543 U.S. 220 (2005).

Court held, the provision of the statute making the guidelines mandatory must be excised. As so modified, the guidelines have now become merely advisory. It would thus appear that Frankel lost, and Martin won. Are we are back to the unfettered discretion of the trial judge with all its pitfalls? Not so.

The Second Circuit held, post *Booker*, that district judges should follow the guidelines or, if they do not, write a convincing opinion stating the reasons why not. So the trial judge must look to the guidelines for ranges of sentence, but may tailor them to other sentencing goals such as the circumstances of the individual defendant. Most Mother Court judges today continue to follow the guidelines slavishly, although not required to do so, and the guidelines continue to have vitality.

There are of course exceptions. In the recent insider trading case involving ex-Goldman Sachs director Rajat Gupta, Southern District Judge Jed Rakoff, a great judicial innovator, sentenced Gupta to two years in prison, although the guidelines would have suggested a sentencing range of six and one-half to eight years. Rakoff was just the right judge for Gupta, as he had been long critical of the guidelines as an unduly simplistic, stripping the federal judiciary of its discretion to fashion a just sentence.

Since 2010, Rakoff had, in cases other than Gupta's, imposed sentences in insider trading cases averaging 21 months, significantly lower than those imposed by other judges on the bench, and 46 percent below the midpoint the guidelines would indicate.

Frankel got it right; his plan needed only some tweaking and retooling. It may need some more. We are where we are.

# CONCLUSION

*There's a battle outside . . .*
*It'll soon shake your windows*
*and rattle your walls*
*For the times they are a changin.*
       **—Bob Dylan**

As Southern District Judge Inzer B. Wyatt, quoting the Good Book, told the jury in the case of *Roy Cohn*, "Better *is* the end of a thing than the beginning thereof."[1] I have enjoyed writing this book, as I have lived with the material for many years. It is a history enhanced by intimacy. Captured with not too little nostalgia are the happenings, the drama, the tomfoolery, the levity, and the business that I saw unfold in the Mother Court almost every day. As Red Smith famously said, "Writing is easy. You just open a vein and bleed."

I have written about the crucible of truth and justice that is the U.S. District Court for the Southern District of New York as I lived and witnessed it. Some of the cases I have described I participated in personally; others I saw unfold, heard about through colleagues, or read about. All are indelibly imprinted in my professional DNA.

I came to the Mother Court after a brief flirtation elsewhere. The "road not taken" was to become a journalist. At Princeton, where I

---

1. Ecclesiastes 7:8.

spent my undergraduate years, I wrote for the *Daily Princetonian*. Hugh Boyd, a Princeton resident, was the publisher of the *Wall Street Journal*. He was also the owner of the *Daily Home News* in New Brunswick, New Jersey. He knew of my work on the "Prince" and out of the blue offered me a summer job on the *Home News* in 1959, after my sophomore year as a "swing shift" reporter working from four to midnight. That summer I began to cover a murder trial in South Amboy, and was swept up in the drama of the law. After some days of trial, the jury convicted the defendant and sentenced him to death.[2] There and then, I decided that the courtroom was where I wanted to spend my life, and I prepared to go to law school.[3] And there and then, it all began.

Each generation produces its own edition of great judges and great lawyers as tough issues are decided in our evolving society. Men (and women) may come and go, but the Mother Court, like Tennyson's *Brook*, will go on forever. John Adams said we are a government of laws, not men. But, as Judge Frankel added, "Men and women count too." It is of these extraordinary men and women that I write. The drier stuff I leave to the scholars and the historians.

The Mother Court today is a very different forum from the court I grew up in. Although some of the recent appointments to the Mother Court have been spectacular—former Supreme Court clerks, court of appeals clerks, and great scholars of the substantive law—I miss the bigger than life personalities who presided over the celebrated trials of the mid-20th century. It was they who projected the law in all its majesty and drama. When the transforming issues in our society required adjudication, the government came to the Southern District as a forum of choice. Sometimes, the FBI waited

---

2. As fate would have it, the Middlesex County prosecutor who tried the case was Warren Wilentz, uncle of my future wife. Of course, I did not know this at the time.

3. My dalliance with journalism was not wasted. I have written over 200 op-eds, on subjects ranging from foreign policy to terrorism to law, for *Forbes*, the London *Times*, the *Los Angeles Times*, and many other publications, both print and online.

for a drug dealer to take the contraband from Kennedy Airport in the Eastern District of New York to the Bronx where the drug deal was to go down, so that the case could be tried in the Mother Court. No more.

Today, the Mother Court is still at the cutting edge of American history. In 1789, when the Fourth Amendment's proscription on illegal searches and seizures was enacted, electronic surveillance of any kind was undreamed. As brilliant a scientist as he was, Benjamin Franklin could not have conceived of the National Security Agency's (NSA) bulk telephony metadata collection program, which Southern District Judge William H. Pauley III said "vacuums up information about virtually every telephone call from or within the United States."

Deciding an issue that may well reach the Supreme Court, Judge Pauley came down on the side of national security and validated the NSA program, contradicting a respected jurist in the District of Columbia who had concluded that the program was "almost Orwellian" and "almost certainly" unconstitutional. Pauley held that "almost" doesn't count, and the Mother Court continues at the epicenter of the national debate.

Yet, the Mother Court is losing business. The biggest case of mass murder since the Israelis caught Eichmann, *United States v. KSM* is heard not in the Southern District of New York, where the crime occurred, but before a military commission in a faraway base off Cuba, under procedures untested by appellate review. Major commercial cases are referred to arbitration, mediation, or negotiation. Judges tell litigants that trials are expensive, outcomes are uncertain, and contentiousness is a bad thing rather than an inevitable thing in a diverse, competitive, and vibrant society.[4] Judge Shira Scheindlin, appointed

---

4. The Chinese prefer mediation to litigation so there is the potential of profitable business relations once the matter is settled.

to the Mother Court in 1994, told Jeffrey Toobin of the *New Yorker*, "I don't love trials. They are not a good way to tell a story. They are not efficient. And they are often so tedious. . . ." I would take issue with this. The crowning glory of our legal system has been the adversary battle, with the canons of ethics requiring "zeal" of the attorneys on both sides, and with assertions put to the rigorous test of cross-examination. The wisdom that comes with experience convinced us that this was the best way to get at the truth.[5]

This trend is dangerous and impacts young lawyers in a bad way. Instead of aspiring to become professional advocates, our law schools, and our large law firms as well, train young lawyers to produce a commodity and not a tailor-made suit.[6]

Southern District Judge Harold Medina said in his preface to Lloyd Paul Stryker's marvelous book, *The Art of Advocacy*:

> When once the spark is fired and a young lawyer becomes thoroughly imbued with a grim determination to see that justice is done as between man and man, and as between man and the state, there is a reasonable basis for hope that this young man will dedicate himself to the cause of justice, as every lawyer should. The phases and compartments of the law are legion; but if a lawyer chooses to devote his talents to the art of advocacy, he may rest assured that there will be ample opportunity to make a lasting contribution to the spirit of justice.

What I saw unfolding daily in the U.S. District Court for the Southern District of New York was a "lasting contribution to the

---

5. The Supreme Court has said, "The very premise of our adversary system of criminal justice is that partisan advocacy on both sides of a case will best promote the ultimate objective that the guilty be convicted and the innocent go free. Herring v. New York, 422 U.S. 853, 862 (1975).

6. See my friend Richard Suskind's provocative book, *The End of Lawyers*, on the commoditization of the legal profession.

spirit of justice." It is essential that this continue in the courts of our nation.

Law school enrollment, however, has declined dramatically. Many regard legal education as expensive and unproductive. The economics have turned away from the legal profession. Students see that they will have to incur as much as $150,000 in student loans to finance a legal education, with little hope of earning enough to satisfy the loan in a reasonable period of time. The lucrative jobs in their perception lie in the financial sector where there is more bang for the buck.

Today, we see fewer criminal cases tried because of the federal sentencing guidelines, which, although no longer mandatory, still give prosecutors greater control over criminal case outcomes. Criminal cases result in plea bargains more often than not because sentencing guidelines "suggest" that the judge go easier on sentence if the defendant admits his guilt.

It's not the same as it was for civil cases, either. Judge Weinfeld refused to participate in or order settlement discussions. He put cases on the trial calendar; the date was firm; and the lawyers, if they didn't want to go to trial, often settled on the courthouse steps. Today, there is a big administrative push to get civil cases disposed of amicably. Cases are routinely sent to a magistrate judge to "knock their heads together" and accomplish a settlement. The push is not so much to achieve a fair and equitable settlement as it is to get the case settled and off the docket. Although equity is said to be equality, splitting the difference does not necessarily mean a just result.

I am uncomfortable that the Mother Court has become too much of a claims administrator. Litigants and cases have become statistics spat out of the computers in the New Streamline Timely Access to Statistics, known by the acronym NewSTATS, project of the Administrative Office of the United States Courts. With all the technological efficiencies of NewSTATS, we have forgotten what Judge Weinfeld taught us: "Litigants are not ciphers—they are people."

I do not intend to minimize technological efficiency, but today's courtroom resembles more the starkness of a computer science laboratory than the thrust stage of old. Perhaps in the digital age this is inevitable. But the trappings of justice are important as well.

I miss the Mother Court of yesteryear, where judges and lawyers ranted, raved, and tilted at one another, where legal principles were, as the great Washington lawyer Thurman Arnold put it, an "argumentative technique" and an "arsenal of weapons to be used in litigation." It was the court where criminals were brought to swift and certain justice; where rascals were acquitted; where eloquence and humor were not misplaced; where obstreperous defendants were bound and gagged; and where dirty movies in obscenity cases were projected on a rude screen in a darkened courtroom for only a few minutes before the judge rang down the curtain, saying something reminiscent of the King's reaction to the play within the play in *Hamlet*, "Give me some light."[7]

It is perhaps trite to lament that the parties are not so good as they used to be or, as storied movie agent Sue Mengers said of Hollywood, "Honey, we used to have fun," and I do not argue that here. But there was rarely a dull moment then, and what happened seemed to matter so much more.

The Southern District of New York, as I knew it, was the best in the justice business; and I hope it still is and always will be. It stayed the course and kept the faith. But I can't help but feel sometimes that something of the special quality and excitement of its "golden age" has been lost. Without being overly elegiac, I hope I have retrieved here some of its essence.

---

7. *Hamlet*, act III, sc. 2.

# ACKNOWLEDGMENTS

As must be true with almost any book, *The Mother Court* reflects the contributions of many people—some in the way of moral support; others more practical.

I thank Jon Malysiak, my editor, for taking me on and raising the questions that mattered. A shout-out to Peter Dougherty, who got it from the start and gave me just the extra push the project needed.

Thanks to my extraordinary agent, Andrew Wylie, who never lost faith in the work, and to my special agent, Ronald Goldfarb, who helped make the project happen.

Special thanks go to my beloved wife, Marlene Hess, to whom I gratefully dedicate this book. It can't be easy to be married to someone who begins his work at five in the morning, but she graciously stayed the course, read the manuscript a number of times, and made many invaluable suggestions.

Thanks to the iconic sportswriter, and my Princeton classmate, Frank Deford for inspiring me to write a book in the first place, and to Thomas L. Pulling, Kate Medina, Susan Mercandetti, and Kate Foley, all of whom read all or part of the manuscript and gave me the benefit of their helpful reactions as the book evolved. Thanks to André Bishop, Charles Rippin, and James Goodale, who provided needed encouragement along the way.

Thanks to my colleagues in the U.S. Attorney's Office, friends for life, who shared a story or a recollection or two: Bob Arum, Tom Baer, John Doyle, Hugh Humphreys, Andy Maloney, Dan Murdock, Paul Rooney, and Jim Tripp. Special thanks to two extraordinary lawyers, also veterans of the office, Mike Armstrong and Frank Tuerkheimer, who gave the book a close reading and imparted a number of helpful suggestions.

And undying thanks to the Boss, Robert M. Morgenthau, who made it all possible.

# INDEX

Abramovic, Marina, 94
Abrams, Creighton, 194
Adams, Sam, 187–188, 190
Adams, Sherman, 166, 166n15
Adler, Irving, 239
African embassy bombings,
    214–215, 290
Agnew, Spiro, 70n20, 111, 121n7
Alfano, Donald, 117, 119
Alien Registration Act of 1940,
    57–59, 60, 63
Allen, Chris, 227
*Allen v. United States*, 35, 36–37
al Libi, Anas, 222
Alo, Vincent, 279–280
al Qaeda, 223. *See also*
    Mohammed, Khalid
    Sheikh (KSM); September
    11 attacks
al-Zawahiri, Ayman Mohammed
    Rabie, 223
American Cyanamid
    Company, 251
American Museum of Jewish
    Heritage, 19n5

Amicus brief, 133n6
Amsterdam, Anthony, 91, 91n44
Anastasia, Albert, 135, 136–137
Apalachin meeting, 20, 131–135,
    137–138
"Arab Spring," 288
Arkin, Stanley, 178
Armstrong, Michael, 14
Arnold, Thurman, 199
Art, obscenity and, 107–109
Arthur Andersen, 154, 167–168
*Art of Advocacy, The* (Stryker),
    306
*Art of Cross-Examination, The*
    (Wellman), 43, 45
Arum, Bob, 20–21
Assange, Julian, 126, 126n17,
    126n18, 127
Atomic Energy Act, 80, 81,
    81n31, 82–83

Badalamenti, Gaetano, 139
Baer, Harold, 19–20
Baghdadi Jews, 179
Barash, David, 274

Barbera, Joe "the Barber," 131,
132, 133
Barr, Tom, 182, 184
*Batson v. Kentucky*, 34
Bauman, Arnold, 2–3, 267
Becker, Charles, 142
*Behind the Green Door* (film), 104
Bell, Daniel, 202
*Bersch v. Drexel*, xvi
Bender, Louis, 253, 274
Berenson, Berry, 219n3
*Bernstein v. Universal Pictures,
Inc.*, 39n14
Betancourt, Jo-Jo, 239
Bethe, Hans, 87
Binger, Carl A., 71
bin Laden, Osama, 214, 223
Birnbaum, Saul, 266–268, 268n25
*Birnbaum v. United States*, 268n25
Black, Hugo
    *Dennis v. United States* and, 62
    free speech and, 59n6
    in *Goldwater v. Ginzburg*, 178n6
    in *Grunewald v. United States*, 86
    as libertarian, 111
    on obscenity, 97
    as textualist, 111–112
    on trials and media, 27
Blacklisting, 56
Blackmun, Harry, 112
Bloomberg, Michael, 226
Boies, David, 196n21
Boise Cascade Sec.
    Litig., *In re*, 39n14

Bolan, Tom, 205, 209
Bonanno, Joseph, xiii, 132, 135
Bordoni, Carlo, 47
Bork, Robert, 250–251
Boroson, Warren, 176, 177
Boudin, Leonard, 133
Boyd, Hugh, 304
*Boys in the Sand* (film), 104
*Brady v. Maryland*, 240–241
Brandeis, Louis, 63, 188
*Brandenburg v. Ohio*, 63
Brecht, Berthold, 84
Brennan, William J., Jr., 86, 93,
96, 231
Breslin, Jimmy, 118
*Brideshead Revisited* (Waugh), 213
Brill, Joseph, 204–205, 204n6
Brodsky, Abe, 133
Brodsky, Reed, 47–48
Brokhovich, Boris V., 87–88
*Brooklyn Inst. of Arts and Scis. v.
City of N.Y. & Rudolph W.
Giuliani*, 107–109
Brooklyn Museum, 107–109
Brown, H. Rap, 243,
244–246, 246n6
Brownell, Herbert, 76, 263
*Brown v. Board of Education*, 279
Bryan, Frederick van Pelt, 157–158
Buchwald, Art, 167
Buckley, William F., 201
Buckner, Emory, 23
Burr, Aaron, 1
Burt, Dan, 196

Buscetta, Tomasso, 139
Bush, George H.W., 298
Bush, George W., 56, 138, 225
Butler, Pierce, 143

Cabell, James Branch, 98n8
Cahill, John, 23, 143, 144
Califano, Joe, 167
*Camelot* (Lerner), 13
Cannella, John, 117–118
Caputo, Luciano, 235
Carson, Edward, 172–173
Carter, Jimmy, 167
Carter, Robert, 278–279
Cartier-Bresson, Henri, 220
Castellano, Paul, 133
*Cast of Hawks, A* (Gould), 183n10
Catalano, Salvatore, xiii, 138
Catholic Legion of Decency, 109
CBS (television station), 187–198
Celler, Emmanuel, 263
Cell phones, 288–289
Cerf, Bennett, 99, 101
Chambers, Whittaker, 48, 64,
    64n14, 65–71, 65n15,
    70n18, 73
Chayefsky, Paddy, 57
*Chem. Bank v. Arthur Andersen*, xvi
Christie, Agatha, 41
Churchill, Winston, 14, 18, 27,
    39, 53, 65, 222
Cicero, 8
Cirofici, Frank, 142

Civello, Joseph, 133
Civil War, 56
Clark, Ramsey, 218, 219n4
Clark, Wesley, 227
Clinton, Bill, 189
Cockran, W. Bourke, 142n2
Cohen, Jacob, 146–147
Cohn, Albert, 211
Cohn, Roy, 70n20, 75, 76, 82,
    171–172, 199–211, 303
Common law, xii
Communism. *See* "Red Scare"
Connelly, John, 217
Conspiracy, 129–131, 139
Continental Vending Machine
    Corporation, 155, 156–157
Contorno, Salvatore, 139
Coolidge, Calvin, 9, 99
Cooper, Irving Ben,
    260–269, 286
Corallo, Anthony "Ducks," xiii, 146
Cornfeld, Bernard, 167–168
Corruption, official, xiii–xiv
Costello, Frank, 135–136,
    135–137, 135n9, 270
Courtroom 318, 5–6
Cowley, Malcolm, 64n14
Crile, George, 188
Criminal law
    jurisdiction in, 3
    jury in, 34–35
    sentencing guidelines in, 3,
        242, 292–301
Crockett, George W., 62

Cross-examination
bias and, 41–42
elements of, 42
Fleming on, 42–43
importance of, 41
jury and, 41–42
in Wellman, 43
Croswell, Edgar, 133n6

Damiano, Gerard, 104
Dan, Uri, 181n8
Dawson, Archie, 202–203
Day, William R., 143
Dayan, Moshe, 180
Day of Terror plot, 214
*DED v. Andersen*, xvi
*Deep Throat* (film), 104–107
Defense of Marriage Act, 110n24
Deloitte & Touche, 154
DeLorean, John, 34–35, 168
Dembitz, Nanette, 133
*Dennis v. United States*, 61–62
DeSapio, Carmine, xiv, 45,
210n9, 250
Deutsch, Seymour, 146
*Devil in Miss Jones, The*
(film), 104
Dewey, Thomas E., 113
Digital courtroom, 284–289, 307
Donovan, William "Wild Bill,"
113, 247, 247n9
Dorsen, David, 90, 103,
195–196, 274n31

Douglas, William O., 59n6, 81,
86, 97, 178n6, 268
Driscoll, Daniel, 205
"The Dry Salvages" (Eliot), xi
Dylan, Bob, 303

Edelbaum, Maurice,
45, 240–241
Edelstein, David, 275–278
Edwards, John, 35
Einstein, Albert, 84
Electronic documents,
284–289
Eliot, T. S., xi
Ellsberg, Daniel, 122–123, 123n12
Enron, 154
*Equity Funding* cases, 164–165
Erdman, Robert, 146, 148
Ernst, Morris, 99
Ernst & Young, 154
Espionage Act of 1917, 76–77,
77n28, 80, 127

Facebook, 289n1. *See also*
Social media
*Fact* (magazine), 176–178
Felsikov, Alexander, 88
Field, Stephen J., 183n10
Fifth Amendment, 1, 203n4
Fitch, Clyde, 98n8
*Fitzgerald v. Westland Marine
Corp.*, 189

Fleming, Peter, 14–15, 42–43,
157, 163
*FOF v. Andersen*, xvi
Foley Square, 4, 4n4
*Fool for a Client, A* (Cohn), 171–172
Ford, Gerald, 165, 250
Foreman, Percy, 132–133
Fortas, Abe, 254–255
Fraenkel, Osmond, 133
France, Anatole, 296–297
Frank, Jerome, 62
Frankel, Marvin, 3, 4, 47,
293–295, 298, 304
Franklin National Bank, 47
Frankfurter, Felix, 81–83,
91, 91n43
Franks, Lucinda, 17
*Freedom for the Thought That We
Hate: A Biography of the
First Amendment*
(Lewis), 58
Friendly, Henry
on accounting, 153
*I Am Curious (Yellow)* case and,
97, 102–103, 105–106
Kaufman and, 90
Keogh and, 150–151, 153
Leval and, 188
McMahon and, 274–275
Pentagon Papers and, 127n19
Rosenberg case and, 87
*United States v. Benjamin*
and, 116

*United States v. Kahaner*
and, 148n9
*United States v. Simon* and, 163
Frost, Robert, 220
Fuchs, Klaus, 77, 79n29
*Fund of Funds* case, 167–168
Fusco, Otto, 6–7

Galella, Ron, 264–266, 264n23
Gambino, Carlo, 119, 132, 135
Garfield, James, 49–51
Garfinkel, Barry, 232
Gates, Samuel, 8n9, 165
Gay marriage, 109–110
Gaynor, Al, 14, 15, 205
Gelb, Les, 153
Gemayel, Bashir, 180, 181,
181n8, 185
Genovese, Vito, xiii, 119, 132,
135, 136–137
Gershon, Nina, 107–108
Gesell, Gerhard, 123n12
Gigante, Vincent "Chin," 136, 137
Gilbert, Cass, 4
Gilbert, W.S., 25, 199, 229
Ginsburg, Ruth Bader, 253n13
Ginzburg, Ralph, 176
Giuliani, Rudolph, 107–109, 138,
140, 269–270, 269n27, 271
Goddard, Henry W., 71, 73
Gold, Harry, 77–78, 79n29
Gold, Jay, 270–271
Goldberg, Arthur, 91n43

Goldfine, Bernard, 166, 166n15
Goldstein, Nathaniel, 113
Goldwater, Barry, 176–178
Goldwater v. Ginzburg, 176–179
Goldwyn, Samuel, 161
Goodale, Jim, 123n12
Gotti, John, 30–31
Gould, Milton, 182–184, 186
Graham, Katherine, 121
Grand, Paul, 14
Greenberg, Jack, 278–279
Greene, Harold, 298
Greenglass, David, 77–78, 79n29, 87, 131
Greenglass, Ruth, 77, 78, 79n29, 85
Gregg v. Georgia, 91, 91n44
Grossman, Marshall, 165
Grunewald v. United States, 86
Guercio, Jo, 14
Guiteau, Charles J., 49–51
Gupta, Rajat, 47–48, 301
Gurfein, Murray, 112–120, 124–127, 126n16, 156, 163–164

Habeas corpus, 86
Halberstam, David, 122n10
Halevy, David, 185
Halley, Rudolph, 135–136, 135n10
Halperin, Morton, 122
Hamscher, George, 191

Hand, Augustus, 100–101, 100n11, 143
Hand, Learned, 143
  on conspiracy, 130, 139
  Dennis v. United States and, 61
  Harrison v. United States and, 129
  Kaufman and, 90, 91
  Smith Act case and, 63
  Ulysses case and, 100n11
  Weinfeld and, 10, 11
Harding, Warren G., 143
Harlan, John Marshall, 10, 97
Harrison v. United States, 129
Haskins & Sells, 164–165
Hawke, Roger, 218–219
Hawkins, Gains, 190–191, 195
Hayden, Michael C., 138
Hayden, Sterling, 56
Hearsay, 130–131
Hearst Corporation, 174–175
Heath, Burton, 144
Henkin, Louis, 103
Herzberg, Ben, 267
Hiss, Alger, 48, 56, 63–74
Hiss, Donald, 48
Hiss, Priscilla, 68, 68n17
Holbrooke, Richard, 122
Holmes, Oliver Wendell, 39n15, 54, 59, 61, 64, 107, 125
Holocaust, 17–18
Holy Virgin Mary, The (collage), 107–109

*Homo Sapiens*
  (Przybyszewski), 98n8
Homosexuals, 28–30, 95
Hoover, J. Edgar, 58, 84, 135,
  135n9, 200
Horowitz, Harry, 142, 142n1
House Committee on
  Un-American Activities
  (HUAC), 57. *See also*
  "Red Scare"
Hughes, Christopher, 28–30
Hughes, Evans, 5
Humphreys, Hugh, 15n2
Hundley, William, 148
Hyde, Henry B., 113

*I Am Curious (Yellow)* (film), xiii,
  97, 101–104, 105–106
IBM, 275–276
*ILC Peripherals Leasing Corp. v.
  Int'l Bus. Machs.
  Corp.*, 39n14
Internet, 289–292
*Iolanthe* (Gilbert), 199, 229
Iran-Contra affair, 46–47
"Iron Curtain Speech"
  (Churchill), 53
Isenberg, Steven, 33

Jackson, Robert, 20, 113, 227
*Jacobellis v. Ohio*, 97
Japanese internment, 56
Javits, Jacob, 116

Johnson, Lyndon, 122, 122n11,
  123, 167
Johnson, Sterling, 20
Jowitt, William 1st Earl
  Jowitt, 55
Joyce, James, xiii, 98–101
Judiciary Act of 1789, ix, 1
Julien, Alfred, 264, 266
*Jurgen, A Comedy of Justice*
  (Cabell), 98n8
Jurisdiction, 3, 4
Jury
  as check on judiciary, 28
  in Constitution, 27, 38
  in criminal trials, 34–35
  cross-examination and,
    41–42
  importance of, 25
  Internet research by, 290, 291
  nullification, 26
  oath of, 26
  origin of term, 26
  selection, 31–34
  skepticism about, 26
  trials without, 38–39

Kahan, Yitzhak, 180–181, 185, 186
Kahaner, Elliott, xiii, 141,
  146–147, 149–150
Kaplan, Robbie, 110n24
Kaufman, Irving P., 74–83, 89–92,
  113, 133, 134, 293
Kaufman, Stephen, 243–245

Kean, Thomas W., 223
Keenan, John, 1n1
Kefauver Senate
   Committee, 135–136
Keller, Bill, 126n18
Kelly, Raymond, 226
Kendall, Edith, 256
Kennedy, Anthony, 297
Kennedy, John F., 13, 89n42, 146,
   250, 263
Kennedy, Robert, 14, 14n1, 20,
   148, 201–202
Kenney, John J., 47
Kenya embassy bombing,
   214–215, 290
Keogh, Eugene, 146, 146n7
Keogh, J. Vincent, xiii, 141,
   145–151, 236
Kimmelman, Michael, 108–109
King, John, 167–168
Kissinger, Henry, 121, 123
Kleinman, Bill, 148–149
Knohl, Larry, 115
Knox, Amanda, 31n6
Koetl, John, 232
Korean War, 78
*Korematsu v. United States*, 56
Kove, Moses, 237–238
KPMG, 154
KSM. *See* Mohammed,
   Khalid Sheikh (KSM)
Kuh, Richard, 210
Kunstler, Bill, 245
Kushner, Tony, 211n10

Lamont, Corliss, 236
Lansky, Meyer, 119, 135n9, 136
*Leaves of Grass* (Whitman), 95
Lebanon War, 180
Lee, Richard Henry, 28
Lehman, Herbert, 232, 233
Leisure, George, 196
Leisure, Peter, 20
Lenox Hill Gang, 142
Lerner, Alan Jay, 13
Leval, Pierre, xiii, 19, 138, 140,
   188–189, 194, 198
Lewis, Anthony, 58
Libi, Anas al, 222
Liman, Arthur, 46–47
Lincoln, Abraham, 56, 84
Lindsay, John, 33
Lipton, Marty, 232
*Lochner v. New York*, 39n15
Lombardozzi, Carmine, xiii, 133
Long, Breckinridge, 17–18
"Love for Sale" (Porter), 95
Lovelace, Linda, 104
Lucas, Malcolm, 165, 165n14
Lucchese, Tommy, 135
Luciano, Lucky, 136
Lumbard, J. Edward, 101–102,
   103, 134, 270
Lybrand Ross Bros. &
   Montgomery, 155,
   155n3, 159

MacMahon, Lloyd, 269–275
Magaddino, Nino, 135

Maitland, F.W., xii
Maloney, Andrew, 254
Mann Act, 268–269
Manning, Bradley, 126n17
Mansfield, Walter, 158–159,
    229, 246–249
Manton, Martin, xiii,
    100n11, 142–145
Marcus, James, 237
Marino, Salvatore, 116–118, 119
Marriage, same-sex, 109–110
Marshall, Thurgood, 4n4, 278
Martenson, Charles, 210
Martin, John, 3, 20, 298–300
Mayer, Jane, 226–227
McCarthy, Joseph, 73, 75, 200
McCarthyism, 73. *See also*
    "Red Scare"
McChristian, Joseph, 191–193, 195
McGinley, Marie, 117, 118
McLean, Edward, 69
McNamara, Robert, 122, 122n10
Medalie, George Z., 23
Medina, Harold, xiii, 59–61,
    89, 306
Meeropol, Michael, 89
Meeropol, Robert, 89
Mengers, Sue, 308
Meredith, James, 279
Meskill, Thomas, 106–107, 106n18
Methyl Tertiary Butyl Ether
    (MTBE) Prods. Liab.
    Litig., *In re*, 290
Metzenbaum, Howard, 251

Military Commissions Act, 225
Military tribunal, 224–226
Miller, Henry, 95
*Mind of the Juror, The*
    (Osborn), 41–42
"Mini-summation," 194
Miranda, Michele, 133
*Miranda* rights, 253–254
Mitchell, John, 14, 123
Mohammed, Khalid Sheikh
    (KSM), 223–228
Mollo, Silvio, 14, 15, 15n2, 140,
    144–145, 155, 271
Montana, John, 133
Moorer, Thomas H., 121
Morgenthau, Henry, Jr., 13,
    17–18, 140
Morgenthau, Robert M., ix–x
    appointment of, 13
    as boss, 16–17
    Cohn and, 199–200, 202,
        208, 210
    family of, 13–14
    Fleming and, 14–15
    home of, 17
    independence of, 20
    Mollo and, 15
    Nixon and, 22
    Oberdorfer and, 20–21
    in World War II, 18–19
"Mother Court," as name, 1, 1n1
Motley, Constance Baker, 278–282
Moynihan, Daniel P., 4n4, 74, 87
Mukasey, Michael, 3, 127

Mulligan, William, 277–278
Mundt, Karl, 202
*Murder on the Orient Express* (Christie), 41
Murdock, Dan, 243
Murphy, Johnny "Fireman," 238
Murphy, Thomas, 48, 68, 70–72, 74, 89, 102, 115–116, 119, 200, 238–246
Muslims, 54
*My Life in Court* (Nizer), 175

Natelli, Anthony, 114. *See also United States v. Natelli*
National Student Marketing Corporation (NSMC), 160–164
*Near v. Minnesota*, 120
Netanyahu, Benjamin, 186
Newman, Jon O., 276
New York City, xii
New York Society for the Suppression of Vice, 98–99, 98n8, 109
*New York Times*, 120–121, 123, 124n14. *See also* Pentagon Papers
*New York Times v. Sullivan*, 176, 182
9/11 attacks, xi, 54, 215–223
Nixon, Richard, 22, 44, 65, 112, 119, 120–122, 121n7, 123, 126n16

Nizer, Louis, 43, 175
North, Oliver, 46–47
Nuremberg Trials, 113

Obama, Barack, 224, 226
Obamacare, 112
Oberdorfer, Louis, 20–21
Obscenity. *See* Pornography; Sex
Odets, Clifford, 56–57
Ofili, Chris, 107–110
Onassis, Jacqueline Kennedy, 264–266, 264n23
O'Neill, James, 89–92, 89n41
Opening statement, prosecutor, 7–8
Osborn, Albert, 41–42

Palestinian Liberation Organization, 180
Palmieri, Edmund, 252–259
Panico, Salvatore, 271
Patient Protection and Affordable Care Act, 112
Patrusky, Bernard, 203, 207
Paul, Randolph, 18
Pearl, Daniel, 223
Peat Marwick Mitchell & Co., 160–164
Peck, David, 155, 157–158, 267
Pegler, Westbrook, 174
*Pegler v. Reynolds*, 174–175
Pentagon Papers, xiii, 88n40, 112–113, 120, 122–126, 124n14

*People v. Shilitano*, 84
Peraino, Anthony,
   Sr., 105
Peraino, Louis, 105
Perjury, 44
Personal electronic
   devices, 288–289
Phalangists, 180,
   185, 186
Phones, 288–289
Pisani, Joseph R., 276–277
Pistone, Joe, 139, 139n13
Pius XII, Pope, 84
"Pizza Connection" case, xiii,
   59, 138–140
Plea bargains, 297–298
Pollard, Jonathan, 77n28
Pomerantz, Abe, 154
Porcellian Club, 9n10
Pornography, 96–97, 104–107. *See
   also* Sex
Porter, Cole, 95
Porter, John K., 50–51
*Praeteritio*, 8, 9–10
Preska, Loretta, 288
PricewaterhouseCoopers,
   154, 155n3
Profaci, Joe, 132, 133, 135
Przybyszewski, Stanislaw, 98n8
Public Accounting Oversight
   Board, 169
Pulling, Thomas, 216
"Pumpkin Papers," 69–70, 70n18

Racketeer Influenced and
   Corrupt Organizations Act
   (RICO), 132n5
Raichle, Frank, 133, 204, 255
Rajaratnam, Raj, 47
Rakoff, Jed, 301
Randall, Cortes, 161
Rao, Vincent, xiii
Rayfiel, Leo, 146n7, 147, 148
Reagan, Ronald, 251
"Red Scare," 200–202
   background of, 53–54
   blacklisting in, 56
   Hiss case and, 63–74
   Odets and, 56–57
   Rosenberg espionage case
      and, 74–92
   Smith Act and, 57–59
   *United States v. Dennis*
      and, 59–64
Reid, Richard, 223
Reuther, Walter, 177
Reynolds, Quentin, 174–175
*Reynolds v. Pegler*, 175, 236
Rifkind, Simon, 2, 243–244,
   263–264, 265
Ritmaster, Alexander, 255
Rivera, Diego, 84
Roberts, Burt, 145
Roberts, John, 112, 188
*Roe v. Wade*, 112
Roosevelt, Franklin Delano, 9,
   13, 14

Roosevelt, James, 167–168
Rosenberg, Louis, 142
Rosenberg espionage case, xiii, 56, 74–92, 113, 131
Rosenthal, Herman, 142
Rostow, Walt Whitman, 122n11
Roth, Harold, 155, 157
*Roth v. United States*, 93, 96
Runyan, Damon, 142
Rusk, Dean, 122n11

Sacco and Vanzetti, 74, 74n24, 75, 81–82
Safire, Bill, 121n7
Same-sex marriage, 109–110
*Sappho* (play), 98n8
Sartre, Jean Paul, 84
Sawers, John, 137
Saypol, Irving, 75, 82, 85–86
Sayre, Francis B., 64, 64n14
Scalia, Antonin, 218, 297
Scalish, John, 133
Scansaroli, Joseph, 114, 161–162
Scheindlin, Shira, 290, 305
*Schenck v. United States*, 59
Seabury, Samuel, 260n18
*Secrecy* (Moynihan), 87
Seeger, Pete, 242–243, 242n4
Seidman, William, 165
Sentencing guidelines, 3, 242, 292–301
Sentencing Reform Act of 1984, 295–296

September 11 attacks, xi, 54, 213–214, 215–223
Settlement, 307
Sex
    ambivalence on, 94–95
    art and, 107–109
    complexity of, 93–94
    *Deep Throat* case and, 104–107
    *I Am Curious (Yellow)* case and, 101–104
    Ofili case and, 107–109
    *Ulysses* case and, 98–101
Seymour, Whitney North, Jr., 22
Sharon, Ariel, 179–187
*Sharon v. Time, Inc.*, 179–187
Sharp, Ulysses, 191
Sheehan, Neil, 122–123
Shultz, George, 3
Sidorovich, Ann, 77
Siegel, Bugsy, 119
Sifton, Tony, 19
Silbert, Earl, 218, 219
Simon, Carl, 155, 159
Sindona, Michele, 47
Singer, Henry, 133, 149
Sixth Amendment, 225, 225n9, 273
Slobodkin, Ralph, 166
Smart phones, 288–289
Smith, Howard W., 58
Smith, Liz, 216
Smith, Rosemary, 217
Smith, William E., 185–186

Smith Act, 57–59, 60, 63
Snowden, Edward, 126
Sobell, Helen, 203n3
Sobell, Morton, 79, 79n29, 80, 86–87, 88, 203n3
Social media, 289–292
Sodomy, 29
Sofaer, Abraham, 3, 20, 179, 182, 184, 186
Solomon, Abe, 258–259
Sotomayor, Sonia, 279n36
Soviet Union, 53–54. *See also* "Red Scare"
Spellman, Francis, 200, 201
Spira, Howie, 252
Spitzer, Eliot, 268
Sprizzo, John, 19, 26, 287–288
Stalin, Joseph, 65
Steinberg, Harris, 178
Stettinius, Edward, Jr., 64
Stewart, Potter, 96–97
Stryker, Lloyd Paul, 71, 306
Student Nonviolent Coordinating Committee (SNCC), 244
Sullivan & Cromwell, 155
Sulzberger, Arthur, 123
Summary judgment, 189
Surratt, Mary Eugenia, 83–84
Suskind, Richard, 305n5
Sutton, Abie, 234–235
*Swain v. Alabama*, 31
Swan, Thomas, 143
Sweet, Robert, 105, 106

Taft, William Howard, 143
Tanzania embassy bombing, 214–215, 290
Tariff Act of 1930, 96
Tebaldi, Renata, 253
Technology, 284–289, 307
Tendy, William, 271
Tenet, George, 223
Tenney, Charles H., 209
*Terminiello v. Chicago*, 227, 227n12
Terrorism. *See* Mohammed, Khalid Sheikh (KSM); September 11 attacks
Terry, David S., 183n10
Thatcher, Margaret, xvi, 168, 220
Thomas, Evan, 166–167
Thomas, Frank, 271
Thompson, Robert G., 61
Thurgood Marshall United States Courthouse, 4, 4n4
*Time* (magazine), 179–187
Tolson, Clyde, 135n9
Toobin, Jeffrey, 305
Treason, 76
*Trial by Jury* (Gilbert), 25
Tripp, Jim, 253
*Tropic of Cancer* (Miller), 95
Truman, Harry, 64, 233
Tuerkheimer, Frank, 232
Tuttle, Charles H., 8–10
Twain, Mark, 162, 292

Tyler, Harold R., Jr., 3, 161, 163, 164, 177–178, 249–252
Tyler, Joel, 104–105

*Ulysses* (Joyce), xiii, 98–101
United States Courthouse (New York), 4
*United States v. A Motion Picture Called I am Curious (Yellow)*, 97, 101–104
*United States v. Aviles*, 273
*United States v. Barash*, 274–275
*United States v. Benjamin*, 153
*United States v. Bentvena*, 271–272
*United States v. Birnbaum*, 54–55, 266–268
*United States v. Booker*, 300–301
*United States v. Bufalino*, 131
*United States v. Dennis*, 59–64
*United States v. First National City Bank*, 20–21, 21n6
*United States v. Friedland*, 255–258
*United States v. Hughes*, 28–30
*United States v. Jones*, 262
*United States v. Kahaner*, 35–36, 148n9
*United States v. Locascio*, 30–31
*United States v. Lombardozzi*, 292, 292n4
*United States v. Natelli*, 114, 156, 160–164
*United States v. N.Y. Times Co.*, 125

*United States v. One Book Called Ulysses*, 98–101, 144n5
*United States v. One Book Entitled "Contraception,"* 99
*United States v. One Obscene Book Entitled "Married Love,"* 99
*United States v. Sacher*, 62
*United States v. Schwimmer*, 54
*United States v. Simon*, 155–160, 161
*United States v. Various Articles of Obscene Merchandise*, 105. See also *Deep Throat* (film)
*United States v. Vincent Alo a/k/a "Jimmy Blue Eyes,"* 280
*United States v. White*, 139n14
Urey, Harold, 84
U.S. Fin. Sec. Litig., *In re*, 39n14

Valley Commercial Corp., 155, 156–157
Venona project, 73, 73n21, 88
Vietnam War, 112, 123, 269n27. See also Pentagon Papers; *Westmoreland v. CBS*
Vinson, Fred M., 81
Vogel, Larry, 14
*Voir dire*, 32

Walker, Jimmy, 260n18
Wallace, Mike, 187. See also *Westmoreland v. CBS*

War Refugee Board, 18
Warren, Earl, 86, 112, 268
*Washington Post*, 120–121,
   123n12, 124n14
Waugh, Evelyn, 213
Weinfeld, Edward, 10–11, 11n12,
   36–37, 141, 146, 148, 149,
   174, 208, 230–238
Weisman, Lawrence I., 204,
   206, 207–208
Wellman, Francis, 43, 45, 49–50
Wells, H.G., 75
Westbrook, Pegler, 174–175
*Westmoreland v. CBS*, 179, 187–198
White, Henry Dexter, 202
White, Mary Jo, 214
Whitman, Walt, 93, 95
Whitney, Richard, 9, 9n10
*Whitney v. California*, 63
WikiLeaks, 126, 126n17, 127
Wilde, Oscar, 172–174
Wilentz, Warren, 304n2
Williams, Edward Bennett, 9,
   32, 166–167
Williams, Stephen, 19, 263
Wilson, Will, 140
Wilson, Woodrow, 13, 142
Windsor, Edie, 109–110, 110n24

Winfield, Dave, 252
*Witness Who Spoke with God
   and Other Tales from
   the Courthouse, The*
   (Gould), 183n10
Wolfson, Louis, 20, 254–255
"A Woman Waits for Me"
   (Whitman), 93
Woodward, Ann, 114–115
Woodward, William, 114–115
Woolsey, John, 99–100, 204
World Trade Center bombing
   (1993), 214, 215
World War II, 17–19, 56, 247–248.
   *See also* "Red Scare"
Wyatt, Inzer B., 204, 204n5, 207,
   208, 267, 303

Yalta Conference, 65,
   74, 74n22
*Yates v. United States*, 63
Younger, Irving, 33
Yousef, Ramzi, 214, 223

Zeibert, Duke, 167
Ziegler, Ron, 22
Zola, Emile, 92